LIBRARY LEADERSHIP IN THE
UNITED STATES AND EUROPE

LIBRARY LEADERSHIP IN THE UNITED STATES AND EUROPE

A Comparative Study of Academic and Public Libraries

PETER HERNON AND NIELS OLE PORS, EDITORS

LIBRARIES UNLIMITED

AN IMPRINT OF ABC-CLIO, LLC
Santa Barbara, California • Denver, Colorado • Oxford, England

Library of Congress Cataloging-in-Publication Data

Library Leadership in the United States and Europe : A Comparative Study of Academic and Public Libraries / Peter Hernon and Niels Ole Pors, Editors.
    pages cm
  Includes bibliographical references and index.
    ISBN 978-1-61069-126-0 (hardcopy : alk. paper) — ISBN 978-1-61069-127-7 (ebook)   1. Library administration—Research.   2. Library administration—Cross-cultural studies.   3. Comparative librarianship.   4. International librarianship.
5. Academic library directors—United States.   6. Academic libraries—United States—Administration.   7. Academic library directors—Europe.   8. Academic libraries—Europe—Administration.   9. Public library directors—United States.   10. Public libraries—United States—Administration.   11. Public library directors—Europe.
12. Public libraries—Europe—Administration.   13. Leadership.   I. Hernon, Peter. editor of compilation.   II. Pors, Niels Ole. editor of compilation.
  Z678.L465   2013
  025.1—dc23   2012041627

ISBN: 978-1-61069-126-0
EISBN: 978-1-61069-127-7

17 16 15 14 13   1 2 3 4 5

This book is also available on the World Wide Web as an eBook.
Visit www.abc-clio.com for details.

Libraries Unlimited
An Imprint of ABC-CLIO, LLC

ABC-CLIO, LLC
130 Cremona Drive, P.O. Box 1911
Santa Barbara, California 93116-1911

This book is printed on acid-free paper ∞

Manufactured in the United States of America

CONTENTS

Part III: Themes

Part IV: Conclusion

ILLUSTRATIONS

FIGURES

TABLES

PREFACE

Academic and public libraries across the world are facing a competitive environment in which their managerial leaders deal with matters related to technological challenges; a climate of austerity (decreased resources) and change, which can be more than merely incremental; staff assuming new roles and functions; more collaboration; new partnerships; greater accountability; and achieving service improvements in part through technological innovations and efficiencies. Amid an environment of dwindling resources and increasing scrutiny and demand to assume new service roles and respond to changing information-seeking behaviors, conferences, institutes, and the literature of library and information science address the concept of managers as leaders in charge of complex organizations. Leadership is often presented in terms of change management, rallying support for a preferred future, and ensuring progress in accomplishing that future.[1] There might be reference to change leadership, when in fact leadership per se denotes change.

There are too many opportunities today for those managing libraries to get caught up in the immediate problems they confront on a daily basis and to ignore the long term. As leaders they should make decisions in the short term based on their understanding of the long term, as established through some type of planning process. To us, managers cope with the short term while leaders reflect on the future and where the organization might head, and they translate that vision into an action plan that everyone works to achieve.[2] As David Kaser, a retired library director and educator, was fond of saying, managers are tempted to react to every blip on the radar screen and to lose sight of all of the images on the screen. Leaders deal with the big picture and marshal resources to accomplish both short-term and long-term needs. Leaders also view change as an opportunity to redirect or redefine the organization.

Numerous books and articles cover leadership, many of which explain the topic, often in simplistic terms, and introduce one or more of the leadership theories. The general literature on leadership might differentiate between management and leadership, identify critical attributes associated with leadership, and encourage more librarians and other workers to become leaders. The assumption seems to be that people are leaders *if* they read the proper literature; participate in leadership workshops, programs, and institutes; and benefit from some mentoring. A further assumption is that leadership adheres to some basic principles (truths) that can be easily conveyed and mastered. The basic writings encourage readers that if they do as instructed they will become effective leaders. However, the more we investigate and read about leadership, it becomes clear how little is actually known about the topic, other than that leadership is a complex concept that is highly valued and sought after, and that defies easy definition or, at least, there is no consensus on a perfect definition. It seems that, as a leader, one knows where the organization needs to go, involves others in accomplishing the needed change, and does not get misdirected. Another way to explain leadership is that it is a process that involves influencing others, setting and accomplishing common goals, and interacting with others on an individual and group basis. Power is associated with leadership because power is the capacity or potential to influence others. There are multiple dimensions to leadership, which have not been fully explored. Clearly, the truths and platitudes conveyed in the general literature are simplistic and have limited value.

An increasing number of scholars and researchers have explored some facet of leadership and add to general knowledge about the topic but they generally cover one location, country, or perhaps region of the world. In the United States, researchers might focus on a particular theory and theorists continue to add to (and modify) established theories on leadership. Furthermore, with the global recession there has been increased interest in the practice of leadership and how leadership functions on an everyday basis.

Turning to the United Kingdom and Europe, there might be coverage of a particular leadership theory or linkage of leadership to national cultures and the deep-rooted values of a culture. These cultural values shape how people expect organizations to be managed. Ideally, employer and employee expectations need to be balanced, while many times the cultural distance between them creates problems for management. Furthermore, cultural values impact institutions and organizations, in particular their norms, value system, behavior, and regulation, as well as their view of leadership and its practice. Both leaders and employees have their own view of the environment in which organizations operate, and cultural values shape their perspective, including the actions that managers take (e.g., their decision-making processes). The perceptions of employees about work and work processes have culturally implications. Complicating matters, both perceptions and values align with national and other cultures, including that of a profession.

Library Leadership in the United States and Europe is the first book in library and information science to present and compare leadership in the United States and throughout Europe. Other than the GLOBE (Global Leadership and Organizational Behavior Effectiveness) Project, which examined 62 of the world's cultures and viewed leadership in terms of those cultures, there are few attempts to view leadership on a large global or cross-national scale. With the GLOBE Project, the societal cultures studied "are not referred to as 'nations' because the researchers were admirably thinking as social anthropologists instead of political scientists."[3]

During the spring of 2011, Peter Hernon spent part of his sabbatical leave at the Royal School of Library and Information Science, Copenhagen, and discussed editing a book on leadership with Niels Ole Pors. At first, they considered editing a book that covered leadership on a global basis, perhaps modeled in part after the *Encyclopedia of Leadership*,[4] but focused on the state-of-art as reflected from the research literature. We decided that such a book was premature and our strength at this time rested more with leadership in academic and public libraries in Europe and the United States, showing issues, trends, and key literature. Our discussions revealed language differences among countries regarding how leadership is conceived and exercised. Other differences relate to the way that libraries interpret management and leadership, perceived differences in trends, and the insularity of the leadership research and other writings on libraries and other cultural institutions. Rarely, is there a broad perspective on leadership in libraries in other countries and regions of the world. We firmly believe that taking the broader perspective might result in a more reflexive practice of leadership.

Library Leadership in the United States and Europe, which is the result of those discussions, is divided into four sections. The first, which lays the foundation for the subsequent chapters, provides an overview of leadership, leadership theories, and the characterization in terms of perceptions of national culture and related concepts (social capital and trust). This and other chapters identify key literature but do not provide a comprehensive analysis of the literature within and outside library and information science. The second section, which includes Chapters 2–7, highlights the United States, the United Kingdom, Europe as a whole, and selected European countries. Chapter 3 complements Chapter 1 and highlights leadership from European perspectives. The European literature focuses more on national cultures than do the literatures in the United Kingdom and the United States. However, when cultures are discussed in the United Kingdom and the United States, the focus is more on organizational culture and perhaps the role of teams. It is also apparent that, in many European countries, there is no distinction between management and leadership, with the focus more on management.

Chapter 5, which offers a perspective from United Kingdom, focuses on appropriate leadership behavior and styles suitable to confront the challenges arising from the widespread financial crisis affecting so many European countries. The chapter also introduces additional leadership models. In Chapters 6 and 7, the question concerning a specific Scandinavian leadership and management style is discussed. The discussion is based on a leadership survey that has been conducted several times and in several countries. The results at least indicate some support for a specific and rather human-oriented leadership practice in the Scandinavian countries and one can contemplate this in the relation to the idea about the so-called welfare state and its relation to issues such as trust and social capital.

The third section concentrates on selected themes. Chapter 8 covers driving forces (forces of change), change management, and a shifting emphasis to innovation and entrepreneurial activities. Chapter 9 addresses organizational recipes, which, for Europe, covers managerial tools for tracking areas of potential change. In the United States, this term is not used. Chapter 10 focuses on managers known to be leaders and their personalities and cultural orientations. In the United States, the equivalent type of research would examine the emotional intelligence of leaders and their relationships with others (see Chapter 1). Chapter 11 moves beyond leaders and discusses employees—in some national cultures they are called followers. In this chapter leadership is viewed in terms of influencing others to accomplish change. Chapter 12, which covers a management issue, focuses on accountability and the gathering and use of evidence to demonstrate organizational effectiveness. This chapter perhaps shows the biggest differences between the United States and

Europe. In the former, impact and assessment have precise meanings and those meanings transcend library and information science. In fact, stakeholders have shaped the perspective on both. In Europe, performance measures are assumed relevant to impact assessment. The exception is the United Kingdom, where there is a stricter view of accountability.

In the final section, Chapter 13 focuses on an international research agenda and shows that there is still much to learn about leadership, especially from an international perspective. Chapter 14 completes the discussion on leadership by highlighting themes that transcend a country or region. In these times of austerity leadership, moving beyond the status quo, becomes important as libraries prepare to assume new roles and offer new services. One goal of that chapter and the book is to offer a foundation from which others can build and another goal is to challenge all of us to look at issues from an international perspective.

The recent global recession underscores the interconnection about regions of the world and how events in one region influence global markets. No region exists in isolation of what occurs elsewhere. *Library Leadership in the United States and Europe* serves as a reminder that library and information science, like other disciplines, benefits from cross-national comparisons made by more than one knowledgeable scholar. We can all learn from each other and deepen the understanding of leadership and library and information science.

This book should appeal to educators in schools of library and information science around the world and classes dealing with change management, organizational development, and leadership. Anyone interested in leadership theories, cultures, styles, and practices, regardless of discipline, should be interested in the content and approach taken in the book and in learning which theories and styles, if any, have the greatest value within a national context. The book should also appeal to anyone conducting research on leadership and wanting to include an international or cross-national perspective.

Peter Hernon and Niels Ole Pors

NOTES

1. Peter Hernon and Joseph R. Matthews, *Reflecting on the Future: Academic and Public Libraries* (Chicago: American Library Association, 2013).

2. Hernon and Matthews, *Reflecting on the Future*.

3. Cornelius N. Grove, "Introduction to the GLOBE Research Project on Leadership Worldwide" (2005), http://www.grovewell.com/pub-GLOBE-intro.html (accessed May 24, 2012).

4. George R. Goethals, Georgia J. Sorenson, and James MacGregor Burns, *Encyclopedia of Leadership* (Thousand Oaks, CA: Sage, 2004).

Part I

INTRODUCTION

1

—◆•••◆—

LEADERSHIP IN CONTEXT: AN OVERVIEW

Peter Hernon and Niels Ole Pors

Leadership is one of those words for which there are numerous definitions, none of which, however, has become the standard against which other definitions are judged. Some of the definitions mention the leader's vision and implementation of that vision, whereas other definitions do not focus on a vision. In the case of managerial leadership, which combines management and leadership and applies them to change management, the vision most likely originates with the director or perhaps the senior management team. Leadership may occur at other levels of the organization and, in such cases, these other staff members—be they managers or not—do not set the vision; rather, they implement the vision or else, in some instances, participate in creating a shared vision.

Complicating matters, not all library directors are leaders. We have all heard about library directors who are invisible to the organization; they are introverts, hide in their offices, and have little direct contact with others in the organization. Given such circumstances, Peter G. Northouse, a professor of communication in the School of Communication at Western Michigan University, notes that such individuals are leaders by virtue of their position in the organization, chief executive officers or, by extension, library directors. These individuals are *assigned* leaders, and they are not always genuine leaders.[1] Further, a director may be a leader within the library but not within the broader organization or institution, or in both the immediate and broader organization.

It is important for managers and staff to possess insight into the very diversified and complex aspects of leadership applicable to the organizations and institutions they are expected to lead. This is probably more important in organizations such

---

A section of this chapter is based on the following: Pors, Niels Ole. "Globalization, Culture, and Social Capital: Library Professionals on the Move," *Library Management* 28, no. 5 (2007): 181–90. We also acknowledge the other articles in the issue on "Globalisation, Culture, and Social Capital: Library Professionals on the Move," in particular Susan McKnight, "The Expatriate Library Director," pp. 231–41.

as universities and libraries characterized by a high educational level among the employees and a general high degree of professional commitment. Managers need to have an intimate knowledge of the different aspects of leadership because such knowledge could make them better and more reflective leaders in their organization. Basically, leaders need to analyze the environment of the organization to be able to adapt the organization to address technological developments; educational, political, and economic trends; and value systems. They also need to focus on the different aspects of internal integration in the organization. Internal integration is not just about organizational cultures but also about power structures, decision-making systems, and the whole structure of the organization. This ability calls for analytical skills, but it is also of paramount importance that the leader be able to analyze and understand people throughout the organization, and to read the climate and cultures of the organization and the values that pervade and shape it. Without understanding factors like these, change processes become arduous and more difficult than necessary and can cause conflict.

Without doubt, it is extremely important that leaders understand the employees or the followers in an organization but it would also be extremely beneficial in relation to change processes if employees had an understanding of leadership and the different kind of cross-pressures leaders face. In all organizations, staff discuss leaders and their behaviors. An understanding of the leadership situation would benefit internal communication and probably make some elements in change processes more relevant for each employee. Open communication about conditions, prerequisites, and leadership styles could minimize many of the stereotypes that tend to guide interpretations of leadership behavior.

SOME DEFINITIONS OF LEADERSHIP

The *Oxford English Dictionary*, which shows the word as first appearing in the 19th century, considers leadership as "the dignity, office, or position of a leader, esp. of a political party; ability to lead; the position of a group of people leading or influencing others within a given context; the group itself; the action or influence necessary for the direction or organization of effort in a group undertaking."[2] Such a definition narrowly focuses on politicians but does connect leadership to influencing others. Northouse concurs that leadership is "a process whereby an individual influences a group of individuals to achieve a common goal,"[3] while Robert J. House and his colleagues refine the definition: leadership "is the ability of an individual to influence, motivate, and enable others to contribute toward the effectiveness and success of the organizations of which they are members."[4] Such a definition confuses the distinction between management and leadership; organizational effectiveness and success involve management, whereas leadership looks long term.

For this book, the definition of leadership guiding the writing of the various chapters is the ability to develop a vision for the organization, get others to support that vision, implement the vision in organizational (or institutional) terms, and ensure that things happen according to some plan. This definition connects leadership with strategic planning and the direction in which the library is going over time. A mission states what the organization does now, whereas a vision conveys what the organization will become. Economic realities impact the achievement of the mission and the timetable for achieving the vision.

Issues

Redesign role/mission of library

Cost savings (use $ for priorities). Dwindling budgets. Close branches, etc.

Collections—digital/print (less print)

Repurposing library space

Shift in reference—from desk to digital

Reengineering staff positions

Managerial leadership
- Vision
- Planning
- Follow-through

More Issues

New service roles (e.g., publishing (open access), e-research)

Organizational agility—shift and change quickly

Collaboration across institutions

Gaining staff support for change (especially for their areas of responsibility)

Accountability

Figure 1.1: Libraries Today and Tomorrow: The Types of Challenges to Overcome

Fundamental change
- challenges that alter the norms and procedures on which organizations rely

Mismatched "cultures" in an organization
- service culture

Technological advances: Problem and part of solution

Empowerment

Organizational fit for change

Competition with other stakeholders

Organizational development

Managing the change process by managing the people involved in the change

Assessment (when really discussing "evaluation")

Levels of change management
- project management
- building the organization that can handle events that have not been thought of and are unpredictable

Change leadership

Uncertainty

Teams/staff training and motivation

Conflict such as organizational resistance

Leadership across the organization
- more than the "assigned" leader

Figure 1.2: Some Terms Associated with Change Management

Whatever definition of leadership members of an organization favor, leadership deals with the types of challenges discussed in the literature of library and information science. The topics covered in Figure 1.1, compiled from an extensive examination of that literature and reviewed by several library directors, comprise major challenges that libraries are coping with as their broader organization or institution recovers from the economic recession of 2007–2009 and its lingering aftermath. As libraries cope with change, some do so in an evolutional or incremental way, while others regard the challenges as opportunities and engage in change that is more fundamental, continuous, and transformational. Either way, they must deal with the types of topics identified in Figure 1.2 and become a learning organization in which the staff "continually expand their capacity to create the results they truly desire, where new and expansive patterns of thinking are nurtured, where collective aspiration is set free, and where people are continually learning to see the whole together."[5]

LIBRARY STAFF PERCEPTIONS OF LEADERSHIP

In the United States, librarians on their blogs or in response to what others write on a blog may comment on leadership and their perception of their director as a leader. Most likely, they are commenting on the director within the immediate organization and not on the role played with outside stakeholders. In a number of instances, it appears that those commenting are unfamiliar with the leadership literature and confuse leadership with management. In other instances, the director may communicate and the staff can recite what they are told, but they do not make the association to leadership. Still, the focus is more on attributes than on particular theories or styles.

LEADERSHIP THEORIES

The focus of this section is on some of the leadership theories often discussed in different literatures. Individual leaders draw on one or more theories to form the approach or style that they apply to leadership and management. A style is based on a combination of one's beliefs, values, personality, and preferences, as well as the organizational culture that collectively encourages some styles and discourages others. Relevant writings on a specific theory might also relate the discussion to leadership styles.[6]

Charisma has been studied as both an attribute and a theory. Charismatic leaders rely on their personality and communication abilities (e.g., convey high expectations) as they focus on the person they are talking to and make that person feel as if he or she is very important. Such leaders scan and read their environment, and pick up on the moods and concerns of both individuals and larger audiences. They then hone their actions and words to suit the situation. In essence, they are strong role models. In summary, the goal of charismatic leadership is to link the self-concepts of leaders to the organizational mission and identity, and to get those who work for them to carry out organizational change.

Together with visionary leadership, charismatic leadership has been prevalent in Europe and is now less prevalent in the United States. Visionary leadership focuses on the vision set and brings that vision to fruition. Leaders give work-

Leadership

Theories

Leaders in formal managerial positions	Adaptive leadership
	Authentic leadership
	Collaborative leadership
	Contingency theory
	Emotional intelligence
leadership as interaction	Entrepreneurial leadership
	Innovation leadership
	Leader–member exchange theory
	Path-goal theory
	Resonant leadership
Staff, followers, stakeholders	Servant leadership
	Shared leadership
	Situational leadership
	Team leadership
	Transformational and transactional leadership

Figure 1.3: Leadership Theories and Styles

ers the opportunity to develop their decision-making skills and learn to trust the application of those skills in making decisions. For the purposes of this book, transformational leadership sufficiently covers visionary leadership.

Figure 1.3 identifies some of the more prevalent leadership theories or styles. Two assumptions in most discussions of leadership and those theories and styles are that leadership is both positive and effective, and that those theories and styles apply across nations. As Barbara Kellerman notes, there is the concept of bad leadership, which encompasses factors such as incompetence, rigidity, callousness, corruption, and cruelty that do not advance the learning organization while neither abusing those being led, nor inflicting pain on them.[7] As a result, we approach leadership from a positive perspective; however, readers should still remember there is a negative perspective as well. The following sections amplify on the theories and styles highlighted in Figure 1.3.

Adaptive Leadership

Adaptive leadership, which involves the mobilization of people to tackle tough challenges and to thrive in such an environment, requires the leader first to determine if a problem is *technical* or *adaptive* in nature.[8] Technical problems have a known solution, can be resolved by clearly stated strategies and action, and are addressed by what an organization already knows and excels at resolving. Typically, a manager defines not only the problem but also the solution and the direct path to success. Adaptive problems are more complex because of uncertainty both about the solution and the path to resolution. In order to resolve them, leaders and their organizations go beyond the current sphere of expertise, knowledge, and skills they have available and seek to adopt new strategies. They may apply different problem-solving strategies throughout the organization. Rather than taking a top-down approach, members of the senior management team might ask staff members to find new ways to achieve organizational success. In addition, the team might consult outside partners as needed. Although the strategies employed do not point to a specific, simple solution and clear destination, the process of solving problems might include innovation, risk-taking, and an investment in staff learning and communication.

Authentic Leadership

Authentic leadership focuses on leaders who are authentic, meaning that they act on their core values and sense of purpose to advance the organization. Northouse notes that "on the surface, authentic leadership appears easy to define. In actuality, it is a complex process that is difficult to characterize. Among leadership scholars, there is no single accepted definition of … [it]. Instead, there are multiple definitions, each written from a different viewpoint and with a different emphasis."[9] For this reason, any of the chapter authors who refer to this theory will explain how they interpret it.

Collaborative Leadership

Collaborative leadership, as the name implies, values collaboration among senior managers and throughout the organization, including members of teams or groups. Ibarra and Hansen explain collaborative leadership thus: "It's not enough for leaders to spot collaborative opportunities and attract the best talent to [take advantage of] them. They might also set the tone by being good collaborators themselves."[10] More specifically, "collaborative leadership is the capacity to engage people and groups outside one's formal control and inspire them to work toward common goals—despite differences in convictions, cultural values, and operating norms," according to them.[11] Collaborative leadership, in essence, works best for organizations engaged in innovation and creativity and working across units and with members outside the organization.

Contingency Theory of Leadership

Contingency theory stresses that no leadership theory or style is best for all situations and that effective leadership depends on a match of one's style to the right setting. In essence, the focus is on the leader and the situation in which that person functions. Situational theory centers more on the behaviors that the leader should adopt in given situations, whereas contingency theory, which takes a broader view, examines the relationship between leaders as well as task structure and position power. Such power involves the ability of leaders to influence the behavior, attitudes, and actions of others.

With contingency theory, organizations can change the performance of leaders as these individuals modify their personality and motivation pattern or as situation factors (e.g., the capabilities and behaviors of followers) change. Thus, leaders who are effective in one organization and at one time may be unsuccessful when transplanted to another situation or when the factors around them change. Further, according to the theory, task-oriented leaders are more effective in extremely favorable or unfavorable situations, whereas relationship-oriented leaders perform best in situations with intermediate favorability.

Emotional Intelligence

We regard emotional intelligence, which emerged in the late 1980s in the study of psychology, as a subtheory since transformational and other types of leaders practice it. Emotionally intelligent leaders regulate their display of emotions, and they communicate effectively with others in the pursuit of organizational goals. They influence how subordinates perceive them and develop effective leader–subordinate relationships. By managing conflict and encouraging supportive interactions with subordinates, they create a nurturing environment.

Entrepreneurial Leadership

Although much of the literature seems to view entrepreneurial leadership from the vantage point of a self-employed individual who creates a new venture or enterprise, this emerging theory can be applied in the not-for-profit sector and the ability of organizations to forge new partnerships that generate revenue and opportunities (e.g., those associated with e-commerce). Key attributes, for instance, are risk-taking, innovation, commitment to taking advantage of opportunities, and team-building skills. With the tight fiscal situation that libraries find themselves, entrepreneurial leadership involves repositioning libraries to compete successfully "in the information marketplace for new business, and for corporate, foundation, and federal investment."[12]

Innovation Leadership

This emerging theory encourages the development of leadership capability for organizations to be innovative and creative and to carry that capacity to fruition. Innovative leaders support innovation, and they challenge the status quo. They also instigate and steer innovation in their organization. Furthermore, they are obsessed with providing superior service to customers. They know how to mobilize their staff behind concrete initiatives, and they do not hesitate to coach innovation project teams personally.

Although research on this theory is only starting to emerge, it seems that adaptive capacity is a critical attribute, as is risk-taking, and that innovation must be accepted throughout the organization; innovation is not left to a single individual. If any of the chapter authors comment on this theory in the context of recovery from the economic recession of 2007–2009, they will clarify their use of the term.

Leader–Member Exchange Theory

Leader–member exchange theory (LMX) examines the interaction and relationship between supervisors and their subordinates. According to the theory, every leader has a unique, individual relationship with each follower, and each of these relationships differs in terms of the quality of the interactions. In essence, two groups of subordinates emerge: an in-group and an out-group. Which group the subordinates end up in determines the quality of the interaction and relationship leaders have with each follower.

The in-group comprises the most trusted individuals. Leaders turn to members of this group when they need something done quickly and correctly. They tend to give this group more attention and support and to provide group members with opportunities for challenging and interesting work. In-group members tend to exceed their formal job descriptions, be more satisfied with their jobs, and be promoted more often. On the other hand, members of the out-group find they are clearly defined by their job descriptions because they are perceived as less motivated or less competent. They also tend to have less direct interaction with the leader.

Path-Goal Theory of Leadership

The path-goal theory describes the way in which leaders assist subordinates in defining and accomplishing their goals. The theory helps leaders to increase the satisfaction and performance level of subordinates. Leaders clarify the path so subordinates know which way to go, remove roadblocks that prevent them from going there, and increase the rewards along the route. In clarifying the path, they may give direction. In removing roadblocks, they may scour the path or help the follower remove the bigger roadblocks. They may give occasional encouragement or offer rewards. The variation in approach depends on the situation, including, for instance, the follower's capability and motivation, as well as the difficulty of the job.

This theory encompasses four styles of leadership:

1. Supportive leadership, which works best when the work is stressful or boring, considers the needs of subordinates and creates a friendly working environment. It increases the self-esteem of subordinates and makes their job more interesting.
2. Directive leadership, which involves letting subordinates know what needs to be done and giving them appropriate guidance along the way. Through such leadership, subordinates receive schedules of specific work to be done at specific times. By telling them what they should be doing, rewards may be increased and role ambiguity decreased. This style may be used when tasks are unstructured and complex, and subordinates are inexperienced.
3. Participative leadership, which involves consultation with followers and taking their ideas into account when making decisions. This approach is best when the subordinates have expertise and their advice is both needed and they expect to be able to give it.
4. Achievement-oriented leadership, which means setting challenging goals, regarding both work and self-improvement. The leader shows faith in the capabilities of the follower to succeed. This approach is best when the task is complex.[13]

Resonant Leadership

Resonant leadership, a companion of emotional intelligence, addresses the renewal of managerial leaders—developing practices related to habits of the mind, body, and behavior that enable them to sustain resonance in the face of constant challenges. Those challenges may result "in a vicious cycle of stress, pressure, sacrifice, and dissonance" for such leaders.[14] Resonant leaders maintain a balance between giving to their organizations and taking care of themselves in the process.

Servant Leadership

Servant leadership places the needs of subordinates before those of the leader. The leader therefore becomes a servant, who is willing to sacrifice self-interest for the good of the group. Leaders listen to what others have to say and value their ideas. The desire to serve is the foundation for the desire to lead. Servant leadership has been criticized for giving rise to unresolved cases of individual goals and values conflicting with organizational goals and values, and resulting in organizational goals remaining unfulfilled owing to employees not giving the attention, priority, or urgency that such goals deserve.

Shared Leadership

This theory views leadership in an organization as broadly distributed throughout the organization and as not limited to the downward influence on subordinates. Shared leadership consists of four general components, each of which has subcomponents. These components are accountability, which consists of owning the consequences that are inherent in one's role and cannot be delegated; equity, which includes mutual recognition of the unique contribution of each individual; partnership, which involves a mutually respectful and trusting relationship among individuals who share a common goal; and ownership, which focuses on the personal commitment that an individual makes to carry out the organizational mission.[15]

Situational Leadership

According to situational leadership, managers use different leadership styles depending on the situation. They analyze the situation and apply the most appropriate leadership style. It is even possible that they may lead someone one way sometimes and other ways at other times.

Four leadership styles emerge from combinations of supportive and directive behavior: directing style, coaching style, supporting style, and delegating style. The directing style emphasizes control and close supervision of workers. The coaching style enables the leader to amplify on what the job entails and to solicit suggestions while still staying in control of the situation. The supporting style involves a team approach between the leader and subordinates with the leader supporting (rather than controlling) the subordinates. In the delegating style, the leader turns over responsibility to workers. The key for the successful situational leader is to know which of the four styles to use in a particular situation with particular people. The situational leader bases the choice of which leadership style to use on the competence and commitment of those being led rather than on the leader's usual or preferred style.

Team Leadership

Much work in academic and public libraries may occur within teams or groups. The effectiveness of that team or group can be judged within three contexts: (1) the quality of its results; (2) socialization or the extent to which members work interdependently; and (3) professional growth or the growth and well-being of its members. The more that staff work within a team or group context over time, the more important it is to view effectiveness as more than mere results.

J. Richard Hackman, an organizational psychologist at Harvard University, adds that effective teams meet five conditions and a set of questions for each condition. First, the team must be real and have clear boundaries and members who work in a coordinated way. Second, the team must have a compelling direction, one that is clear and complete, and operate in an efficient manner. Third, there must be an enabling structure and sufficient staffing. Once these three baseline conditions are met, the final two come into play, namely a supportive organizational context (i.e., a support system in place and any changes in the organization structure or support systems to improve the effectiveness of teams) and expert coaching (e.g., assistance regarding the development of effort, knowledge-based skills, and performance strategies).[16]

Susan E. Kogler Hill adds a new dimension to effective teams when she underscores the importance of leadership. She introduces a model that connects internal and external leadership actions to leadership decisions and team effectiveness.[17]

Transactional Leadership

In transactional leadership, the leader motivates subordinates by appealing to their self-interest and establishes a series of transactions or exchanges to accomplish goals. Leaders and subordinates do not seek opportunities to advance joint efforts or collective interests, but rather they bargain to advance individual interests. There are four types of transactional leadership: laissez-faire, passive management-by-exception, active management-by-exception, and contingent reward. A laissez-faire relationship really represents the absence of leadership, since leaders do not take a stand on issues, do not follow employee performance, and do not appear to care if the organization, or a part of it, meets its goals. In passive management-by-exception, the leader uses corrective action and punishment when errors occur. The leader only becomes involved when a mistake is found. In contrast, active management-by-exception, the leader actively monitors subordinates, sets standards, and uses corrective action to address work concerns. Although more involved in the unit of the organization, the leader emphasizes negative rather than positive behavior. In contingent reward, the leader delineates expectations and uses rewards to recognize accomplishments. In this more positive approach, the leader actively monitors performance and looks for positive results to reward.

Transformational Leadership

In contrast to transactional leadership, transformational leadership unites the leader and subordinates in the pursuit of common goals. The leader may assume a teaching role in order to shape, alter, and raise the values and goals of subordinates. Key behaviors of transformational leadership that motivate subordinates to transcend self-interests, promote staff morale, and promote higher achievement are individualized consideration, intellectual stimulation, inspirational motivation, and idealized influence. Individualized consideration refers to the compassionate leader who cares about subordinates and maintains personal contact with them. Intellectual stimulation is a behavior that leads to creative thinking and encourages risk-taking. Inspirational motivation involves a clarification of the mission and vision as needed and inspiring others to achieve more than they thought they could do. Idealized influence ensures that actions match the vision. Leaders develop trust among subordinates, who in turn exhibit great commitment to the organization, its mission, and its vision.

Summary

None of these theories is completely independent of the others, and some such as emotionally intelligence have evolved into new theories such as social intelligence, which refers to the human capacity to navigate and negotiate complex social relationships effectively. Still, the attributes associated with emotional intelligence apply to the management of complex organizations. After all, managerial leaders need to recognize their feelings and those of others, manage emotions in themselves and in their relationships with others, and motivate themselves and others.

Joan R. Giesecke notes that

one challenge in leadership theory is to find ways to bring the leadership theories together in models that can be used to describe a wide range of actions. Many models distinguish leadership theories by looking at leaders concern for performance or tasks versus the leaders concern for followers. These models are used to argue that leadership is most effective when leaders are concerned about both tasks and people.[18]

"Another way to look at leadership models," she explains, "is to look at how power is distributed. When power is viewed as the core of the relationship among leaders and followers as the influencing factor in the theory, then power can be used to distinguish the different theories." She also points out that "adding in the level of concern by the leader for the followers and by the followers for the leader can further differentiate the leadership theories."[19]

However, in this context, it is important to emphasize that the different theories on leadership are not mutually exclusive. They differ in approach and each gives a unique perspective on the specific situation. Insight into the different theories and leadership models will help leaders, managers, and staff members to build a more reflective approach to many organizational problems and will also provide them with a valuable understanding of factors that shape the single organization.

LEADERSHIP ATTRIBUTES

Numerous leadership theorists and researchers suggest assorted attributes that leaders, alone or in combination with the senior management team, should possess. Among these are adaptive capacity, strong communication skills combined with active listening, the ability to motivate or influence others, trustworthiness, displaying good judgment on a consistent basis, the ability to benefit from criticism, integrity, having a vision, and honesty. Managerial leaders should possess key attributes associated with emotional intelligence,[20] and they should also have good organizational development skills, the ability to identify and analyze problems, and the skills associated with problem solving. Problem solving involves the application of evaluation and assessment research to the planning process and decision making. In a study of 25 different societies around the world, Jagdeep S. Chhokar, Felix C. Brodbeck, and Robert J. House identify other key attributes; given the particular society, some are more important than others.[21]

THE CONCEPT OF NATIONAL CULTURE

A major study that compares national cultures is *Culture, Leadership, and Organizations*, which is based on the Global Leadership and Organizational Behavior Effectiveness Research Program (GLOBE). Its authors cover selected European countries but do not consider specific leadership theories, disciplines, or fields of study.[22] They conclude that some countries (e.g., the United States) romanticize leadership, examine its impact, and equate leadership with status, whereas, in other countries, there is skepticism about leaders and a concern that they will accumulate and abuse power. Such a characterization is simplistic. More germane to this book is their focus on culture; House et al. provide a relevant framework for a multi-country comparison. They view culture as consisting of two factors:

1. Practices or "the way things are done in the culture;" and
2. Values or "judgments about 'the way things should be done'."[23]

They define culture as "shared motives, values, beliefs, identities, and interpretations or meanings of significant events that result from common experiences of members of collectives that are transmitted across generations."[24] GLOBE operationalizes this definition by means of indicators that reflect cultural manifestations of the extent of agreement among different societies with respect to the psychological attributes contained in the definition and to factors such as economic and legal systems, political institutions, and work organizations. In essence, GLOBE compares societies on cultural dimensions that have cross-cultural validity.

House et al. discuss culturally implicit leadership behaviors (e.g., charismatic/value-based and team-oriented behaviors) and cultural constructs (e.g., assertiveness, future orientation, performance orientation [innovation], and gender egalitarianism). Not surprisingly they note differences in cultural influences among different countries. In essence, they create the impression that a country does not contain different, significant cultures.

GLOBE documents similarities and differences among national cultures, and the Management Research Group® shows that "in Europe, country culture heavily influences leadership style, approach, and expectations."[25] Cheryl A. Metoyer points out that in the United States, "leadership in American Indian communities then and now is rooted in culture. Leadership as a cultural activity has been and continues to be a powerful force in shaping tribal communities." Further, she points out that "the designation of 'American leadership' does not account for possible differences represented by culturally diverse leaders in America."[26] "This distorted view," she indicates

> is evident in Bernard Bass and Ralph Stogdill's limited and erroneous discussion of leadership and American Indians. In the 1990 third edition [*Handbook of Leadership: Theory, Research, & Managerial Applications* (The Free Press)], the authors wrote, "Little can be said about this country's most impoverished minority, whose members are undereducated and live mainly under tribal councils that discourage participatory democracy and collaborate with state bureaucracies to maintain the status quo." The leadership of their many famous chiefs of the past is only a memory.[27]

The quotations from the Metoyer article are important for three reasons: (1) they reinforce a focus on culture; (2) they indicate that the United States and probably other countries as well have more than one significant culture; and (3) prevailing leadership theories and styles may not apply across all cultures. Linda Warner and Keith Grint's study of American Indians supports Metoyer's perspective as well as reinforces that the prevailing theories and styles have limitations.[28] There is a need for a more complex understanding of leadership and the role of culture as a critical component. This book recognizes that more than one national culture exists but addresses the issue from the perspective of library and information science and the existing body of research.

Northouse identifies other weaknesses to the GLOBE approach. Among these are:

- The "research does not provide a clear set of assumptions and propositions that can form a single theory about the way culture relates to leadership or influences the leadership process;"
- Leadership is viewed as "what people perceive to be leadership and [the research] ignores a larger body of research that frames leadership in terms of what leaders do (e.g., transformational leadership, path-goal theory, ... [and so on]."[29]

Any discussion of national cultures would be incomplete without mention of the Dutch sociologist Geert Hofstede, whose groundbreaking work on cultural differences appears to be especially relevant to organizational management.[30] His detailed analysis operates on several levels, from the individual to country. Furthermore, his theory is based on national characteristics, and it is important to emphasize that he warns against generalizations or stereotyping. In the single country, there exists diversity based on social class, gender, educational level, and other background factors.

Hofstede introduces the idea of a shared set of values held by a society. These values result in behavioral patterns. He further defines culture as "the collective programming of the mind which distinguishes the member of one group or category of people from another." Hofstede sees the following dimensions for categorizing values and behavior:

- *Power distance.* Many western countries have a small power distance, which means that equality, decentralization, and democracy are appreciated values, whereas submission, centralization, and hierarchy have less appeal.

- *Collectivism vs. individualism.* The collectivist emphasizes organizational harmony, employee loyalty, and identity to a group. The individualist, on the other hand, stresses honesty and truth more than harmony and loyalty, and everyone has his or her own identity.

- *Masculinity versus femininity.* This dimension reflects a societal preference for competition and achievement, heroism, assertiveness, and material reward for success (masculinity). Femininity stands for a preference for cooperation, modesty, caring for the weak, and quality of life. Society is consensus-oriented.

- *Uncertainty avoidance.* This is the extent to which members of a society feel uncomfortable with uncertainty and ambiguity. Furthermore, this dimension distinguishes between weak and strong uncertainty avoidance. If someone possess weak uncertainty avoidance, that person seeks to thrive on chaos, which is understood as, for example, fast and discontinuous change, unstructured and muddy situations, action on insufficient information, few or no riles, unknown risks, and basic uncertainty.[31]

- *Long-term orientation.* This dimension deals with society's search for virtue. Societies with a short-term orientation generally have a strong concern with establishing truth. They respect traditions and a focus on achieving quick results. In societies with a long-term orientation, people believe that truth depends on the situation and context. There is an ability to adapt traditions to changed conditions, a strong propensity to save and invest, and perseverance in achieving results.

Later, another dimension, indulgence versus restraint, was added; indulgence stands for a society that allows relatively free gratification of basic and natural human drives related to enjoying life. Restraint stands for a society that suppresses gratification of needs and regulates it by means of social norms.[32]

Hofstede's theory has many similarities to a model forwarded by Fons Trompenaars and Charles Hampden-Turner.[33] They identified seven cultural dimensions, several of which are similar to Hofstede's dimensions. It is probably fair to state that the perspectives on the ways to identify the essentials of national culture do not differ very much. Both approaches are based on a belief that culture consists of values and preferred behavior related to the values.

It merits mention that Golnaz Sadri, Todd J. Weber, and William A. Gentry probed empathy, a basic quality associated with leadership that enables leaders to share emotions with others. They concluded that power distance is "a significant cross-level moderator of the relationship between empathic emotion and performance." In essence, empathy is "an important international leadership behavior" that subordinates prize.[34]

It appears that ranking cultures using Hofstede's classification is similar to ranking countries based on social capital and trust, which are concepts central to leadership and organizational change. Social capital, an elusive concept, has been a popular topic in the literature of the social sciences for the last couple of decades.[35] This is not the place to discuss the concept in detail; it suffices to say that relevant literature comes from economics, political science, and sociology. Economists tend to view it as a feature that can decrease economic transaction costs because of the inherent trust among the actors, whereas other social scientists see the concept in relation to the development of common norms in different types of group settings.

Trust is normally examined through the use of questionnaires that measure an individual's trust in relation to other individuals and to public institutions. Investigations into general and institutional trust are not directly related to other strands of research into cultural differences among nations and subgroups in nations.[36] Several studies using the same methodology have ranked countries based on the amount of trust, which is measured in relation to a general interpretation of the concept and to different social institutions such as the legal and political system.[37] Trust is gauged therefore in terms of generalized trust and institutional trust. Trust is also an indicator of the coherence of the society and the cohesiveness of the different parts of society. In this way, trust is closely connected to value systems, norms, and behavior in a society, and it implies reciprocity. Reciprocity means that people trust each other and that a dominant value and behavior are that nobody cheats and receives, for example, welfare benefits if they are able to provide for themselves. In the same way, institutional trust is shaped by the same type of rules. We have to believe that public institutions work for the common good in a legal and efficient way according to societal values.

Trust, however, can take negative forms. Too much of it in a group and too much cohesiveness in a group cause a group to close its boundaries, excluding others, and, in that way, contribute to an overall decrease in general trust.

It is evident that culture consists of many factors that are shared by nations and by social groups, and that these factors serve as guidelines for behavior and the interpretation of the environment and human interrelationships. At the very least, the concept of culture consists of both values and norms, including basic assumptions that affect behavior.

Table 1.1 is derived from Hofstede's dimensions and the ranking from the surveys of values and trust in different countries. In the original tables, Hofstede reports on 74 participating countries and describes the results in terms of specific dimensions, whereas the World Values Survey, which explores people's values and beliefs, how they change over time, and what social and political impact they have, ranks 86 countries.[38]

Table 1.1   Ranking according to Hofstede and SoCap*

COUNTRY	POWER DISTANCE	INDIVID- UALISM	MASCULINITY	INSECURITY AVOIDANCE	GENERAL TRUST
United Kingdom	64	3	12	67	21
Canada	60	5	33	61	7
Australia	62	2	20	56	8
Netherlands	61	6	72	53	5
Belgium	40	8	21	10	28
Denmark	51	9	51	51	1

*This table was created by compiling data that appeared in different tables in Geert Hofstede, *Culture and Organisations: Software of the Mind* (London: McGraw-Hill, 1991) and Tinggaard Gert Svendsen and Gunnar Lind Haase Svendsen, *Social Kapital: En Introduktion* (Copenhagen: Hans Reitzel, 2006).

KEY LITERATURE

The leadership literature, in general and in library and information science, tends to focus on the topic from the perspective of one country. In Europe, however, there are some exceptions that offer limited comparisons across countries, or, as various writers explain, comparisons among cultures. GLOBE surveyed approximately 17,000 managers from 951 organizations in 62 countries.[39] On a smaller scale, the Management Research Group® compares the leadership style of 4,000 managers in both the private and public sectors "(from first line department supervisors to company president) in eight European countries," using the Leadership Effectiveness Analysis™ questionnaire. That instrument measures 22 leadership practices, the role of vision in the organization, and orientation toward achieving results.[40] On the other hand, Dynamic Learning Inc. (Halifax, Nova Scotia) provides the Leadership Effectiveness Analysis (LEA) 360°™ (http://www.dynamiclearning. ca/courses/gov_leadershipeffectiveness.html), which examines the approach of managers to leadership (actual behavior as opposed to personality variables or traits). This instrument contains 84 questions, which gauge a person's current leadership role.

In *Making a Difference*, Peter Hernon and Nancy Rossiter review the literature on leadership, and in *Shaping the Future*, Hernon updates that review through 2009.[41] Niels Ole Pors documents the development of a survey instrument to monitor the practice of management and leadership in Denmark and the rest of Scandinavia. This instrument can be applied to other countries as well. He notes a gender difference regarding the perception of future challenges and job requirements, and he shows that organizational culture influences leadership:

> Leadership is an important element in the configuration of organisational culture and both leadership styles and the leaders' approach to innovation, change, and competency development are of importance in relation to the directions of the organisation. Leaders are both part of an organisational

culture but they also have the possibility to act as change agents . . . within the culture. The relationship between leadership priorities and organisational culture is important.[42]

Only a few studies compare library leaders and directors in different countries. One of these studies uses Hofstede's concepts and compares Danish and British library leaders and managers.[43] This research, which centers on the employment of management tools or organizational recipes (see Chapter 9), indicates different preferences for tools. British libraries employ tools and organizational recipes (solutions for resolving problems) much more than do Danish libraries, and the management tools British leaders and managers prefer are much "harder" than the "softer" and more human-oriented management tools preferred in Denmark.

Different countries implement management tools and approaches to problem solving in different ways. National culture can probably offer a tentative explanation for many of the variations observed. The concept of national culture could provide an explanation for the way that new ideological movements, such as reinventing government and new public management, are implemented as institutional imperatives in different countries.[44] The culture of evaluation and assessment is much more pervasive in the United Kingdom than it is in Denmark. Such a culture is something that permeates the organizational culture and the beliefs and assumptions embedded therein.

Based on the nature of the culture of evaluation and assessment in Britain, an assumption is that institutional imperatives are stronger in the United Kingdom. Evaluation and assessment tools and strategic managerial approaches are more embedded in the culture of organizations. The differences in discourse and in tools employed probably are related to differences in national culture. The leader's position in relation to the cross-pressure between institutional imperatives and freedom of decisions and actions also plays a role, at least regarding factors such as the sense of job security, workload, and well-being at the job. This is also part of organizational culture, which is important as a zone of acceptance in relation to which tools and managerial approaches are conceivable and legitimate in a given institution. Another culture-related finding in the study is that job satisfaction among leaders was significantly higher in Denmark owing to the perception of a higher degree of freedom in the job.

Another study, based on 30 interviews with library directors and leaders from Ireland, the United Kingdom, and the United States, explores perceptions on different leadership issues.[45] The authors of this qualitative study emphasize the limitations owing to the small number of respondents. However, several interesting and important results emerge from the research. Overall, leaders are the most important factor in shaping and changing the organizational culture; the research indicates differences in this perception based on country. This perception is lowest in the United Kingdom, and it was hypothesized that this is connected to the more bureaucratic organizational structure there. Most of the respondents also agree with the statement that leaders are the most important and determining factor for the success of the organization.

In 2007, *Library Management* published a special issue focusing on eight library directors who describe their changing jobs and the challenges they faced. Most of the job changes involved moving from one country to another (e.g., Australia,

Canada, and the United Kingdom), and most of the professional moves described are between the United Kingdom, Canada, and Australia. Since these countries do not differ much in their value systems, moves among these countries probably do not raise huge cultural problems. There are, of course, differences in legislative systems, the status of professions, institutional traditions, and use of the English language. The articles also reflect that the cultural differences are much more complicated when one takes a position in a country with a very different value system.[46]

Some of the articles in that issue of *Library Management* discuss the relationship among national values, behavior, and organizational culture. It seems that organizational culture tends to correlate with the national culture and the dominant structures of organizations. There may also be a correlation between the value system in a country and the preferred ways to structure organizations.

Susan McKnight, one of the authors in that issue, emphasizes the problem of language differences even where there are insignificant differences in dialects. The main challenges for "an expatriate senior manager," a manager who has moved to a new organization but in another country, associated with a new culture, she thinks, are "national stereotypes, understanding the organisational environment and, importantly, understanding yourself and how your behaviours and attitudes can influence those around you."[47] Further, local differences and the organizational culture, she emphasizes, are important to note.

CONCLUDING THOUGHTS

Leadership has gained the attention of researchers and scholars worldwide. This statement is perhaps less true in library and information science, where the number of those engaged in research on the subject is much less than in other disciplines and fields. Some of the writings do not distinguish between management and leadership, and leadership seems to represent more of a future expectation for managerial leaders than it has in the past. Given the types of challenges identified in Figure 1.1, leadership is something that cannot be neglected. Complicating matters, leadership is a complex process having multiple dimensions, and there are varying expectations of leaders in different countries, one of which is the extent to which leaders are expected to engage in donor relations. Furthermore, a number of writings on leadership romanticize the topic of leadership and attribute organizational success to the effectiveness of the leaders and organizational failures to the ineffectiveness of leadership.[48] Clearly, such depictions are simplistic and fail to appreciate the complexity of leadership as a set of both theories and styles and their practical application in organizations.

Some managers have formal positions as leaders, but many managers have more operational responsibilities such as head of a department or team; and it would be beneficial if they were able to place their work in a broader context. In general, they are the people who are responsible for implementing the changes that often follow leadership initiatives.

In professional, expert-driven organizations, it is necessary that academic professionals identify with the vision and change processes and ideas put in place. If they are unable to relate to new ideas, different types of resistance can occur with unfortunate results. Communicating in a respectful way with staff is necessary. The communication process becomes more fruitful if staff members know about the conditions, obligations, and responsibilities of leadership, including the limitations and constraints under which leaders operate.

Finally, as this chapter illustrates, there is a need for the literature of library and information science to explore national culture as a part of leadership and to broaden the discussion and comparison of leadership across countries. In the case of this book, the focus is on the United States and Europe.

NOTES

1. Peter G. Northouse, *Leadership: Theory and Practice*, 6th ed. (Thousand Oaks, CA: Sage, 2013), 8.

2. *Oxford English Dictionary* (Oxford University Press, 2010), a subscription data base, http://www.oxforddictionaries.com.

3. Northouse, *Leadership*, 3.

4. Robert J. House, Paul J. Hanges, Mansour Javidan, Peter W. Dorfman, and Vipin Gupta, *Culture, Leadership, and Organizations* (Thousand Oaks, CA: Sage, 2004), 15.

5. "Peter Senge and the Learning Organization," http://www.infed.org/thinkers/senge.htm (accessed May 20, 2011).

6. See, for instance, Paul Hersey, Kenneth H. Blanchard, and Dewey E. Johnson, *Management of Organizational Behavior: Leading Human Resources*, 9th ed. (Upper Saddle River, NJ: Prentice-Hall, 2008).

7. Barbara Kellerman, *Bad Leadership: What It Is, How It Happens, and Why It Matters* (Boston: Harvard Business School Press, 2004).

8. See Ronald A. Heifetz, Marty Linsky, and Alexander Grashow, *The Practice of Adaptive Leadership: Tools and Tactics for Changing Your Organization and the World* (Boston: Harvard Business School Press, 2009).

9. Northouse, *Leadership*, 254.

10. Herminia Ibarra and Morton T. Hansen, "Are You a Collaborative Leader?" *Harvard Business Review* 89, no. 7–8 (2011): 72.

11. Ibarra and Hansen, "Are You a Collaborative Leader?" 73.

12. James G. Neal, "The Entrepreneurial Imperative Advancing from Incremental to Radical Change in the Academic Library," *portal: Libraries and the Academy* 1, no. 1 (2000): 2.

13. Robert J. House, "A Path-Goal Theory of Leadership Effectiveness," *Administrative Science Quarterly* 16, no. 3 (1971): 321–38.

14. Richard Boyatzis and Annie McKee, *Resonant Leadership: Renewing Yourself and Connecting with Others through Mindfulness, Hope, and Compassion* (Boston: Harvard Business School Press, 2005), 9. See also Annie McKee, Frances Johnston, and Richard Massimilian, "Mindfulness, Hope, and Compassion: A Leader's Road Map to Renewal," *Ivey Business Journal* 70, no. 5 (2006): 1–5.

15. Sandra Jackson, "A Qualitative Evaluation of the Shared Leadership Barriers, Drivers, and Recommendations," *Journal of Management in Medicine* 14, nos. 3–4 (2000): 169.

16. J. Richard Hackman, *Leading Teams: Setting the Stage for Great Performances* (Boston: Harvard Business School Press, 2002). See also J. Richard Hackman and Richard E. Walton, "Leading Groups in Organizations," in *Designing Effective Work Groups*, edited by P. S. Goodman and Associates (San Francisco: Jossey-Bass, 1986), 72–119.

17. Susan E. Kogler Hill, "Team Leadership," in Northouse, *Leadership*, 244.

18. Joan R. Giesecke, "Modeling Leadership Theories," in *Making a Difference: Leadership and Academic Libraries*, edited by Peter Hernon and Nancy Rossiter (Westport, CT: Libraries Unlimited, 2007), 56.

19. Giesecke, "Modeling Leadership Theories," 56–57.

20. Daniel Goleman, *Emotional Intelligence* (New York: Bantam Books, 1995), 317. For an identification of the relevant attributes, see Peter Hernon, Joan Giesecke, and

Camila A. Alire, *Academic Librarians as Emotionally Intelligent Leaders* (Westport, CT: Libraries Unlimited, 2007). For a discussion of other attributes, see Peter Hernon, ed., *Shaping the Future: Advancing the Understanding of Leadership* (Santa Barbara, CA: Libraries Unlimited, 2010).

21. Jagdeep S. Chhokar, Felix C. Brodbeck, and Robert J. House, eds., *Culture and Leadership across the World* (Mahwah, NJ: Lawrence Erlbaum Associates, 2008).

22. House et al., *Culture, Leadership, and Organizations.*

23. House et al., *Culture, Leadership, and Organizations,* xv.

24. House et al., *Culture, Leadership, and Organizations,* 15. See also Chhokar, Brodbeck, and House, *Culture and Leadership across the World.*

25. Helen Peters and Robert Kabacoff, "GLOBAL or LOCAL: The Impact of Country Culture on Leadership Style in Europe" (Dublin, Ireland: Management Research Group®, 2010), 7, http://www.mrg.com/documents/Euro_Culture.pdf (accessed May 22, 2011).

26. Cheryl A. Metoyer, "Leadership in American Indian Communities: Winter Lessons," *American Indian Culture and Research Journal* 34, no. 4 (2010), 10.

27. Metoyer, "Leadership in American Indian Communities," 2.

28. Linda Warner and Keith Grint, "American Indian Ways of Leading and Knowing," *Leadership* 2, no. 2 (2006): 225–44.

29. Northouse, *Leadership,* 359–60.

30. Geert Hofstede, *Culture's Consequences: International Differences in Work-Related Values* (London: Sage, 1981); Geert Hofstede, *Culture and Organisations: Software of the Mind* (London: McGraw-Hill, 1991).

31. Geert Hofstede, "The Influence of Organisational Culture on Business," http://geert-hofstede.com/organisational-culture.html (accessed May 28, 2012). For a list of publications of Geert Hofstede, see http://geert-hofstede.com/publications.html (accessed June 11, 2012).

32. Hofstede, "Influence of Organisational Culture;" Grovewell LLC, "Leadership Style Variations across Cultures: Overview of GLOBE Research Findings" (2005), http://www.grovewell.com/pub-GLOBE-leadership.html (accessed May 29, 2012).

33. Fons Trompenaars and Charles Hampden-Turner, *Riding the Waves of Culture: Understanding Cultural Diversity in Business* (London: McGraw-Hill, 1997).

34. Golnaz Sadri, Todd J. Weber, and William A. Gentry, "Empathic Emotion and Leadership Performance: An Empirical Analysis across 38 Countries," *Leadership Quarterly* 22 (2011): 818.

35. Gert Tinggaard Svendsen and Gunnar Lind Haase Svendsen, *Social Kapital: En Introduktion* (Copenhagen: Hans Reitzel, 2006).

36. Ronald Inglehart and Wayne E Baker, "Modernization, Cultural Change and the Persistence of Traditional Values," *American Sociological Review* 65, no. 1 (2000): 19–51.

37. Stephan Dahl, "Intercultural Research: The Current State of Knowledge," Middlesex University Discussion Paper no. 26 (January 12, 2004), http://www.alanisguzman.com/archivos/Culture.pdf (accessed July 21, 2011).

38. See, for instance, World Values Survey, http://www.worldvaluessurvey.org/ (accessed May 19, 2012).

39. House et al., *Culture, Leadership, and Organizations.*

40. See Management Research Group®, Management & Leadership Development, http://www.mrg.com/Solutions/Management.asp (accessed May 19, 2012).

41. Peter Hernon and Nancy Rossiter, *Making a Difference: Leadership and Academic Libraries* (Westport, CT: Libraries Unlimited, 2007), chapters 3 and 6; Hernon, *Shaping the Future.*

42. Niels Ole Pors, "Management Tools, Organisational Culture, and Leadership: An Exploratory Study," *Performance Measurement and Metrics* 9, no. 2 (2008): 143. See also Niels Ole Pors, "Dimensions of Leadership and Service Quality: The Human Aspect in Performance Measurement," in *Proceedings of the Fourth Northumbrian International Conference on Performance Measurement in Libraries and Information Services: Meaningful*

Measures for Emerging Realities, edited by Joan Stein, Martha Kyrillidou, and Denise Davis (Washington, DC: Association of Research Libraries, 2002), 245–53.

43. Niels Ole Pors, Pat Dixon, and Heather Robson, "The Employment of Quality Measures in Libraries: Cultural Differences, Institutional Imperatives and Managerial Profiles," *Performance Measurement and Metrics* 5, no. 1 (2004): 20–28.

44. John Mullins and Margaret Linehan, "The Central Role of Leaders in Public Libraries," *Library Management* 26, nos. 6–7 (2005): 386–93; Tauno Kekäle and Jouni Kekäle, "A Mismatch of Cultures: A Pitfall of Implementing a Total Quality Approach," *International Journal of Quality and Reliability Management* 12, no. 9 (1995): 210–20.

45. Brian P. Mathews, Akiko Ueno, Tauno Kekäle, Mikko Repka, Zulema Lopes Pereira, and Graça Silva, "European Quality Management Practices: The Impact of National Culture," *International Journal of Quality and Reliability Management* 18, no. 7 (2001): 692–707.

46. Niels Ole Pors, "Globalisation, Culture and Social Capital: Library Professionals on the Move," *Library Management* 28, nos. 4–5 (2007): 181–90.

47. Susan McKnight, "The Expatriate Library Director," *Library Management* 28, nos. 4–5 (2007): 231–41.

48. Michelle C. Bligh, Jeffrey C. Kohles, and Rajnandini Pillai, "Romancing Leadership: Past, Present, and Future," *Leadership Quarterly* 22, no. 6 (2011): 1058.

Part II

OVERVIEW OF LEADERSHIP IN THE UNITED STATES AND EUROPE

2

LIBRARY LEADERSHIP IN
THE UNITED STATES

Peter Hernon

As Joan Giesecke explains, "to change from collection-centric to user-centered . . . libraries and to survive in tough economic times, libraries face . . . [two] major challenges." First, their constituents must regard them "as indispensable," and, second, library staff must "change their own mental models of their roles to remain relevant in these changing times." Resolving both these challenges will require effective leadership and, she advises, new ways to envision libraries and "seek connections that will help people see libraries as something other than warehouses for books."[1] She recommends the use of metaphors that reflect new ideas. After all, "librarians have been using metaphors to describe libraries and librarians since the modern library movement began in the late 19th century." Some of the more recent metaphors that reflect shifts within libraries include feral professionals, members of the workforce who do not have a master's or any degree in library and information science (LIS);[2] "libraries without walls," which emphasizes digital access to collections; and "embedded librarians," which involves shifting librarians from desks within the library to outside computer laboratories and working with faculty on research and teaching teams. The goal is to develop partnerships and relationships and to view the library system as a set of relationships. Metaphors therefore can be used to depict a service vision to guide the organization, and managerial leaders can enact leadership practices to work toward the accomplishment of that vision.

Any metaphors must show the transformation of libraries from the past to the future. As Karin Wittenborg argues, the biggest challenge for libraries today is to be "open to change, rapid change." She continues, "We need to be ready to serve the fast-changing needs and demands of today's—and tomorrow's—students and faculty [for public and other libraries there are other communities]. The comfortable, predictable routines are gone. The only routine now is change, and if you're going to survive, you need to learn how to thrive in it."[3] Change and managing that change involve leadership.

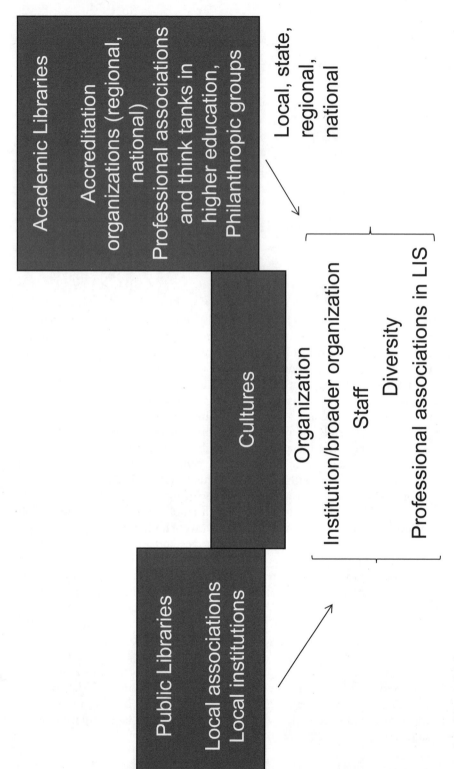

Figure 2.1: Types of Cultures

CULTURES

As discussed in Chapter 1, a national culture is one of many types of cultures with which academic and public libraries deal. Figure 2.1 indicates that both academic and public libraries encounter cultures within the organization, the broader organization or institution, and professional associations, some of which focus on a particular type of library. Academic and public libraries also deal with other cultures as depicted in the figure.

At the organizational level, organizational culture represents a common set of beliefs, assumptions, behaviors, and attributes that are established and agreed on, but they still evolve over time. As Edgar H. Schein states,

> A culture contains components such as mental models, shared habits of thinking and cognitive frames that guide perceptions and thoughts, and the language that members of the organization use; metaphors; rules, the implicit and unwritten rules and assumptions of how things occur in the organization, and these rules are conveyed to new members to assist in orienting to the culture; and formal rituals, the celebrations that reflect the important values that the organization recognizes and deems important.[4]

The literature might approach cultures from the perspective of global leadership, which involves the capacity to function across national cultures and forge a vision that will motivate others around that single vision. Global leaders are team-oriented and forward-looking. Commenting on leaders in business and industry, Nancy Rossiter points out that "the idea of a leader can be culturally embedded." A leader in a U.S. organization "takes . . . [that] organization to new levels of performance, achieving impressive short-term goals, and spinning the organization off to the highest bidder." In contrast, leaders in France, for instance, reach their "position owing to their national examination scores, the schools they attend, and their roles in national networks."[5] At any rate, global leadership pays attention to intelligence such as that associated with emotional and cultural intelligence. Rossiter discusses the history and use of the term *cultural intelligence*.

Library directors may assume a global position when the universities to which they are affiliated have campuses in other countries and the libraries in these locations are under their management. They may be leaders on both the main and satellite campuses. Through international, professional organizations, they (and others) might assume leadership positions, or they might engage in global collaboration. Furthermore, issues such as those associated with scholarly communications most likely have an international component and leaders need to understand key issues and guide the profession to their resolution. Global leadership, as a result, includes information policy and the ability to influence government and other policies on a national or an international basis.

MINORITY LEADERSHIP

When library directors are asked to define leadership, they often mention having a vision around which to motivate staff—followers. As explained in Chapter 1, Native Americans, when they reflect on their culture and life within their communities, associate leadership with a special set of attributes, including, for instance, spirituality, demonstrating generosity and kindness, honoring all living things, and being humble servants to the community, which might cease to follow them. When tribal leaders meet to deliberate on a matter, they seek understanding and consensus through mutual inquiry. As a result, when a library director, for instance, heads a tribal organization, that person practices the cultural view of leadership revolving around respect for elders. If that director is in charge of a nontribal library, then other types of leadership would be practiced.

In her study of African American women who direct academic research libraries, Sharon K. Epps adds that the skill set for successful leaders in academia, be they from minority or nonminority racial groups, need not differ. Leaders from both groups, for instance, need experience in donor relations. Nonetheless, African American women, and presumably other minority directors, "may need additional attributes or more of certain attributes in order to overcome negative stereotypes and successfully navigate invisible barriers in the work environment."[6] It merits mention that, for some types of libraries, women are no longer in the minority as directors. The best example is the set of libraries whose institutions have membership in the Association of Research Libraries; more than half of the directors are now women.

The Epps study also serves as a reminder that a commitment to diversity involves more that the recruitment of individuals to the profession. It is important to create an organizational culture that values diversity and ensures that everyone has and demonstrates respect for the views and experiences of others, as well as to retain and promote talented individuals. "For . . . [these leaders] to be successful, they need experience and opportunities to learn and grow. Minority leaders need the opportunity to 'sit at the table'."[7] Leadership development is critical to the success of future library directors and other members of the senior management team. At the same time, there must be efforts to move leadership development down the organization.

Camila Alire issues an important reminder: "Minorities themselves view differences between white and minority leadership. These include factors such as a two-pronged leadership agenda, dispelling stereotypes, and proof of self."[8] Amplifying on these differences, she notes that "White leaders perceive themselves as leading all followers no matter who they are. Minority leaders assume that same position but also assume the additional responsibility of identifying and developing emerging minority leaders."[9]

Although they do not address libraries, Sylvia A. Hewlett, Carolyn B. Luce, and Cornell West emphasize "that the lives of minority professionals are rich with experience that goes unleveraged by their employers." However, their "lives remain invisible largely by choice." For many reasons, "minority professionals are reluctant to speak of their outside pursuits and accomplishments to colleagues and managers."[10] In essence, they may operate "under the radar."[11] The issue is to determine whether this situation applies to libraries and, if it does, which of those experiences apply to organizational change and how to take advantage of those experiences. Furthermore, are there hidden biases in a library's organizational cultures, and, if there are, how might they be prevented from retarding the development of leadership talent? As Hewlett, Luce, and West remind us, "think of the extraordinary energy and purpose that will be released when minority professionals are finally able to speak openly and proudly of their lives, their core values, and their skills. It might well be transformative—of individuals, of companies, and of society."[12]

LEADERSHIP CHALLENGES

Figure 1.1 characterizes the types of challenges that academic and public libraries face as reflected in the literature of LIS. The recent economic recession and its aftermath have led to a number of academic and public libraries entering a sustained period of budget cuts that are likely to last for the next three to five years, or perhaps even longer. These libraries are searching for the proper balance in expenditures in their infrastructure (facilities, collections, information technologies, and staffing).

Some communities that are or are not undergoing financial stress have outsourced library services or privatized public libraries. Library Systems & Services, a for-profit company in Maryland, provides management services for 14 library systems and 63 branch libraries. The services seem to focus on cost-cutting. For instance, the biggest expense for any library is the staff, their salaries and benefits (e.g., pension plans and health care coverage). By releasing staff and trimming hours of operation, cost savings occur. Because economic efficiency is clearly of great concern in the management of a company, the focus is more on management than leadership. In fact, leadership may be marginalized; however, the outsourcing of public library services and the privatization of public libraries themselves merits investigation. Service may be more reactive to the demands of the public and far less anticipating future information needs and information-seeking behavior.

Some libraries are using the tight fiscal situation to redefine their role and develop new services to meet new and changing information needs. As James G. Neal explains,

> Academic libraries are assuming new roles as traditional boundaries shift. Libraries are learning how to be better consumers, often negotiating and licensing content and software collectively. Libraries are aggressive intermediaries and aggregators of information, and, as publishers, are creating new innovative modes of scholarly communication. . . . Libraries are more entrepreneurial organizations, more concerned with innovation, business planning, competition and risk, leveraging assets through new partnerships to produce new financial resources.[13]

At the same time, some research university libraries are reconfiguring their reference departments and having reference librarians interact with faculty and students outside the library. These libraries have seen a 70–80 percent decline in the number of questions that people ask by approaching the physical desk. The concept of reference service as described by Samuel Rothstein is definitely changing. These libraries do not merely provide "personal assistance to readers in search of information." They may play a preservation role for data sets generated as part of federal grants as they expand on their responsibility and the specific organization for providing reference service.[14]

In coping with the types of issues highlighted in this section, libraries benefit from having leadership and a vision of service to the communities served. The challenge for public libraries that are privatized (i.e., library services shifted to the private sector through transference of library management and/or assets to a commercial company) will be to build for the future and engage in more than cost-effective management of resources. After all, information needs and expectations of community residents will continue to change, perhaps dramatically so.

LEADERSHIP DEVELOPMENT

In the United States, there are numerous centers for the study of leadership associated with institutions of higher education. Students might engage in research, and the faculty might engage in consulting as well as offer courses and workshops. In addition, nonprofit organizations offer leadership development. One example is the Greenleaf Center for Servant Leadership, which Robert K. Greenleaf founded in 1964, and which "holds conferences, publishes books and materials, sponsors speakers and seminars, and provides information and services for its members."[15] Within LIS, there are also numerous leadership programs and institutes, and writings about the various options.[16] Such opportunities make it possible for libraries not to engage in succession planning,[17] which involve planning for the future and matching employee skill sets, knowledge, and experience with the future needs of the organization. Succession management involves implantation of that plan and therefore libraries might not cultivate staff talent at the higher levels of management from within the organization, other than supporting key individuals when they engage in external leadership development. These opportunities, however, tend not to be available for nonmanagers or low-level managers. Still, as Teresa Y. Neely observes, "the impact of leadership institutes on participants appears to be much more personal in the arenas of confidence gained and self-awareness realized." Further, as she explains, "mentoring relationships are critically important for some, depending on the emphasis and effort placed on this element by program coordinators, and long-lasting relationships with cohorts, colleagues and fellow participants, provide long-term, much-needed and appreciated support."[18]

As an alternative to these institutes and workshops, the Graduate School of Library and Information Science, Simmons College, initiated the PhD Program in Managerial Leadership in the Information Professions in 2006 with funding from the Institute of Museum and Library Services (IMLS). The program has research expectations for all students and covers leadership through courses taught by professors of practice, who are leaders in the profession with in-depth knowledge and experience in meeting leadership challenges and opportunities in the academic and public libraries.[19]

THE COVERAGE OF LEADERSHIP IN THE LITERATURE OF LIBRARY AND INFORMATION SCIENCE

The literature of LIS contains numerous essays that explain or mention leadership in general terms and discuss leadership issues, perhaps including those associated with the recent economic recession. *Library Lit & Inf Full Text*, for instance, contains more than 1,300 entries on leadership published since January 2000. Refining the search to "leadership" and "research" reduces the pool of citations to slightly more than 220 entries (searched June 16, 2012). However, the word *research* is a generic word that does not limit the search to original investigations applying quantitative or qualitative techniques of data collection. There are biographies, book reviews, and general discussions, not all of which provide an accurate portrayal of leadership as presented in the literature highlighted in Chapter 1. Furthermore, there are a variety of textbooks on library management that might provide an overview of leadership.[20]

In the early 1980s, Donald E. Riggs edited a work on library leadership in which he laments the dearth of writings on leadership in LIS. Libraries, as he notes, need leaders and leadership, and leaders need more than the mere possession of the attributes discussed in the broader literature. He comments,

> It is not especially difficult to find persons who are leaders. It is quite another matter to place these persons in situations where they will be able to function as leaders. It becomes clear that an adequate analysis of leadership involves not only a study of leaders but also of situations.[21]

Still, today there remains an inadequate understanding of how leaders and leadership function in different situations and on a daily basis. For instance, are some situations more critical than others, which leadership theories or styles occur most frequently in those situations, and how might leadership (as opposed to management) be observed? The research needs to go beyond self-reporting.

In the late 1990s, Terrence F. Mech and Gerard B. McCabe edited an important work on leadership in academic libraries that, among other topics, covered visionary leadership, the role of the library director as a campus leader, and leadership in the profession that called attention to assorted issues related to leadership.[22] Chapter authors show how the roles of librarians have changed over time from that of a steward of books to the purveyor of services to the communities served. Librarians, as they show, play more of an institutional role, one that requires leadership.

Donald L. Gilstrap "provides a historiographical analysis of the major leadership and organizational development theories that have shaped our thinking about how we lead and administer academic libraries."[23] He notes that leadership can be connected to organizational development by viewing leadership as occurring "any time one attempts to influence the behavior of an individual or group, regardless of the reason. It may be for one's own goals or for those of others, and they may or may not be congruent with organizational goals."[24] However, this book takes a more limited view of leadership, namely its connection to a vision and follow-through on that vision.

Few research studies on transformational leadership, as well as on most other leadership theories, exist in the LIS literature. Gilstrap, who identifies and summarizes some of them, concludes that the research on leadership theories is "becoming more complex" and moving "from only looking at one aspect of . . . leadership, such as behavior or trait theory, to investigating the interaction of multiple aspects of organizational dynamics and leadership as processes."[25] Although not a research study, Mary Ann Mavrinac's work provides an excellent companion presentation of transformational leadership and how it contributes to a learning culture, which places learning at the center of change management. She sees peer mentoring "as an example of a learning process that is in harmony with the values-based transformational leadership and change process, the professional values of librarianship, and the democratic nature of a learning culture."[26] In a review of transformational leadership and management, James Castiglione expands on their linkage to organizational learning and adaptation.[27] To this, we add that a learning organization must be agile and respond quickly and flexibly to environmental changes and the information needs and expectations of stakeholders.

Adele Barsh and Amy Lisewski introduce ethical leadership, which places ethical behavior at its core and relates it to business ethics. Ethical leaders think about ethical values, include it in their decision making, and foster an ethical climate in the organization.[28] Barbara I. Dewey discusses leadership from a cultural perspective, noting that librarians work "more adeptly" at the interface of a "diverse set of campus and academic cultures." She concludes "that the success of research libraries demands that we aggressively support the complete spectrum of academic cultures existing and forever emerging on our campuses."[29]

The largest number of the research studies in LIS on leadership perhaps relates to emotional intelligence (EI), which focuses on self-knowledge and interpersonal relationships. Yet, those works predominantly deal with "the skill sets of library directors with EI and how those skills affect organizational success"[30] and might deal less with organizational success than with articulation of vision and follow-through on it. To a lesser extent, research examines a few aspects of "recruitment efforts to hire staff with EI skills." Still, "there is recognition that any library staff member with EI skills can contribute to organizational effectiveness and increased morale."[31]

The Simmons MLIP program may have a large impact on the literature on managerial leadership in LIS. Some of the writings pertain to management, and others examine the application of leadership, including emotional intelligence and shared leadership. With Anne Marie Casey, the program has produced its first dissertation (see Table 2.1).

Table 2.1   Literature on Managerial Leadership, Simmons MLIP Program

Articles

Carpenter, Maria. "Cheerleader, Opportunity Seeker, and Master Strategist: ARL Directors as Entrepreneurial Leaders," *College & Research Libraries* 73, no. 1 (2012): 11–32.

Carpenter, Maria, Jolie Graybill, Jerome Offord, Mary Piorun, and Gary Shaffer. "Employee Onboarding: Identification of Best Practices in ACRL Libraries," *Library Management*, forthcoming.

Carpenter, Maria, Jolie Graybill, Jerome Offord, Jr., and Mary Piorun. "Envisioning the Library's Role in Scholarly Communication in the Year 2025," *portal: Libraries and the Academy* 11, no. 2 (2011): 659–81.

Casey, Anne Marie. "Distance Learning Librarians: Their Shared Vision," *Journal of Library & Information Services in Distance Learning* 3, no. 1 (2009): 3–22.

Cawthorne, Jon E. "Leading from the Middle of the Organization: An Examination of Shared Leadership in Academic Libraries," *The Journal of Academic Librarianship* 36, no. 2 (2010): 151–57.

Chadwick, Cynthia, Renee DiPlato, Monique LeConge, Rachel Rubin, and Gary Shaffer. "The Future of the FDLP in Public Libraries," *Public Libraries* 51, no. 4 (2012): 40–47.

DeLong, Kathleen. "The Engagement of New Library Professionals in Leadership," *The Journal of Academic Librarianship* 35, no. 5 (2009): 445–56.

Herold, Irene M. H. "Digital Image Archival Collections: Who Are the Users?" *Behavioral & Social Sciences Librarian* 29, no. 4 (2010): 267–82.

Hunter, Ben. "The Effect of Digital Publishing on Technical Services in University Libraries," *The Journal of Academic Librarianship* 39, no. 1 (2013, forthcoming).

Kreitz, Patricia A. "Best Practices for Managing Organizational Diversity," *The Journal of Academic Librarianship* 34, no. 2 (2008): 101–20.

Kreitz, Patricia A. "Leadership and Emotional Intelligence: A Study of University Library Directors and Their Senior Management Teams," *College & Research Libraries* 70, no. 6 (2009): 531–54.

(*Continued*)

Table 2.1 (*Continued*)

Lim, Adriene. "The Readability of Information Literacy Content on Academic Library Web Sites," *The Journal of Academic Librarianship* 36, no. 4 (2010): 296–303.

Piorun, Mary. "Evaluation of Strategic Plans in Academic Medical Libraries," *Library & Information Science Research* 33, no. 1 (2011): 54–62.

Seaman, David. "Discovering the Information Needs of Humanists When Planning an Institutional Repository," *D-Lib Magazine* 17, nos. 3–4 (2011).

Walter, Tyler. "The Future Role of Publishing Services in University Libraries," *portal: Libraries and the Academy* 12, no. 4 (2012): 425–54.

Dissertations

Casey, Anne Marie. *Strategic Priorities and Change in Academic Libraries*, PhD diss., Simmons College, 2011.

DeLong, Kathleen. *True North: Journeys in Leadership of Women Library Directors in Canadian Academic Libraries*, PhD diss., Simmons College, 2012.

Herold, Irene. *An Examination of Leadership Programs for College Library Directors Associated with ACRL's College Libraries Section*, PhD diss., Simmons College, 2012.

Lim, Adriene. *Assigned Leaders in Unionized Environments: Coping with the Economic Recession and Its Aftermath in Academic Libraries*, PhD diss., Simmons College, 2012.

In conclusion, Maureen Sullivan points out that

the theories of leadership that inform and guide effective practice call for the engagement of followers; building relationships based on trust and authentic behavior; diagnosing the situation and choosing a response that will result in the best approach for the organization, its staff, and its future; and paying continuous attention to the development of self and others. The work of leadership is to listen, learn, empower, respect, inspire, motivate, and engage followers in the accomplishment of meaningful results for the organization. This work is necessarily done in a context of uncertainty, ambiguity, and challenge.[32]

The LIS literature recognizes that effective leaders generate higher employee satisfaction. Higher satisfaction saves organizations' scarce resources in terms of absenteeism and turnover and results in a staff that is empowered, motivated, and future-oriented. Satisfied individuals tend to be more loyal and align their own goals with those of the organization. The literature also recognizes that organizations should see that leaders gain the necessary renewal to continue to play significant leadership roles.

LEADERSHIP ATTRIBUTES IDENTIFIED IN THE LITERATURE OF LIBRARY AND INFORMATION SCIENCE

Attributes associated with leadership in general or with a particular theory appear in various sources. Those producing emotionally intelligent library leaders have been probed the most.[33] Still, among the key attributes are adaptability and flexibility, trust, having a service vision, having integrity, having effective communication skills, being able to motivate others to carry out that vision, developing relationships with others, and building an effective management team. Leaders now need the courage to act in situations where results are not assured and to initiate new services while refining existing ones. They are willing to risk failure.

Around 140 attributes have been identified that might characterize a successful library leader.[34] This is not to say that all of them are of the same importance or that particular individuals need to possess each one. It only means that here is a list from which managerial leaders can select. Those in the position of library director might possess some and expect others in the management team to have complementary knowledge, skills, and abilities. Still, they probably do not need or have all 140.

Earlier in this chapter, some leadership programs in library and science education have been mentioned. However, worldwide such programs are few, and the majority of library leaders and directors have not completed leadership courses even if a small majority had a management course or module in their educational program. Maureen L. Mackenzie and James P. Smith have recently analyzed library directors' responses to a survey concerned with how library directors obtained the relevant qualifications and competences for their position. Even if it is a small-scale study, the majority of the library directors learn the tools of their trade through other means than formal education.[35]

CONCLUDING THOUGHTS

In his final commencement speech as secretary of defense to the graduates of the U.S. Naval Academy, Robert Gates spoke about the importance of leadership and essential attributes associated with leadership. His list complements the one presented above. The first attribute is a vision that looks "beyond tomorrow and discern[s] a world of possibilities and potential." A deep conviction, the second attribute, refers to "strength of purpose and belief in a cause that reaches out to others, touches their hearts and makes them eager to follow." The next two attributes are self-confidence and courage, which includes moral courage: "the courage to chart a new course, the course to do what is right and not just what is popular, the courage to stand alone, the courage to act, the courage . . . to 'speak truth to power'." It takes "real courage," he notes, to stand alone and be willing to say "because I have the responsibility, this is what we will do." The final attributes he highlights are integrity and common decency. In conclusion, Gates remarks,

> Remember that the true measure of leadership is not how you react in times of peace or times without peril. The true measure of leadership is how you react when the wind leaves your sails, when the tide turns against you.[36]

The reference to times of peril and peace do not pertain to libraries, but his insights can apply to change (beyond incremental change) and engaging in planning and evidence-based management.

NOTES

1. Joan Giesecke, "Finding the Right Metaphor: Restructuring, Realigning, and Repackaging Today's Research Libraries," *Journal of Library Administration* 51, no. 1 (2010): 54, 55.

2. James G. Neal, "Raised by Wolves: The New Generation of Feral Professionals in the Academic Library," ACRL Twelfth National Conference, http://www.ala.org/ala/mgrps/divs/acrl//events/pdf/neal2-05.pdf (accessed June 3, 2011); James G. Neal, "Raised by Wolves: Integrating the New Generation of Feral Professionals into the Academic Li-

brary," Library Journal.com (February15, 2006), http://www.libraryjournal.com/article/ CA6304405.html (accessed June 3, 2011).

3. "Karin Wittenborg—Future of Librarians Interview," http://www.collegeonline. org/library/librarians-online/karin-wittenborg (accessed June 12, 2011).

4. Edgar H. Schein, *Organizational Culture and Leadership*, 4th ed. (San Francisco: Jossey-Bass, 2004).

5. Nancy Rossiter, "Global Leadership," in *Making a Difference: Leadership and Academic Libraries*, edited by Peter Hernon and Nancy Rossiter (Westport, CT: Libraries Unlimited, 2007), 40.

6. Sharon K. Epps, "African American Women Leaders in Academic Research Libraries," *portal: Libraries and the Academy* 8, no. 3 (July 2008): 270.

7. Epps, "African American Women Leaders."

8. Camila Alire, "Diversity and Leadership: The Color of Leadership," *Journal of Library Administration* 32, nos. 3–4 (2001): 102.

9. Alire, "Diversity and Leadership." See also Mark D. Winston, *Leadership in the Library and Information Science Professions: Theory and Practice* (Binghamton, NY: Haworth Information Press, 2001).

10. Sylvia A. Hewlett, Carolyn B. Luce, and Cornell West, "Leadership in Your Midst: Tapping the Hidden Strengths of Minority Executives," *Harvard Business Review* 83, no. 11 (2005): 76.

11. Hewlett, Luce, and West, "Leadership in Your Midst," 77.

12. Hewlett, Luce, and West, "Leadership in Your Midst," 82.

13. James G. Neal, "Advancing from Kumbaya to Radical Collaboration: Redefining the Future Research Library," *Journal of Library Administration* 51, no. 1 (2010): 67.

14. Samuel Rothstein, "Reference Service: The New Dimension in Librarianship," *The Reference Librarian* 11, no. 25–26 (1989): 24; Samuel Rothstein, "Development of the Concept of Reference Service in American Libraries, 1850–1900," *Library Quarterly* 23 (January 1953): 1–15.

15. The Greenleaf Center for Servant Leadership, "About Us," http://www.greenleaf. org/aboutus/ (accessed June 1, 2011).

16. For a list of training programs associated with leadership development in libraries, see American Library Association, "Library Leadership Training Resources," http://www.ala. org/ala/aboutala/offices/hrdr/abouthrdr/hrdrliaisoncomm/otld/leadershiptraining.cfm (accessed June 1, 2011). See also American Library Association, "ALA Emerging Leaders Program," http://wikis.ala.org/emergingleaders/index.php/Main_Page (accessed June 1, 2011); Association of Research Libraries, "Leadership Development" [Research Library Leadership Fellows (RLLF) Program], http://www.arl.org/leadership/rllf/index.shtml (accessed June 1, 2011).

17. See also Duane E. Webster and DeEtta Jones Young, "Our Collective Wisdom: Succession Planning and the ARL Research Library Leadership Fellows Program," *Journal of Library Administration* 49, no. 8 (2009): 781–93.

18. Teresa Y. Neely, "Assessing Diversity Initiatives: The ARL Leadership and Career Development Program," *Journal of Library Administration* 49, no. 8 (2009): 832. See also Robert D. Stueart and Maureen Sullivan, *Developing Library Leaders: A How-to-Do-It Manual for Coaching, Team Building, and Mentoring Library Staff* (New York: Neal-Schuman, 2010).

19. See Peter Hernon, ed., *Shaping the Future: Advancing the Understanding of Leadership* (Santa Barbara, CA: Libraries Unlimited, 2010).

20. See, for instance, Robert D. Stueart and Barbara B. Moran, *Library and Information Center Management* (Westport, CT: Libraries Unlimited, 2007). See also Winston, *Leadership in the Library and Information Science Professions*.

21. Donald E. Riggs, *Library Leadership: Visualizing the Future* (Phoenix, AZ: Oryx Press, 1982), x.

22. Terrence F. Mech and Gerard B. McCabe, *Leadership and Academic Libraries* (Englewood, CO: Libraries Unlimited, 1998).

23. Donald L. Gilstrap, "A Complex Systems Framework for Research on Leadership and Organizational Dynamics in Academic Libraries," *portal: Libraries and the Academy* 9, no. 1 (2009): 57.

24. Gilstrap, "Complex Systems Framework for Research," 58; see also Paul Hersey and Kenneth H. Blanchard, *Management of Organizational Behavior* (Englewood Cliffs, NJ: Simon & Schuster, 1993).

25. Gilstrap, "Complex Systems Framework for Research," 72.

26. Mary Ann Mavrinac, "Transformational Leadership: Peer Mentoring as a Values-Based Learning Process," *portal: Libraries and the Academy* 5, no. 3 (2005): 391.

27. James Castiglione, "Organizational Learning and Transformational Leadership in the Library Environment," *Library Management* 27, nos. 4–5 (2006): 289–99.

28. Adele Barsh and Amy Lisewski, "Library Managers and Ethical Leadership: A Survey of Current Practices from the Perspective of Business Ethics," *Journal of Library Administration* 47, nos. 3–4 (2008): 27–67.

29. Barbara I. Dewey, "Leadership and University Libraries: Building to Scale at the Interface of Cultures," *Journal of Library Administration* 42, no. 1 (2005): 42, 43.

30. Brandi Porter, "Managing with Emotional Intelligence," *Library Leadership & Management* 24, no. 4 (2010): 199.

31. Porter, "Managing with Emotional Intelligence."

32. Maureen Sullivan, "Leadership Theories That Lead to Effective Practice," in Hernon, *Shaping the Future*, 31–32.

33. Examples of these sources include Peter Hernon, Ronald R. Powell, and Arthur P. Young, *The Next Library Leadership: Attributes of Academic and Public Library Directors* (Westport, CT: Libraries Unlimited, 2003); Hernon and Rossiter, eds., *Making a Difference*; Peter Hernon, Joan Giesecke, and Camila A. Alire, *Academic Librarians as Emotionally Intelligent Leaders* (Westport, CT: Libraries Unlimited, 2008); Hernon, *Shaping the Future*.

34. Gilstrap, "Complex Systems Framework for Research," 60.

35. Maureen L. Mackenzie and James P. Smith, "How Does the Library Profession Grow Managers? It Doesn't—They Grow Themselves," in *Advances in Librarianship* 33, edited by Anne Woodsworth (Bingley, UK: Emerald, 2011), 51–71.

36. Robert Gates, "In Commencement Speech, Gates Shares Thoughts on Leadership," *Washington Post* (May 30, 2011), http://www.washingtonpost.com/politics/gates-on-leadership-a-rare-and-precious-commodity/2011/05/27/AGNamIEH_story.html?wprss=rss_politics (accessed July 22, 2011).

3

LEADERSHIP IN EUROPE

Niels Ole Pors

This chapter does not provide a history of all parts of Europe, but it is important to be aware of the different legacies, traditions, and values throughout Europe. A huge part of Europe consists of countries that have been part of the Soviet Union–dominated Eastern Europe, and it can be hypothesized that southern Europe is Catholic whereas the northern part of Europe is dominated by a Protestant culture. Until fewer than 40 years ago, Spain and Portugal were dictatorships. Further, Europe has been characterized by conflicts and civil wars. This chapter, which builds on Chapter 1, provides an overview of the diversified leadership situation and leadership styles employed and preferred in different countries in Europe. The chapter also contextualizes the following chapters on library leadership in a number of European countries.

FRAMEWORKS

There exists a multitude of cultural frameworks employed for research into the diversity of norms, values, and behavior across nations and cultures. One of the most well-known of these cultural frameworks is probably that developed by Geert Hofstede.[1] His research discussed in Chapter 1 started in the late 1960s and continued into the 1980s and covers more than 80 countries. Shalom H. Schwartz's research,[2] conducted around 1990, covers 31 countries. His basic approach is similar to the one employed by Hofstede, but his operationalization is different. He identified 45 different values that he groups into seven dimensions. Fons Trompenars and Charles Hampden-Turner, who studied managers in 54 countries, cover seven cultural dimensions.[3]

One of the most interesting and promising studies about leadership in national and cultural contexts is the series of GLOBE (Global Leadership and Organizational Behavior Effectiveness Research Program) studies (see Chapter 1).[4] Conceived in 1993 by Robert House, the GLOBE project "has evolved into a multiphase, multi-method research project in which some 170 investigators from over 60 nations representing all major cultural regions in the world collaborate to examine the inter-relationships between societal culture, organizational culture, and organizational leadership."[5]

The GLOBE studies, partly based on Hofstede's theories, generate numerous hypotheses about the relationship between national culture and leadership.[6] One of the hypotheses is that transformational leadership is easier and more effective in collectivist cultures than it is in individualistic cultures. Cultures with a propensity for high uncertainty avoidance tend to emphasize rules and procedures as tools to reduce uncertainty. Cultures that score high on the feminine dimension tend to prefer leaders who are consultative and considerate more than strong and directive. The power distance also influences the preferences for leadership attributes. Authoritarian leadership is more common and accepted in cultures with a high power distance.

Studies such as the GLOBE research have helped to create a richer picture of leadership. The growing interest in differences and similarities has called into question prevailing assumptions on leadership, often based on U.S. studies that emphasize characteristics such as individuality and rationality, incentives oriented toward individuals rather than groups, and a focus on follower responsibilities and not so much on follower rights. Further, many of the motivation theories focus on hedonistic motives rather than, for example, on altruistic motives.

These different frameworks have all been both praised and criticized, but Hofstede's framework has demonstrated its usefulness as a benchmark for cross-cultural studies. Some of his dimensions are of special interest. For example, power distance is important together with the index for uncertainty avoidance.[7] The GLOBE studies try to expose both values and practices.

A high power distance tends to be associated with decision structures that are centralized in a hierarchical structure. Formal rules and regulations frequently exist and managers often make decisions with little or no consultation with staff. Staff often expect to be told what they have to do. A small power distance is often associated with decentralized structures and a flat structure, often in the form of a matrix organization, a type of management system in which people who have similar skills work together on particular assignments. Managers and leaders rely on staff, and the type of leadership they practice is often consultative. Information flows rather freely in the organization.

Low uncertainty avoidance is often associated with a belief in generalists and common sense. Countries with low uncertainty avoidance tend to prefer a transformational and consultative leadership role, and top managers and leaders are heavily involved in strategy work. There is also a high tolerance for ambiguity in structures and procedures, just to mention some of the more important issues. High uncertainty avoidance is often associated with directive and transactional leadership behavior, and there is a strong belief in the role of specialists. Further, there is an inclination toward hierarchy and bureaucratic structures, and management is highly structured. Managers are often involved in operations.

There are also organizational implications for the degree to which femininity or masculinity is a societal value. The so-called feminine countries value equality, solidarity, and quality in the work life; they consider leaders and managers as employees just like everybody else; and they normally consider good working conditions as the most important factor in achieving job satisfaction. Conflict resolution is often based on discussion, negotiation, and compromises. The so-called masculine societies are associated with valuing equity, pay, and performance as important elements in the job, and they tend to resolve conflict through conflict resolution. Leaders and managers are often considered as cultural heroes. Job satisfaction is a result of the content of work, security in the job, and the level of salary.

In the GLOBE study's coverage of leadership in Europe, different countries are clustered, and two separate clusters, each with subclusters, emerge from the comprehensive set of data and the analyses.[8] The two main clusters are North/West and South/East. The North/West cluster has subclusters encompassing England and Ireland. A Nordic subcluster includes the Netherlands, Sweden, Denmark, and Finland, and a German subcluster consists of Germany, Austria, and Switzerland. The South/East cluster is divided into a subcluster for Latin countries, such as France, Italy, Spain, and Portugal. Another subcluster is made up of Near Eastern countries, such as Greece and Turkey, and the last subcluster consists of Central and East European countries, such as Hungary, the Czech Republic, Slovenia, Poland, Russia, Albania, and Georgia.

The results from the study of European cultures and leadership are in many ways similar to the results that Hofstede obtained. The former communist countries are not a part of his research, and their inclusion in the GLOBE studies somewhat alters the picture, but overall the cultural issues and dimensions employed by Hofstede are robust.

When examining the elements in leadership that are judged important, there are some marked differences between the North/West cluster and the South/East cluster. Inspirational leaders believe passionately in the vision and mission of the organization. They share that passion in a way that enables others to feel passionate and value integrity. These attributes are considered more important in North/West than in South/East. In the South/East cluster, the following are more important: administrative competence, autocratic style, conflict-inducer, face-saver, procedural, status consciousness, diplomatic, and nonparticipative. It is important to emphasize that the data were collected in the 1990s, indicating that the enormous societal changes, especially in Eastern Europe, influenced the results, as these countries were in a transition from a planned society to a more market-oriented and liberal society.

In summary, the preferred leadership style varies according to cultural orientation. In the single cluster, the research also points to marked and significant differences. For example, in the North/West cluster, the Nordic cluster ranks team orientation as more important than does the German cluster. The clustering coincides with factors such as geographical proximity, language or language group, and religion. The factor related to the degree of modernity, as measured by indicators of economic development, income, life expectancy, educational level, health care systems, and social security, also influences cultural values: individualism, uncertainty avoidance, and gender equality.

The clustering of countries is also found in other GLOBE studies. One of them concerns elements of emotional intelligence and other leadership types of preferences, values, and behavior.[9] The authors form four cultural clusters to study the relationship between emotional intelligence and leadership effectiveness. The clusters are named Anglo, Latin European, Eastern European, and Southern Asian. Three clusters cover at least some of the countries that this book focuses on. In the GLOBE study, managers worldwide are placed in 10 different cultural clusters. The present study uses a subsample of the total GLOBE data.

All leaders and managers consider attributes associated with emotional intelligence as very important across the clusters. In general, social skills and attributes associated with transformational and charismatic leadership also score high. There are some differences between the clusters when the researchers look at the different leadership attributes, but the differences do not appear to be major, indicating that at least that the way people talk about leadership and leadership attributes is similar cross-culturally. One of the more distinct differences is that, in the Eastern European cluster, an attribute, being empathetic, scores low in comparison to the other cluster. In Latin Europe, team skills are also ranked low compared to the Anglo cluster. This is probably the result of a combination of different management practices and a general and normative way to talk about leadership and leadership attributes.

The study, which considers both similarities and dissimilarities, emphasizes that the way managers and leaders discuss leadership concepts and attributes can be identical. Attributes and behaviors, however, can take very different forms. For example, both President John F. Kennedy and Mahatma Gandhi are considered visionary and charismatic, but the ways they presented problems, and the ways they spoke and persuaded, differed, and the differences were culturally determined.

Based on the GLOBE studies, Omar E. M. Khalil and Ahmed Seleim analyze the relationship between national cultures and information dissemination practices, which is an important area for library leaders and directors to know.[10] They compare data from the GLOBE studies to indicators provided by the World Bank[11] and analyze nine hypotheses about the relationship between different elements of national culture and societal dissemination capacity and practices. The findings point to interesting and important relationships. Countries that possess high information dissemination capacities tend to have high uncertainty avoidance, high institutional collectivism, and low gender egalitarianism practices. Information is primarily used to regulate the environment and reduce the uncertainty through rules and written procedures. On the other hand, countries with a high power distance correlate negatively with information dissemination practices. This means that countries with a low power distance—ceteris paribus—are more inclined to adopt technological solutions and information technology (IT) systems that may disturb the existing power structure.

Authentic leadership is one of the newest leadership theories.[12] Authentic leadership behavior has the following key aspects that also define transformational leadership. Idealized influence indicates that employees identify themselves with the leader. The second aspect, individualized consideration, suggests that each individual is treated uniquely and fosters individual growth. The third key aspect, inspirational motivation, means that the leader articulates goals and a mutual understanding about the most important phenomena, objectives, and means in the organization. Finally, intellectual stimulation means that the leader succeeds in getting employees to question their beliefs, values, and assumptions and look at problems in a new way.

The notion of authentic leadership also incorporates the ethical aspect of transformational leadership. The ethical aspect means that leaders act according to their values, and that their values are transparent to the organization and its staff. The ethical aspect of authentic leadership has to do with transparency, self-awareness, morality, and balanced processing. Balanced processing means that leaders are open to solutions proposed by other people, listen to those solutions, and consider them in decision-making processes. Overall, the main point concerning authentic leadership is the will and ability to create trust and trustful relations both inside and outside the organization.

An interesting study uses the classification scheme of Shalom H. Schwartz to analyze gender gaps[13] but departs from his cultural models and improves other existing models. He analyzes culture from three pairs of value types:

1. Conservatism versus autonomy. The conservative value type emphasizes social order, respect for tradition, family, status quo, and actions that disrupt the existing order are avoided. The autonomy value types emphasize the pursuit of individual desires. The pair of values is similar conceptually to Hofstede's dimension of collectivism and individualism.
2. Hierarchy versus egalitarianism can be compared to Hofstede's measure of power distance. Hierarchy implies a culture in which unequal distribution of power, roles, and resources is legitimate, whereas egalitarianism corresponds to equality, social justice, freedom, and responsibility.
3. Mastery versus harmony, where mastery is associated with self-assertion, success, ambition, and competence and it contrasts with harmony, which emphasizes the acceptance of the world as it is and unity with nature.

The study was conducted as a macro-, cross-cultural level in more than 50 countries. The macro-level analyses indicates that the gender gap correlated significantly with two of the three value types Schwartz puts forward, namely conservatism and hierarchy. The gender gap is defined in terms of four aspects or indicators: economic participation and opportunity, educational attainment, political empowerment, and health and survival. The study, which controls for different socioeconomic variables, concludes that cultural values have a significant and independent effect on the gender gap. This study is important for several reasons. First, it is cautious in its conclusions about intervening factors and possibilities, including theories of modernization and even if the authors find that gender gaps are closely associated with conservatism in societies, they also indicate that policy-makers and leaders can remedy or change the situation. Gender issues apply to the library and information sector as, on certain levels, it is feminine-dominated. This is an issue that it is important to consider in the context of European leadership.

LEADERSHIP IN SELECTED COUNTRIES

It is not surprising that leaders and managers from the United Kingdom (UK) and Germany are among the most compared and analyzed executives in Europe as they come from two of the most influential economies and are important actors on the political and economic scene of Europe. Some of the differences between general leadership preferences and practices in Germany and the UK have been studied, and it is important to emphasize that at least some of the research results are contradictory. Research indicates that German managers and leaders are reluctant to formulate visions and goals and could be more comfortable with day-to-day management practices. Many German leaders and managers prefer to a greater degree than UK leaders an authoritarian management style. Teamwork is a practice that only recently has been introduced in a more widespread manner.

German leaders are highly qualified especially in professional and technical areas. Several researchers have pointed to difficulties associated with the introduction of change and innovations in German organizations, and they have associated this with a high degree of uncertainty avoidance and reluctance in relation to risk-taking decisions.[14] However, when decisions are taken, they will often be introduced and implemented in a systematic and serious manner. Implementation has a huge impact because the implementation process involves consultation with employees.

Overall, there appears to be many similarities and dissimilarities between leadership preferences and practices among German and UK leaders and managers. Grace McCarthy and Richard Greatbanks point out some more differences, such as German managers interacting more with their suppliers and the local community than do their British counterparts.[15] There were also indicators that point to the fact that German organizations are more inclined to recognize team efforts more than individual efforts among employees. The study further compares German and British companies that use the leadership model named EFQM (European Framework for Quality Management) and find that the difference between leadership preferences is between companies that either use or do not use the framework. This indicates a convergence over time as a result of the employment of the same kind of unspecified management frameworks.

There is possibly a need to study the context of leadership in further detail. Context can be conceptualized in different ways, but Doris Jepson advances a logic model that consists of three overlapping and interconnected layers.[16] One is the cultural layer that consists of the national culture and organizational culture. The second layer is the institutional context, which consists of issues, such as history, education, regulation, and socialization. The third layer is the immediate social context that consists of topics, such as organization, technology, group, job, hierarchy, industry, and department. She notes that the interaction among the layers is seldom the subject of the research literature and that it would be of theoretical and practical significance to know about the relative influence of the different contexts. She uses the conceptual model and an interpretivist methodology to study chemical companies in Germany and the UK. She studied more than 100 employees in the two countries who come from different departments and different levels in the companies.

The interviews in the chemical industry were conducted in several thematic waves, and they offer a rich picture of perceptions on leadership. One finding is that there are many similarities in the perception of leadership behavior at the departmental level between employees in the two countries. In the research and development (R&D) departments, it is important that leaders have a participatory style drawing on the expertise of staff and that leadership should be conducted by example. In the R&D departments it is also appreciated if the leader protects the working environment against wider organizational aims and targets. This perception of leadership behavior contrasts to the perception put forward in production units where the leader has expertise in the production process, on products and machinery, and employees expect supportive management and directions when things go wrong. The leadership styles are dependent on the actual work, indicating that leaders' behavior is related to their area of responsibility.

This study indicates that the actual work, be it research, development, or production, plays a significant role in shaping leadership behaviors and perceptions of leadership. Further, this finding probably has more significance than can be associated with national cultures. The research points to an issue about an intermediating factor of national culture and behavior, namely the effect of what could be named occupational culture. Occupational culture is the values, norms, and beliefs that are connected and learned during a person's education. These values and norms differ from discipline to discipline and are often transnational in character, meaning that they have more significance than the national or organizational culture. Professional norms interact with both national and organizational culture. In this context, occupational culture is of paramount importance if a leader or a manager in a library or in an information center has an overriding identity connected to the information profession or if that person has an identity that is more determined by the profession of leadership. To a certain degree, it is a question of loyalty toward the discipline and practice or toward objectives and goals, which often conflicts with norms and values embedded in the values and beliefs of the profession.[17]

In 2003, a study that compared leadership preferences among German and English managers found significant differences between the two national groups.[18] At the time of the study, it was obvious that German industry and business generally were more compartmentalized than was the UK business, and placed less emphasis on teamwork. It is also seen as a national cultural trait that German managers appear to be more specialty-oriented than are the British and are often appointed to management positions because of their expertise rather than their general management capabilities. This difference is pronounced at the level of mid-level managers. German mid-level managers consider the most important basis for authority to be their technical expertise. General traits in German management culture can be described in terms of professionalism. Nonetheless, authority and respect are gained on the basis of professional status more than hierarchical position. Bureaucracy still plays a significant role as an organizational structural principles and rules, and roles are precisely defined and documented. Planning is an important element in the work process as are punctuality, discipline, accuracy, and order. There are often close bonds among managers, workers, and owners.

Romie F. Littrell and Lapadus N. Valentin compared the preferred leadership behavior in England, Germany, Romania, and Albania.[19] This is just one of the many studies done in these nations, and many of the studies point to the same conclusions. It must be remembered, however, that such studies were conducted a few years after the change in the economic and political system, and they reflect on management and leadership in a turbulent period that was difficult in economic terms for these countries. Romania is one of the former satellite states of the Soviet Union, and much research into leadership has been conducted in these countries. Managers and leaders who worked in the totalitarian system had difficulties making decisions, and they were reluctant to adopt a participatory style of leadership. They also had difficulties fostering creativity and taking initiatives.

There is one common feature in the former Eastern European nations, and it is the absence of a private sector during the communist period. This has probably meant that the public sector has been unable to learn and adopt principles of efficiency and market orientation. A good example of this lack of efficiency is that, judged by standards from western countries, many public institutions, such as libraries, are overstaffed in comparison to libraries in, for example, the UK.

Romania is, in Hofstede's terms, characterized by a high power distance, high uncertainty avoidance, collectivism, and a moderate degree of masculinity. Romania has a low degree of trust on the societal level. The view on leadership of the few Romanian leaders who were interviewed was embedded in the actual context. They consider it a leadership attribute to be able to think in a systematic and system-oriented way, very much like solving an engineering problem, and they noted that their situation is different from that in other countries as they spent much time offering remedies for an infrastructure in society that makes planning, strategies, and innovation extremely difficult. Some of the managers express the sentiment that change since the revolution only has been on the rhetorical level and that the

procedures and processes have not improved. This is not a result of missing management education. The interviewed leaders all participated in different western-
oriented management courses, but they found them totally unfit for the Romanian
infrastructure, economic and political climate, and the missing interaction between
the different parts of the societal infrastructure. Overall, they find themselves in a
chaotic situation that should not be judged by western standards.

It was apparent that Romanian leaders, in contrast to leaders from the UK and
Germany, placed a greater emphasis on the ability to reconcile demands, be they
external or internal, and, in contrast to the other two countries, they have a low
preference for persuasive behavior directed at the staff, indicating this is a result
of a more command-oriented culture with less involvement from staff in decision
processes.

A rather comprehensive study explores the problem of the adoption of standards
and management ideas in four countries in South East Europe.[20] The study investigates managers' perceptions of the concept of total quality management (TQM)
in Greece, Romania, Bulgaria, and Serbia. TQM is a management philosophy and
a framework that has been studied widely, even in the context of national cultures,
and it has been shown that national culture has a direct influence on the implementation of TQM. The investigation consists of an analysis of nearly 1,000 questionnaires and more than 30 interviews. The investigation analyzed data from over
120 service companies from both the public and the private sector in the region.

Hofstede's research is important for this kind of research, and especially the dimensions of uncertainty avoidance and power distance have been predictive in relation to the interaction between national culture and the implementation of TQM.
There is also preference for different leadership styles in countries, and the dominating leadership style influences the specific implementation of that framework.

TQM consists of both soft and human-oriented concepts and practices and
harder concepts and practices. Some of the softer aspects of TQM are concerned
with issues, such as employee involvement, continuous improvement, continuing
professional development, teamwork and empowerment, top-management commitment and support, democratic management style, customer satisfaction, and
cultural change processes. The harder side of TQM deals with issues, such as statistical process control, quality function deployment, critical path analysis, adherence
to ISO (International Organization for Standardization, www.iso.org/iso/iso_
catalogue.htm) standards, and other quantitative accountability tools and ideas.

The research about the attitudes to TQM in South Eastern Europe indicates that
the educational background of managers and leaders and the sector of employment
are the two variables that really distinguish between the attitudes to the softer
aspects of TQM. These results are independent of organizational size, country of
operation, organizational life cycle, gender, and age. The level of educational background correlates positively in these four countries with the perception of need for
continuous professional development, empowerment and involvement, and the
wish to establish quality-oriented cultures. The study also indicates that managers
in the public sector in these countries have less awareness of the framework and
may be less inclined to implement it in comparison to the private sector.

The research also indicates that the knowledge about the so-called softer aspects
of TQM is superficial and that these softer aspects do not play a significant role
in the improvement processes concerning service delivery. This fact is probably
connected to an overall authoritarian management culture in the region of South

Eastern Europe. Most of the interviewed managers and leaders indicate that change processes often were forced upon employees in order to increase productivity and quality. Some of the managers characterize the people-oriented aspects of TQM as ideal in organizations that have nothing to do with the reality in which they operated.

The obvious lack of belief in the softer aspects of TQM can also been seen in the striking absence of human resource management and as an important factor in the business culture. Most of the managers can name the technical side of TQM. The authors link the emphasis with this aspect in relation to uncertainty avoidance. The South European countries possess a high degree of uncertainty avoidance and focus on processes and procedures reduce uncertainty. This must be seen in context that the interviews with leaders and managers indicate that the TQM process is a top-down process implemented in an authoritarian manner, and many managers and leaders at the middle level find the control now stricter than before. In summary, there is no doubt that the leadership style in relation to general national cultural preferences explains the way that TQM is perceived and implemented.

Some researchers argue that the East European states possess some underlying commonalities imposed on their different national culture owing to the centralized form of government.[21] It is argued that it is the ideology of the centralized communist regime and its practical implications that formed a common value system that has been in existence for generations. One important factor in this imposed value system is that managers and leaders in the former communist states were more concerned with their standing in and possibility of advancement in the power structure of party and society than they were in managing the institutions and organizations they led.

Newer research indicates a change in preferences for desired leadership behavior among Romanian leaders.[22] This change, which is related to age cohorts and to gender, indicates that females and younger managers and leaders tend to prefer a more transformational leadership behavior than do older people and male leaders. It might be surprising that younger managers favor transactional leadership behavior, but the authors explain this fact by Romania's troubled history. The younger leaders did not operate during the communist period, and they now function in a turbulent and difficult situation where they are forced to make tough decisions.

It is important to know that preferences are affected by national culture, but preferences also change in relation to economic situation, history, and political development of a society. Further, it is important to consider the intermediating role that organizational culture plays in this context. Some of the more important characteristics in Romanian organizational culture are standard bureaucratic structures and values. Hierarchical structures, rigid and nonflexible organizational boundaries, and a mechanistic view of people working in organizations are the norm, and it correlates with another finding in the study, namely an overall preference for transactional behavior.

TRUST AND CORRUPTION

Trust is important in relation to leadership and motivation. Leaders have a great influence on employees' motivation, but it is also important to remember that people are primarily motivated by the possibility to obtain what is valued. Trust has been studied in global-oriented studies and in European value studies and has been compared to, for example, the UK and Germany, and the North Western nations, especially those in Scandinavia. Romanians, by the way, have a rather low degree of interpersonal trust.

A certain amount of both interpersonal trust and trust in institutions in society is a prerequisite for economic growth and flexibility and for stable social institutions. Trust cannot be overestimated as an important factor in organizations and societies. In business, transaction costs are reduced when partners who trust each other conclude the deal. In organizations, trust contributes to the reduction of expensive control mechanisms and procedures.

Trust is an expectation about behavior. People expect others to behave according to norms and rules in a society or in an organization. If people do, that trust is reinforced, but if people do not behave according to norms, trust decreases. Francis Fukuyama associates lack of trust in a society with corruption.[23]

There are strong indicators that Romanian society as a whole is more corrupt than, for example, Germany and the UK. Corruption makes commerce and the establishment of companies more difficult to discuss in terms of the interaction with the official infrastructure in a society. Littrell and Valentin indicate a certain cynicism about leadership among some managers in Romania.[24] The managers point to the fact that they feel they are judged by western standards, even if they work in situations in which there is a constant struggle for resources and cooperation from the authorities. They obviously believe that their performance is judged by a standard that views them as wrong.

Trust, which is normally measured in terms of trust in other people or interpersonal trust, is important to institutions in a society.[25] There is a strong statistical association or covariation between interpersonal or general trust and institutional trust. It is also important to note that the concept of trust, often in connection with concepts concerning social capital, characterizes cooperation patterns in organizations and companies. This is the case in studies of knowledge sharing and its relations with structures and decision-making strategies.

Gert Tinggaard Svendsen and Gunnar Lind Haase Svendsen combine rankings from the World Values Survey with their own international measures of trust and the combined ranking yields interesting results covering 86 countries. The ranking for general or interpersonal trust includes, for instance:

1 Denmark

2 Norway

3 Sweden

4 Finland

5 Netherlands

10 Iceland

11 North Ireland

12 Switzerland

13 United States

16 Ireland

21 Great Britain

22 Germany

23 Spain

24 Montenegro

25 Austria

27 Italy

28 Belgium

32 Bulgaria

34 Czech Republic

37 Luxembourg

39 Albania

40 Hungary

42 Lithuania

45 Estonia

46 Serbia

47 Greece

50 France

51 Poland

58 Slovakia

59 Croatia

65 Latvia

68 Slovenia

69 Portugal

70 Romania

76 Macedonia[26]

The most remarkable feature is that the Nordic countries, together with the Netherlands, occupy the first five positions in the ranking. These countries are followed closely by New Zealand, Canada, and Australia. At the bottom of the list, countries, such as Brazil, Costa Rica, and Uganda appear. Most of the Central European and Eastern European countries occupy the middle of the ranking. However, there are some remarkable results. It is difficult, for instance, to explain the difference between Spain and Portugal. It also appears a bit surprising that France is placed at rank 50 and Poland at 51.

As stated earlier, there exists a rather marked correlation between institutional trust and general trust. There is no doubt that institutional trust is connected with perceptions, for instance, of the degree of fairness, nepotism, equal treatment, and corruption. This could explain the remarkable fact that all measurements place the Nordic countries at the top. One could hypothesize that the fact is connected to the structure of the so-called welfare states. The prerequisite for a welfare state is trust in institutions and a certain degree of equality in economic, political, and social matters.

Arguably, trust can be related to values and behavior in the sense that is presented by Hofstede, Tromepenars, and Hampden-Turner, and the World Values Surveys, including the GLOBE surveys. Ahmed Seleim and Nick Bontis depart from the conceptualization formulated in the GLOBE studies.[27] Research into corruption indicates that both cultural and national values influence the perception of ethical problems the same way that studies of organizational behavior indicate a relationship between organizational behavior and the individual. Corruption is important in relation to trust because corruption at different levels in society tends to minimize trust directed at people and institutions.

In public institutions, corruption refers to dishonest and partial exercise of official functions, and it is also a misuse of public power for the sake of private benefit. In a library setting, it is difficult to define corruption, but one can think about a library buying technology. There could be bribes involved or there could be forms of nepotism. Just like trust, corruption is a concept that is important as both a value and a practice. Further, it is influenced by culture, the structure of society, values, and norms. As a result, there is no single way to reduce corruption. Depending on the exact relationship with norms and values, different types of treatment must be considered.

Trust is also a concept that has influenced the information profession, and there is research that investigates the relationship between libraries and trust-building in society. Trust-building will often consider social capital, and it is hypothesized that libraries as a kind of neutral meeting area engaged in many activities that contribute to trust-building. It is a phenomenon that library directors should be aware of when they plan services, physical facilities, and service agreements.[28]

CONCLUDING THOUGHTS

Given the number of countries and national cultures comprising Europe, as well as the diverse history of those countries, it is not surprising that the concept of national cultures offers an important perspective to view leadership. This does not mean that the leadership theories and styles presented in Chapter 1 are devoid of value to European settings. Together, national cultures and leadership theories and styles offer a more complete picture of leadership and its effectiveness. National cultures also offer a perspective for making international comparisons about the status and composition of leadership across the globe. Increasingly leaders must understand and be competent in cross-cultural awareness and practice, especially if they manage a multicultural workforce and if some of them move from country to country.

NOTES

1. Geert Hofstede, *Culture's Consequences: International Differences in Work-Related Values* (Thousand Oaks, CA: Sage, 1980).

2. Shalom H. Schwartz, "Beyond Individualism/Collectivism: New Cultural Dimensions of Values," in *Individualism and Collectivism: Theory, Methods and Applications*, edited by Uichol Kim, Harry C. Triandis, Cigdem Kagitcibasi, Sang-Chin Choi, and Gene Yoon (Thousand Oaks, CA: Sage, 1994), 85–119.

3. Fons Trompenaars and Charles Hampden-Turner, *Riding the Waves of Culture: Understanding Cultural Diversity in Business* (London: McGraw-Hill, 1997).

4. Robert J. House, Paul J. Hanges, Mansour Javidan, Peter W. Dorfman, and Vipin Gupta, *Culture, Leadership, and Organizations: The GLOBE Study of 62 Societies* (Thousand Oaks, CA: Sage, 2004).

5. Paul L. Koopman, Deanne N. Den Hartog, Edvard Konrad, et al., "National Culture and Leadership Profiles in Europe: Some Results from the GLOBE Study," *European Journal of Work and Organizational Psychology* 8, no. 4 (1999): 505.

6. One study maintains that Hofstede's framework still possesses a high degree of validity. See P. Magnusson and Richard T. Wilson, "Breaking through the Cultural Clutter: A Comparative Assessment of Multiple Cultural and Institutional Frameworks," *International Marketing Review* 25, no. 2 (2008): 183–201.

7. See Gillian Oliver, *Organisational Culture for Information Managers* (Oxford, UK: Chandos, 2011).

8. Koopman et al., "National Culture and Leadership Profiles in Europe," 503–20.

9. Anne H. Reilly and Tony J. Karounos, "Exploring the Link between Emotional Intelligence and Cross-Cultural Leadership Effectiveness," *Journal of International Business and Cultural Studies* 1 (February 2009), http://www.aabri.com/manuscripts/08134.pdf (accessed July 15, 2011).

10. Omar E. M. Khalil and Ahmed Seleim, "National Culture Practices and Societal Information Dissemination Capacity," in the *Proceedings of the 2009 International Conference on Information Science, Technology and Applications* (New York: AMC, 2009), 104–13.

11. *World Development Indicators 2004* (Washington, DC: World Bank, 2004), 294–97.

12. Bruce J. Avolio, William L. Gardner, Fred O. Walumbwa, Fred Luthans, and Douglas R. May, "Unlocking the Mask: A Look at the Process by Which Authentic Leaders Impact Follower Attitudes and Behaviors," *Leadership Quarterly* 15, no. 6 (2004): 801–23.

13. Hamid Yeganeh and Diane May, "Cultural Values and Gender Gap: A Cross-National Analysis," *Gender in Management: An International Journal* 26, no. 2 (2011): 106–21; Shalom H. Schwartz, "A Theory of Cultural Value Orientation: Explication and Applications," *Comparative Sociology* 5, nos. 2–3 (2006): 137–82.

14. Grace McCarthy and Richard Greatbanks, "Impact of EFQM Excellence Model on Leadership in German and UK Organisations," *International Journal of Quality and Reliability Management* 20, no. 9 (2006): 1068–91.

15. McCarthy and Greatbanks, "Impact of EQFM Excellence Model."

16. Doris Jepson, "Leadership Context: The Importance of Departments," *Leadership and Organization Development Journal* 30, no. 1 (2009): 36–52.

17. Oliver, *Organisational Culture for Information Managers.*

18. Judith Schneider and Romie F. Littrell, "Leadership Preferences of German and English Managers," *Journal of Management Development* 22, no. 2 (2003): 130–48.

19. Romie F. Littrell and Lapadus N. Valentin, "Preferred Leadership Behaviours: Exploratory Results from Romania, Germany and the UK," *Journal of Management Development* 24, no. 5 (2005): 421–42.

20. Alexandros G. Psychogios, "A Four-Fold Regional-Specific Approach to TQM: The Case of South Eastern Europe," *International Journal of Quality & Reliability Management* 27, no. 9 (2010): 1036–63.

21. Bruno Grancelli, ed., *Social Change and Modernization: Lessons from Eastern Europe* (New York: Walter de Gruyter, 1995).

22. Erich Fein, Aharon Tziner, and Cristinel Vasiliu, "Age Cohorts Effects, Gender, and Romanian Leadership Preferences," *Journal of Management Development* 29, no. 4 (2010): 364–76.

23. Francis Fukuyama, *Trust: The Social Virtues and the Creation of Prosperity* (New York: Free Press, 1995).

24. Littrell and Valentin, "Preferred Leadership Behaviours."

25. Gert Tinggaard Svendsen and Gunnar Lind Haase Svendsen, *Social Kapital: En Introduktion* (Copenhagen: Hans Reitzel, 2006); Ronald M. Inglehart, Michael Basanez, Jaime Dies-Medriano, Loek Halman, and Ruud Luijkx, *Human Beliefs and Values: A Cross-Cultural Sourcebook Based on the 1999–2002 Values Surveys* (Mexico City: Siglo XXI, 2004).

26. Svendsen and Svendsen, *Social Kapital.*

27. Ahmed Seleim and Nick Bontis, "The Relationship between Culture and Corruption: A Cross-National Study," *Journal of Intellectual Capital* 10, no. 1 (2009): 165–84.

28. Ragnar Audunson, "The Public Library as a Meeting-Place in a Multicultural and Digital Context: The Necessity of Low-Intensive Meeting-Places," *Journal of Documentation* 61, no. 3 (2005): 429–41.

4

LIBRARY LEADERSHIP IN EUROPE

Niels Ole Pors

The international research literature on leadership in libraries and information centers in Europe is limited in both number and scope. One reason for this is probably a combination of the different types of libraries in the countries and the educational systems that differ from the models in, for example, the United Kingdom (UK) and the United States. Another important reason is the diversity of languages in Europe. For example, the European Union (EU) has 27 member states, and nearly every state has its own national language. Further, not all of the European countries are EU members. In total, there are more than 50 different nations in Europe.

In many European countries, there is a marked difference between academic and public libraries. Public libraries are often small and badly financed whereas academic libraries connected to universities and other institutions of further or higher education are in better shape. One has to be careful, however, of making generalizations because in some countries, especially those from Eastern Europe, the tradition of good public libraries that support education has been strong.

Education for library and information science is also much diversified and based on different traditions. Implementation of the so-called Bologna charter, however, has modified this diversified situation, and most of the countries have changed or are in the process of doing so, the educational system into the well-known bachelor's, master's, and PhD structure. In some countries the program for degrees in library and information science is outside the university system. The education is often placed in higher education institutions with only a limited research obligation and without an option for a PhD degree. In some of the countries, the education is placed in both universities and higher education institutions.

This complicated picture has its roots in very different educational traditions, and they have been reformed through the Bologna process, an EU declaration. The Bologna declaration set guidelines for the educational structure and most European countries have adopted those guidelines; nonetheless, there are national variations. The declaration's prescriptions are directed at universities and institutions of higher education, promoting a structure with a three-year bachelor's program, a two-year master's program on top of that, and a three-year PhD program.

The EU plays an important role in the educational scene. In the 1990s, the EU financed many library development programs and eased the cooperation among the countries, including countries that are not members of the Union. Many of these projects concerned development through knowledge transfer. It is nearly impossible to cover European library leadership in total as the cultures, languages, managerial traditions, and contexts of libraries and information centers vary.

Accordingly, this chapter introduces some of the important players in the European library scene and discusses different values, preferences, and leadership behaviors. The chapter draws on studies concerned with cross-cultural leadership, and it refers to some of the frameworks used in other studies. Next, there is an exposition of different types of values, perceptions, and behaviors among leaders in different countries. Finally, there is a discussion about the relationship between the general frameworks and leadership in libraries and information centers.

IMPORTANT ORGANIZATIONS AND ASSOCIATIONS

In Europe, there is a long tradition of cooperation among libraries and different library associations and organizations. EBLIDA (www.eblida.org) and LIBER (www.libereurope.eu) are important associations. The former is the European Association for the National Library Associations, and the latter is the Association of European Research Libraries. There exist other associations, such as EUCLID (www.euclid-lis.eu), which organizes European institutions engaged in library and information science education, and this organization promotes an annual conference known as Bobcatsss. The main organizers of this unique, annual conference are students from two different European library and information science education institutions. The conference attracts around 200 students, educators, and researchers every year.

The different national authorities on public libraries in Europe have formed an umbrella organization named NAPLE (www.naple.mcu.es), which works on transnational strategies and cooperates with some of the other aforementioned organizations and associations. There are also many regional networks and cooperation partners. An example is the Nordic–Baltic Research School in Information Studies (NORSLIS), a body consisting of 14 Nordic and Baltic educational institutions associated with library and information science. It organizes PhD courses and facilitates cooperation between researchers and PhD students in the Nordic and Baltic countries. The network organizes joint doctoral courses.

The activities of LIBER are the most interesting and relevant to this book. LIBER organizes seminars, working groups, and conferences, and the association also produces a journal, *LIBER Quarterly*. The main focus of the association is digitization and open access. Management issues such as those related to human resources, however, are of interest to the organization. A perusal of the last decade of journal issues shows just a few papers on leadership issues and topics. This does not mean that leadership issues are a topic absent from the agenda of European libraries. It just means that most of the literature on leadership issues in Europe exists in one of the many languages found in Europe.

The changing landscape of Europe during the last 25 years has put the EU in a central place, and the EU has also played an important role in facilitating the development of public libraries in Europe. EU development programs are used widely, and many of them expect partners to come from northern and southern

Europe; the partner for which the development should take place, however, is normally from Eastern Europe. Many of these programs have secured cooperation among libraries, universities, and other players in networks, last up to three years, and provide interaction that results in practical developments. Program topics are far-ranging, from implementation of online catalogs to curriculum development, the establishment of a structure for facilitating strategic planning, and so on. (Some of the challenges in this cooperation are touched upon later in the chapter.)

The EU also facilitated a number of state-of-the-art reports on the situation that public libraries in Europe face, and some of these reports advocate a strong strategic direction. They were produced in the 1990s and at the beginning of the new century, and one of them merits mention. Published in 1996, this comprehensive report, edited by Jens Thorhauge and Monika Segbert, maps the European library scene.[1] The study, part of the European Commission's Libraries Program, is the most complete study of the public libraries of Europe. The study consists of 11 country studies, five case studies of innovative public libraries, and a case study of regional cooperation. It also includes six papers on different aspects of the public library in the information society. The study presents European public libraries in the mid-1990s, and it deals with the development and challenges facing them in the information society.

The report sees the main role of public libraries as giving access to published information, offering lifelong learning opportunities, safeguarding cultural identity in a changing world, and ensuring that citizens can cope with information technology and have access to the equipment and systems they need. The role of public libraries is seen as an extension of their traditional values, enlightenment, learning, and access. The philosophy behind the report reflects traditional democratic values, and the report defines the future key roles of public libraries in relation to existing barriers. The barriers are identified as insufficient political awareness or a lack of confidence in the potential of the public library. This is, to some degree, connected with the lack of plans and strategies for networking and technological support. The report also lists barriers related to professional development because of the insufficiency of continuing education throughout most of Europe, and discusses mental barriers and managerial problems as obstacles. The report was influential, and the discussions and meetings following its release have facilitated intensive library cooperation and the foundation of NAPLE. Leadership issues were only implicitly analyzed and discussed in the report and investigations that followed its publication.

The diversity in Europe is also reflected in the public funding of public libraries. Of course, the data cannot easily be compared because of the differences in cost of living in the countries, but they indicate the amount of public support. The data, most likely, are from an EU-funded project named LibEcon in 2002.[2]

The funding measures cost per inhabitant for public libraries. Some countries have a structure for the library system in which different forms of educational libraries play a more significant role in the national library scene. The spending per inhabitant is calculated in Euros and placed in parentheses. The figures are rounded. If we look at a group of countries with similar economies in terms of income, price levels, and so on, the group consists of countries such as Denmark (€65), Switzerland (€50), Iceland (€50), Finland (€50), Sweden (€40), the Netherlands (€35), Norway (€30), UK (€30), Belgium (€20), and Germany (€10). Countries such as Greece, Spain, Portugal, and the former Eastern Europe states all spend less than €10 per inhabitant, but these countries also had a much smaller gross national product (GNP) than the other countries. Overall, the data indicate different national funding and strategies for public libraries. The ranking has not changed much during the last 10 years.

LIBRARY LEADERSHIP IN SELECTED COUNTRIES

It is important to probe the degree to which mediating factors exist between the national culture and leadership in libraries. One such mediating or intervening factor could be a kind of professional culture embedded in the profession of library and information science. This is not the place to expand this discussion, but librarianship without doubt has some internationally accepted values.

During the last couple of years LIBER, an umbrella organization for many European research libraries, has held leadership courses for European library managers and leaders. Their most striking feature is that they are extremely oriented to Anglo-American values and leadership practices. Leadership courses are designed not to replicate national leadership programs but rather to supplement them, and they are directed at leaders who intend to assume a senior position in a couple of years. The courses include some coaching and mentoring between modules. Each module only lasts a couple of days. The international trend concerning self-awareness is prominent in the first module built around the Myers-Briggs Type Indicator (MBTI) that all participants are supposed to take and use in the course.

United Kingdom

It is not surprising that the literature on leadership and management is rather comprehensive when one looks at UK. John Mullins and Margaret Linehan have conducted empirical and comparative research into leadership in different countries.[3] Their study is based on interviews employing a grounded theory approach with 30 library directors from England, Ireland, and United States. Half of the respondents came from Ireland and all of them are leaders in the public library sector. One of the interview questions concerned how the respondents valued the central role of leadership as part of organizational success. Two-thirds of them agreed to the statement but modified it with explanations that pointed to the fact that they tend to view leadership as a shared activity and not something that is embedded just in the library director. Many of the library leaders pointed to the importance of staff and staff motivations as important for organizational success and effectiveness.

The majority of the respondents also saw the library leader as the dominant factor in the organizational culture. Irish library directors, in contrast to English directors, were more positive in relation to the leaders' possibility to influence and change the culture. The explanation for the difference was that English public library leaders operate in an environment that is bureaucratic and driven by central control. The American directors, to a higher degree, emphasized a more democratic view emphasizing the contribution of the staff in changing the culture.

In another article based on the same research the authors explore the relationship between leaders and followers—or rather the leaders' perception of their relationship with followers.[4] There appears to be a high agreement among the library leaders about staff and that the relationship between leaders and followers is a symbiotic one or, as some of the respondents express, a partnership between leaders and staff. Interviewed leaders were aware of their dependency on the so-called followers. It is dangerous to use a rather small sample of statements from directors and evaluate tendencies based on limited research. However, the authors find what they term three different forms of the leader–follower relationship. The Irish leaders were more concerned with setting an example for their staff through their mode of behavior and communication. The American leaders had a more collegial approach, and some of them suggested that leaders must serve their followers, thereby introducing the concept of servant leadership. The English directors were more concerned with what they saw as an excessive amount of regulations they have to follow.

Nearly all the interviewed leaders emphasized the necessity of serving staff members through empowerment, development of self-leadership, the establishment of a learning culture, and the importance of giving credit and recognition. Further, it became evident that library leaders, to a high degree, perceived leadership as a question about developing teams and staff members as these were seen as the most important elements to achieve organizational effectiveness and success. This implied a high degree of delegating responsibilities and focusing on the leader as a motivator.

A third study based on the same data collection analyzed how library leaders interpreted and perceived difficulties and serious challenges in their job as leader of a library.[5] Several problems were raised during the interviews. One of the more pertinent problems was the paucity of leadership in libraries. This is partly an effect of the unwillingness of many librarians to take on leadership responsibilities. This problem was especially mentioned among the English library leaders and to a much less degree among leaders from Irish libraries and U.S. libraries. It is a problem if many professionals deliberately choose not to become leaders, and it seems that the position as leader in a library is considered as not attractive enough. The interviews with the library leaders about working conditions indicate that library leaders work long hours in comparison with their staff members. Some of the respondents stated that their weekly work hours amounted to more than 70. Further, some of the leaders find that their job is so diversified that it can be difficult to focus. None of the library leaders from the United States, however, saw long hours as a problem. Many of the respondents also emphasized that it is difficult to start a career as a leader as there is no formula to support actions. The respondents talked much about the pressures of starting a leadership career and about the importance of gaining experience from the job and through reflection. It is also evident that leaders need a kind of robust personality to cope with difficult situations, dissatisfied staff members, and the pressure of making unpopular decisions.

The library leaders also saw the negative stereotyping of librarians and library leaders as a problem. It is mostly a question about status, but it also affects the possibilities for a career change. British library leaders expressed to a higher degree than did the Irish and Americans about bureaucratic restrictions causing frustrations. The library directors also mentioned that it is a problem when external commitment to libraries is low.

Without doubt, it is difficult to lead, and it is probably more than difficult to lead public institutions that have stereotypes attached to them. Further, if there is a kind of mismatch between library goals and the bureaucratic structure surrounding it, the situation becomes complex and filled with obstacles.

A fourth study by the same authors explores how leaders interpret and perceive the relationship between management and leadership.[6] It is not surprising that the distinction between leadership and management is blurred when leaders talk about the distinction. Overall, the majority of the respondents emphasized that leadership is change-oriented and people-oriented, and management is more task- and procedure-oriented. Irish and American library leaders appear to be similar, and English public library leaders are different and act in accordance with a hierarchical structure. For instance, who is allowed to communicate with the media? Both Irish and American library leaders have no problems with staff members communicating externally, in contrast to the English library leaders, who follow strict rules put forward by the local council.

Overall, the results of the studies are similar to those from a comparative analysis done by Niels Ole Pors, Pat Dixon, and Heather Robson.[7] Their study was based on a survey including nearly 200 questions and statements covering all areas of leadership and management in libraries, and marked differences were found in a number of areas. Some of the main results from this study were that there was less leeway for decision making in English libraries than there was in Denmark and, combined with bureaucratic structures, workloads, and external requirements, English library directors were more dissatisfied with their job situation than were Danish library directors. The level of perceived stress was higher among English leaders. Another interesting result was that the knowledge and use of different management tools differed in the two cultures. The preference in Denmark was for human-oriented tools, whereas in England, it was for more economy-oriented ones.

In the comparative study, British library leaders possessed a much higher knowledge of management tools than did their Danish colleagues. This was probably a result of the requirements for constant measurement and assessment especially in England. At the time of the analysis, these requirements were less pronounced in Denmark. The analysis also indicated a correlation between the knowledge of library directors and their amount of use of management tools and other forms of quality assurance instruments. Another issue was that British leaders spent more time on strategic work than did their Danish colleagues and less time on staff development than did the Danish directors.

Further, the perception of job security and work–private life balance was low in the UK compared to the perceptions Danish library directors expressed. British library directors found that they had less freedom in decision-making processes, and this result supports the findings from the research of Mullins and Linehan, the conclusion of which is as follows:

> The findings gave a confirmation of the relevance of the tentative model. It is observable that the differences in discourse and in tools employment probably are related to differences in the national culture. The manager's position in relation to the cross-pressure between institutional imperatives and freedom of decisions and actions also plays a role, at least in relation to factors like the sense of job security, workload and well-being at the job. This is, of course, also part of the organisational culture. This culture is important as a zone of acceptance in relation to which tools and managerial approaches are conceivable and legitimate in a given institution.[8]

Finally, the analytical framework for the comparison between English and Danish library leaders was based on the categories from Geert Hofstede and one striking difference between UK and Denmark is the score on the dimension characterized as masculinity versus femininity.

There are not many published books in Europe on leadership in the information sector, including libraries. There are a number of books on management of libraries that include some coverage of leadership. One of the few books devoted to leadership in the information profession is by Sue Roberts and Jennifer Rowley,[9] which introduces many issues and new trends in the leadership discourse such as those associated with entrepreneurship and innovation. The book also includes some case studies and interviews with leading leaders in libraries and information management. Naturally, they approach leadership from an Anglo-Saxon perspective, but they offer a broad outlook that presents many facets of leadership theories and practices. Similar to other countries, for example, Denmark,[10] central initiatives concerning the development of leaders and leadership skills have been enacted.[11] The general problems appear to be issues concerning recruitment of leaders and the transformation of managers into leaders. Libraries will continue to operate in an increasingly competitive environment for the coming years, while external funding will likely decrease; the political, technological, and economic environment becomes more complex; and the capabilities of a library leader are an extremely important factor in the positioning of libraries in society. Managerial skills do not suffice. Leaders must give direction and inspiration. They have to be able to build teams, lead by example, and be accepted both internally in the organization and externally in relation to other stakeholders.

It seems that British leadership programs succeed at several levels. One of the most important results of participating in leadership programs can be an increase in self-confidence and self-awareness, together with insight in strategy tools and knowledge about how organizations operate and develop. The programs also build confidence, which is important for any leader.

The Baltic States and Eastern Europe

The Baltic states and some of the Eastern European states are interesting for the study of leadership as they have been engaged in a radical transformation process. The changes that have taken place at all levels in society since 1990 are paramount and radical, and this transformation has greatly affected the libraries.

There is no doubt that libraries in Eastern Europe have come a long way in a rather short time. There are several reasons for this quick change. The most important are probably that the staff as a whole are well-educated and that the EU, especially in the 1990s, ran numerous programs that included Eastern European organizations.

A professional viewpoint from 2000 focuses on EU's Tempus program, which, among other goals, supports modernization of higher education and cooperation among EU countries and their partners, and draws attention to the extent of cooperation among European countries. To benefit the international readership of this chapter and book, we present some of the findings from this program. First, librarians and librarianship have a low standing in many of the Eastern European countries. This might be due to the fact that librarianship is even more female-dominated as a profession than librarianship is in the rest of Europe. Second, many of the Eastern European libraries have a good legacy from the time of communist regimes as many of the libraries played an important role in education and library staff are well-educated. However, there is still a lack of a structure for incentives linked to achievements and not to seniority or the number of years in employment. In university libraries, one of the striking features was a marked lack of cooperation with the academic staff at the educational institution, but this situation has changed for the better during the last decade. The last issue is that decision-making styles differ. Overall, they tend to be slower and more indirect or less clear-cut. The mode of discussion is more polite, philosophical, and theoretical than is common in, for example, British libraries.[12]

This characterization, however, is more than 10 years old, and much has happened since then. The transformation of a society and its institutions is a long-term project, especially to change values and beliefs.[13] An indication of this can be seen from the report of a cooperation project between some Norwegian and Polish public libraries.[14] The cooperation is not directly oriented to leadership but to library development and networking. The challenges, however, facing the libraries have immense leadership implications. In the cooperation project, the challenges facing Polish public libraries were outlined. Some of the challenges focus on the modernization of the Polish libraries, including a broadening of the traditional role of libraries, the establishment of a national interlibrary loan system, and the creation of joint and digitalized cataloging processes. The article also points to management issues, such as professional development in such areas as flexibility, change management, and cooperation with stakeholders. Another challenge is to establish promotion systems in libraries and work with the qualification structure of employee. The Polish participants in the project that ends in 2013 have found that the interaction with Norwegian colleagues has been fruitful in addressing management issues because the participants were exposed to new ideas about management. The Norwegian partners became aware of other cultures and traditions and emphasized the common European heritage as an important part of the system. The interaction with the Polish colleagues also provided insight into the limitation of the standard description of a strategy process for planning and change. The Norwegian librarians noted the formalized and hierarchical organizational structures existing in Polish libraries.

Henryk Hollander has written a passionate article about the library situation in Eastern European nations, with a special emphasis on Poland, and he points to several problems of high relevance for leadership and innovative management.[15] One of them is the lack of cooperation in the national library systems and the huge diversity in quality of the different libraries. This lack of cooperation indicated by the lack of interlibrary loan systems, national networked library services, and portals reflects poor funding, the way that libraries are managed, and how directors are appointed and viewed by stakeholders. Hollander emphasizes that library positions in most of the Eastern European countries are feminine-dominated, and he discusses how this fact contributes to low prestige and salaries one sees in these countries. The main problem, as he sees it, is the need for a much more determined leadership and a more modern management culture that employs and adopts newer management methods and incorporates them in the daily routines.

Ane Landøy and Angela Repanovici compare library leadership in Norway and Romania.[16] They look at how library directors perceive future challenges, and they find marked differences between the situation in Norway and Romania. They examine two challenges, open access and bibliometrics. It is not surprising that the majority of Norwegian academic library directors find both challenges important when they consider the place that bibliometrics has in research assessment and the libraries' role in that context. Bibliometrics can be used as an instrument for collection development, be it digital or printed. The situation is different in Romania, where fewer library directors or leaders put much significance on these challenges. The rather low importance put on these two challenges contrasts with the academics' evaluation of how good libraries are in fulfilling document needs. Many of the library's acquisitions come from funds obtained by researchers, who use project funds to buy material for addition to the library collection. This is not a strategic way to develop and manage collections, and it means that the coverage of the different scientific disciplines varies greatly. Academic knowledge of open access and digital repository is limited, and it does not appear that libraries have promoted researcher use of digital material. Yet, Romanian researchers support the idea of digital repositories and open access. Because the Romanian sample in the study was small, firm conclusion cannot be drawn. Still, a challenge for university libraries is to develop and maintain the support of different user groups.

Another study by Ane Landøy and Angela Repanovici examines decision-making processes in Norwegian and Romanian libraries.[17] They provide demographic data about library directors. In Romania, university librarians and library directors are part of the academic staff, which means that it is common for library directors to obtain their position by coming from outside the library community. When it comes to strategic decisions, it is obvious that Romanian university libraries rely more on decisions made by the university than by the library itself. The delegation of decisions in the libraries is also less than it is in the Norwegian libraries. The same study also examines how leaders perceive the basis for their influence or their power base. In Romania, nearly 40 percent of the respondents think that their ability to reward or punish staff is important. Only 7 percent of the Norwegian leaders agree and, overall, they find that, to a higher degree, their influence comes from a persuasive and consultative leadership style.

Another striking difference between the leadership positions in the two countries can be seen in answers to questions concerning how well the leadership job is described. Romanian library directors perceive that they have clearly defined responsibilities and authority; the majority have a written job description, and most of them are never in doubt where a task belongs. The leadership authority and boundaries are much clearer than we often see in other countries, and this is without doubt connected to a more bureaucratic and hierarchical structure. It is not easy to connect these observations to a national cultural framework, but the results indicate that academic libraries in Romania are more isolated than in other countries, and it is also obvious that a high degree of power distance is reflected in at least some of the perceptions of the library directors. The formalization of job descriptions and clear duties and tasks also point to a more bureaucratic and hierarchical structure, and at the same time it indicates uncertainty avoidance. In these studies, however, there is similarity to some of the results from the more general studies on Romanian leadership. It would be beneficial to have further research on this situation.

Germany

Germany is a major player in the European library scene. An interesting study, which focuses on the role of library directors as movers of innovation, indicates that staff in research libraries are becoming more willing to engage in innovation and in change and innovation processes as long as the library director is communicative, candid, and open to staff involvement in decision-making processes.[18] Further, it is beneficial if library directors participate in the processes as equals and are cautious in their exercise of formal power. They should demonstrate initiative, set clear goals, and solve conflicts in a sensible and sensitive manner. Technical, organizational, and managerial competences are necessary, but success requires the presence of other competencies (e.g., social competencies) as well. Together, these competences constitute the basis of professional authority. The study also emphasizes the important role that library directors play in setting and maintaining the organizational climate.

The German study, which is based on a dissertation, is an extensive investigation of staff and leaders in more than 30 academic libraries in Berlin and in close proximity to the city. Conducted in the late 1990s, some of the study findings are now outdated, but nevertheless some of the main findings still apply. The study emphasizes that leadership cannot be meaningfully discussed without taking staff and changing staff attitudes into account. Gerd Paul, the author, states that changing attitudes, and rapid changes within the information technology (IT) infrastructure, present challenges for library directors and their leadership styles.

Paul, who used the concept of organizational climate to analyze some of the data, classified the libraries in three groups ranked after the quality of the organizational climate, and he used the ranking to determine the most effective leadership behavior.[19] Using the respondents' evaluation of the work climate as the tool for classification, he found great diversity among the academic libraries concerning the degree of adoption of IT. Libraries that scored low on IT had much more traditional and silo-oriented structures, and they tended to have a low customer-oriented focus. Staff were change-oriented and had high intrinsic motivation, which, in turn, calls for a certain kind of leadership behavior. Some directors had difficulties coping with both IT developments, however, and a highly change-oriented staff, because the combination of these two factors impacts the whole organization.

The leadership styles and behavior differed according to the quality of the organizational climate. The directors in libraries with a positive climate were willing to integrate staff across divisions in the library, and they used a broad spectrum of tools to enrich the communication between management and staff. They succeeded in making the procedures transparent and facilitated participation in decision making. Further, the directors in these types of libraries often participated as equals in the professional work. In this role, they acted professionally in a nonhierarchical manner, and they balanced this type of act with the maintenance of their formal authority. In a soft manner, they could enforce the rules and ensure that the rules apply to everyone. The directors also showed a high degree of emotional intelligence, detected upcoming conflicts, analyzed the underlying motives, and dealt with the conflicts in a fair and moderating manner. Finally, the directors working in libraries with a positive climate induced and allowed enthusiasm at work as well as inspired and instilled joy and fun in the workplace.

The situation in libraries with a mediocre work climate is different in relation to leadership behavior, even if the working conditions in terms of freedom in the job are probably the same. It is also noteworthy that the rather small power distance in the German society is reflected in this research, and a careful reading of the dissertation also indicates that a main task still is to avoid too much uncertainty. This uncertainty is reduced by having clear goals, directors' participation in processes, and clear and comprehensive communication structures and channels. Paul's dissertation also indicates that the occupational culture embedded in the library and information workforce plays an important role that modifies some elements in the national culture.

The procedures for thorough and comprehensive planning before taking action is are important element in the German management culture. An example of this kind of careful and conscientious processes is described in an interesting article.[20] Digitalization and introduction of digital libraries are the rationality behind the re-engineering and changes made in the organization of work processes. The change is a kind of participative top-down process. It is organized from the top but done in consultation with teams, and a new matrix structure is implemented. The interesting thing is that the traditional workflow bureaucracy that characterizes much of German organizational life is still in place and can accomplish organizational change.

Many of the changes that have taken place in European libraries can be seen as a result of the movement often named new public management (NPM). NPM is a management movement that incorporates many of former trends in management thinking (e.g., total quality management, customer orientation, optimizing of processes, evaluation and assessment, organizational structures (e.g., flatter structure), and the empowerment of staff). NPM can take different forms and emphases depending on a specific mixture of national and organizational culture. One element, or tool, is the balanced scorecard originally developed by Robert Kaplan and David Norton.[21] A number of libraries in Europe use the balanced scorecard, and Roswitha Poll, among others, has promoted it as a suitable framework for performance measurement.[22] The scorecard has all the characteristics of an organizational recipe (see Chapter 9). The promises of the balanced scorecard are twofold. First, it is a simple performance measurement system that measures the whole of the organization by means of a limited number of indicators. Second, it is a strategic planning tool based on a belief in causation between the different elements in an organization.

It is interesting to see how a large German university library has implemented the balanced scorecard as the process enlightens some of the leadership issues touched upon in this chapter. Petra Düren analyzes the implementation of the balanced scorecard in the German National Library of Science and Technology (TIP).[23] He states that introduction of NPM will have consequences for the organizational structure, management, leadership, customer relations, benchmarking, and operations. For instance, organizational structures must be changed from traditional centralized ones to decentralized ones characterized by teamwork and delegation of responsibilities. Management must put strategic visions, missions, and goals forward in the organization and measure the effectiveness and efficiency of the processes. In such situations, the leadership style becomes participatory.

The process was in many ways top-down, at least in the beginning, starting with a leadership seminar in which participants analyzed the strengths, weaknesses, opportunities, and threats. Once they identified strategic areas, they formulated and implemented the balanced scorecard. The process they followed was thorough and detailed, and use of the balanced scorecard correlated with indicators of trust in the organization and transformational leadership. In summary, throughout the entire process, library staff were involved.

This section of the chapter concludes with a short case study demonstrating that some of the countries are alike, and that change can be rather easy to accomplish. Mel Collier, former library director of University of Leicester, described his personal experiences transferring from a position as library director in the UK to one of library director in the Netherlands and in Belgium.[24] He found it relatively easy to transfer professional skills and expertise because the UK and the Netherlands are similar. It appears that the transition has been rather smooth. Still, indications in the article point to difficulties in integrating the libraries and other support services with the academics at the university. Collier also emphasizes the democratic and consultative decision-making processes. He indicates that convergence of services is more difficult to implement, probably owing to a high regard for professionalism in the different departments and work areas, which would be a point that relates closely to the situation in Germany.

Southern Europe

General interest in Greek public libraries has been low in comparison to many other European countries, as reflected in the fact that funding is under the average in comparison to the rest of Europe. However, some of the library programs initiated by the EU have changed this situation for the better, and one element in this change is the implementation of different forms of strategic thinking and planning. In an illuminative article, Petros Kostagiolas and Maria Korkidi surveyed the directors of 100 municipal libraries.[25]

Being a library leader in Greece creates challenges different from those found, for instance, in the UK. For example, the Greek language represents a kind of barrier among users, the Internet, and publishers. This barrier is simply a result of the Greek alphabet, which is different from the dominating Roman alphabet used in nearly all other European countries. At the time of the survey (2007), the majority of Greek libraries had not worked with long-term planning instruments. It must be emphasized that the municipal libraries are funded by the municipalities and in accordance with this they must approve formal strategic planning. In most cases the municipal library was not on the top of the list prioritized by the local authorities. The size of the municipal libraries in Greece is small. A quarter of them do not have a professional librarian among the staff, and only one-fifth of the libraries had more than two librarians on the staff. This adds a new dimension to the implementation of leadership theories and practices. This is accentuated by the finding that over 70 percent of the library directors perceive long-term planning as necessary for the development of the municipal libraries in Greece. Obstacles to widespread use of strategic planning center on low funding, the lack of qualified librarians, and, in some cases, authoritarian control of the supervising local and regional authorities.

Implementation of management strategies and leadership is complex and cannot be characterized as a simple textbook exercise. On the other hand, leadership qualities and capabilities are probably necessary to change the situation for the better. But again, a library director with a small number of staff also needs to be an effective and efficient manager.

In many European countries there exist a deep and profound difference between academic and public libraries. In many of the countries, academic libraries are much better funded than public libraries. This is the case in many of the southern Europe countries. This becomes evident in Spain. Spanish public libraries, in general, are not well-funded, but it appears that academic libraries are advanced and modern institutions. Nuria Balague and Jarmo Saarti compared a Finnish and a Spanish academic library, and they analyze how the ISO 2001 standard has been implemented in the libraries from 2000 and what the consequences have been.[26]

Introducing a management system in a library is an important part of leadership and continuing the system is even more important. It is necessary for the leadership to reflect on the consequences for staff, processes, and customers before the implementation process begins. It is also important to be goal-oriented in order to harvest possible profits to the organization and gains from the implementation of the management system. It is critical to translate the system or the standard in a form suitable to the organizational culture and to be aware of the changes one wants from the system. ISO 9001, a holistic approach to quality management, is a comprehensive quality system that requires an implementation throughout the organization.

The system requires the involvement and commitment from the top management and leadership in the organization. In the Balague and Saarti study, a quality committee with top management involved was established and met regularly to discuss and decide on upcoming issues. The ISO standard is oriented toward customers, but this orientation involves optimization of resources and processes. A successful implementation is also about internal communication and knowledge sharing. This knowledge sharing is necessary with the embedded process approach in the standard because the different processes are interlinked and dependent on each other. An optimization of one part of the system will normally involve changes in other processes. It is interesting that the system in Spain has been in use for more than nine years and that the harvest of benefits increases every year. This persistence of a management system calls for a strong and strategically oriented leadership.

It appears that the group of Spanish academic libraries that implemented the system has benefited, but the benefits occurred because of the involvement of leaders and the change of organizational structures, staff development, and the possibility to make decisions. This case also illustrates that the boundary between leadership and management is fluid and that leadership with a good management system can lack the necessary persistence and diligence. Persistence and diligence are important because otherwise there is a risk that organizational cynicism and hypocrisy might emerge among staff members. It is also an important part of leadership to follow up on implementation of systems.

Leadership is about strategic decisions concerning networks and cooperation with other partners as information technology increasingly calls for solutions based on a national or regional level. Lluis Anglada has examined external cooperation among Spanish academic libraries.[27] Spanish university libraries have been through the same process as other academic libraries and they are integrated into the strategy and goals of the university. Anglada describes the transition of Spanish university libraries in the following way. In the 1980s, there was a movement toward centralization, which resulted in the consolidation of separate service units into a single university library. In the next decade, university library became the university library system, which indicates a radical shift in focus from internal library matters to users and services. The last step in the process, which started in the new century, looks like radical transformation as it is a consequence of a higher integration in the academic life and the digital information revolution that calls for new solutions and competencies. In this phase, the libraries strive to adopt new roles within universities.

The last stage calls for an active and inspiring leadership as the new roles in universities involve much more interdisciplinary work and the need to cooperate with other university libraries, especially concerning information and communication technologies. This is becoming an increasingly important element for library leadership. Libraries are increasingly becoming organizations with flexible and, in some cases, nonexisting boundaries that force cooperation at different levels. This calls for a certain kind of social intelligence because leadership in a networked and cooperative environment requires abilities, knowledge, and skills different from running an autonomous library. Some of the Spanish university libraries would not have made such transformations without some visionary leadership.

CONCLUDING THOUGHTS

This chapter must be seen in relation to the previous chapter that introduces some issues and principles concerning leadership in general in Europe based on different cultural frameworks. The chapter has also drawn a more distant or indirect relationship to the analytical framework presented in Chapter 3. However, the chapter raises some important issues concerning leadership and the possibilities to exercise leadership. In Europe, on a general level, there exist rather deep differences between public libraries and academic libraries in relation to funding, prestige, and placement in a wider structure. This variety of extremely different situations makes it difficult to put forward specific recommendations for the appropriate leadership behavior that covers the variety of institutions and situations.

There are some interesting challenges and obstacles in the different parts of Europe. There is no doubt that English leaders and directors in public libraries encounter a rigid and centralized management structure embedded in the local authorities, and they have less room for decision making due to a high degree of regulation. The situation is different in the British university libraries, where the directors and leaders expressed a high degree of knowledge of leadership issues at the verbal level, and they expressed a keen interest in transforming their institutions into team-oriented and customer-focused libraries. They also shared a common vision of making a difference in society and they are clearly committed to the profession of librarianship. Overall, the impression one gets from the British public libraries is that the rigid structures imposed on many of them hinder the full blossom of existing potential.

German libraries appear on the surface to be less modern. One of the reasons for this is the way organizational changes are implemented. The process is often slow, but normally it involves the whole organization and the process also seeks to reduce uncertainty, for example, by discussing possible positive and negative outcomes. Library leaders in Germany often have strong relations with the profession, and many staff members expect a certain degree of professional competence in the leader. In a leadership context, Germany has a mixture of pronounced regulations and bureaucratic structures combined with a relaxed relationship between leaders and followers due to the low power distance.

The leadership situation in the Baltic and former Eastern European states is also different. The obstacles here relate to funding, but it is also difficult to change the heritage of the former system, which had vastly different organizational cultures and educational structures. This in itself presents a difficult task, but in some of the countries, the library profession also has to cope with image problems. However, the development has been radical and fast. This is partly a result of funding from the EU, but it could not have happened if library directors in these countries did not participate in projects and partners with libraries in other countries.

The situation in southern Europe is also diversified and in the public library system the situation is dependent on the local authorities. The example from

Spain clear shows that academic libraries play an important role in the life of the universities.

In summary, funding differs from country to country, but overall there is a process of convergence and increasing European cooperation as evidenced from the number of European agencies and organizations fostering joint projects and initiatives.

NOTES

1. Jens Thorhauge and Monika Segbert, eds., *Public Libraries and the Information Society* (Luxembourg: European Commission 1997).

2. LibEcon, "Database," http://www.libecon.org/database/default.asp (accessed June 13, 2012).

3. John Mullins and Margaret Linehan, "The Central Role of Leaders in Public Libraries," *Library Management* 26, nos. 6–7 (2005): 386–93.

4. John Mullins and Margaret Linehan, "Leadership and Followership in Public Libraries: Transnational Perspectives," *International Journal of Public Sector Management* 18, no. 7 (2006): 641–47.

5. John Mullins and Margaret Linehan, "It Can Be Tough at the Top: Some Empirical Evidence from Public Library Leaders," *International Journal of Business and Management* 3, no. 9 (2006): 132–40.

6. John Mullins and Margaret Linehan, "Are Public Libraries Led or Managed?" *Library Review* 55, no. 4 (2006): 237–48.

7. Niels Ole Pors, Pat Dixon, and Heather Robson, "The Employment of Quality Measures in Libraries: Cultural Differences, Institutional Imperatives, and Managerial Profiles," *Performance Measurement and Metrics* 5, no. 1 (2004): 20–28.

8. Pors, Dixon, and Robson, "Employment of Quality Measures."

9. Sue Roberts and Jennifer Rowley, *Leadership: Challenges for the Information Profession* (London: Facet, 2008).

10. Niels Ole Pors, "Changing Perceptions and Attitudes among Danish Library Managers and Directors: The Case of Environmental Factors," *New Library World* 106, nos. 3–4 (2005): 107–15.

11. Kerry Wilson and Sheila Corrall, "Developing Public Library Managers as Leaders: Evaluation of a National Leadership Development Programme," *Library Management* 29, no. 6 (2008): 473–88.

12. Vilas Edwards and Niels Ole Pors, "International Co-operation: The West-East Relationship in EU Funded Projects," *Library Management* 22, no. 3 (2001): 124–30.

13. Elisabeth Simon and Karl A. Stroetmann, "Managing Courses in Countries of Central and Eastern Europe: Experiences during Two German Seminars about Library and Information Management," *Library Management* 16, no. 2 (1995): 40–45.

14. Arne Gundersen and Magadalena Kubecka, "Polish-Norwegian Cooperation on Strategies for Regional Libraries," *Library Management* 33, nos. 1–2 (2012): 104–11.

15. Henryk Hollander, "Who Will Take over the Libraries of the New Europe," *LIBER Quarterly* 17, nos. 3–4 (2007), liber.library.uu.nl/publish/issues/2007–3_4/index.html? 000207 (accessed June 12, 2012).

16. Ane Landøy and Angela Repanovici, "What Challenges Are Library Leaders Facing?" in *Information in e-Motion*, Proceedings BOBCATSSS 2012, 20th International Conference on Information Science, Amsterdam, edited by Wolf-Fritz Riekert and Ingeborg Simon (Bad Honnef, Germany: Bock+Herchen Verlag, 2012), 213–18.

17. Ane Landøy and Angela Repanovici, "Managing and Managers of e-Science," in *E-Science and Information Management: Third International Symposium on Information Management in a Changing World, IMCW 2012, Ankara, Turkey, September 19–21, 2012*, the publisher of this work is Berlin: Springer-Verlag, 2012, and the editors of the work are Serap Kurbanoğlu, Umut Al, Phyllis Lepon Erdoğan, Yaşar Tonta, and Nazan Uçak, 119–27.

18. Gerd Paul, "Mobilising the Potential for Initiative and Innovation by Means of Socially Competent Management: Results from Research Libraries in Berlin," *Library Management* 21, no. 2 (2000): 81–85; Gerd Paul, *Leitung und Cooperation in Wissenschaftlichen Bibliotheken Berlins: Eine Empirische Untersuchung*, Dissertation des Grades eines Doktors der Philosophie, Humboldt-Universität, Berlin, 1999.

19. Paul, "Mobilising the Potential for Initiative and Innovation."

20. Hildegard Schäffler, "How to Organize the Digital Library: Reengineering and Change Management in the Bayerische Stattsbibliothek, Munich," *Library Hi Tech* 22, no. 4 (2004): 340–46.

21. Robert Kaplan and David Norton, *Balanced Scorecard: Translating Strategy into Action* (Boston: Harvard Business School Press, 1996).

22. See Roswhita Poll, "Managing Service Quality with the Balanced Scorecard," *Advances in Library Administration and Organization* 20, no. 67 (2001): 213–27; Roswhita Poll, "Performance, Processes, and Cost: Managing Service Quality with the Balanced Scorecard," *Library Trends* 49, no. 4 (2001): 709–17.

23. Petra Düren, "Public Management Means Strategic Management: How Can Libraries Fulfil the Requirements of the New Public Management," *Library Management* 31 no. 3 (2010): 162–68.

24. Mel Collier, "Moving On: Transferability of Library Managers to New Environments," *Library Management* 28, nos. 4–5 (2007): 191–96.

25. Petros Kostagiolas and Maria Korkida, "Strategic Planning for Municipal Libraries in Greece," *New Library World* 109, nos. 11–12 (2008): 546–58.

26. Nuria Balague and Jarmo Saarti, "Benchmarking Quality Systems in Two European Academic Libraries," *Library Management* 30, nos. 4–5 (2009): 227–39.

27. Lluis Anglada, "Collaborations and Alliances: Social Intelligence Applied to Academic Libraries," *Library Management* 28, nos. 6–7 (2007): 406–15.

5

LEADING LIBRARIES THROUGH CUTS: A PERSPECTIVE FROM THE UK

Jennifer Rowley

In a time of indefinite austerity, with uncertain economic conditions, the United Kingdom (UK) government, similar to many other governments in Europe, is in an ongoing cycle of tightening the public purse through cuts in funding to public services. Public libraries have been on the frontline for such cuts because they are viewed as discretionary services, compared, for example, with care and other services for the elderly, disabled, or disadvantaged. All libraries, but particularly academic libraries and the extensive network of medical libraries in the National Health Service, are laboring under an increasing public skepticism as to their value in the face of growing public engagement with the attractive alternatives being offered and increasingly adopted in the growing digital space. In recent times, the increasing use of virtual learning environments (VLEs), social networking, better-quality open access content, and, most significantly of all, the rapid innovation and adoption around eBooks and eBook readers, smart phones, and tablet computers is revolutionizing information and reading behavior. In the face of these advances, it is not difficult for hard-pressed governments to persuade themselves that physical libraries no longer serve a useful function. In such a climate, leadership in libraries has become even more challenging than it was when I coauthored *Leadership: The Challenge for the Information Profession.*[1] Steve O'Connor's comment is particularly apt: "The future is often not continuous with or in a linear relationship to the present or the past. We do not have only one future; we have many and we are, in our personal lives, constantly choosing between them. Organisations are the same; they are not what they were; they will not be the same into the future."[2]

Under a perpetual threat of imminent or longer term cuts, or worse, the actuality of managing reduction in services and staffing levels, and working through the uncertainties, and the insecurities and tensions experienced by a staff group, even more is demanded of library leaders. Yet, the leadership literature rarely addresses leadership in volatile and unpredictable environments. Further, there is an underlying assumption that good leadership will lead to success, and that success will be measured in terms of sustainable and continuing growth for the organization, and recognition and career development for the effective manager. In times of cuts, expectations of personal or organizational success need to be realistic without being defeatist.

Further, with potential further rounds of cuts on the horizon, coupled perhaps with outsourcing, mergers, restructuring and culture change, an uncertain future frustrates the leader seeking to develop and communicate a clear vision. Accordingly, this chapter contributes to thinking about the leadership of libraries in the UK in the climate in which they find themselves, and it reflects on and proposes leadership behaviors that are most appropriate at this time. The chapter starts with a review of two leadership theories that are particularly appropriate in informing thinking about leadership, the Warren Bennis and Burt Nanus model of 21st-century leadership and contingency theories of leadership.[3] The chapter then considers some of the key challenges with which library leaders are presented in the early 21st century in the UK and offers proposals for appropriate leadership styles and behaviors.

LEADERSHIP THEORIES

Two leadership theories seem particularly appropriate in the difficult and challenging times that face many libraries and their staff in the UK and elsewhere. First, the model proposed by Bennis and Nanus is introduced. Next, there is discussion of the contingency theory, which proposes that leadership style and behaviors depend on the context. Related to the discussion are the concepts of transformational and dispersed leadership, and the contingent nature of leadership styles and behaviors, which act as a foundation for the third section of the chapter, which addresses leadership style and behaviors in times of austerity.

Bennis and Nanus's Model

This model is relevant for two reasons here. First, given that it was proposed in 1985, it is surprising how prescient it still remains today. Unfortunately, many of the items in the first list, *From* (see Table 5.1), still apply in libraries in the UK

Table 5.1   The Bennis-Nanus Model of 21st-Century Leadership*

FROM	TO
Few top leaders	Leaders at every level, few managers
Leading by goal setting	Leading by vision, new directions
Downsizing, benchmarking, quality	Create distinctive competencies
Reactive, adaptive to change	Creative, anticipative future change
Design hierarchical organizations	Design flat, collegial organizations
Direct and supervise	Empower, inspire, facilitate
Information held by few decision makers	Information shared with many
Leader as boss, controlling	Leader as coach, creating learning organization
Leader as stabilizer, balancing conflicts	Leader as change agent, balancing risks
Leader develops good managers	Leader develops future leaders.

*This table is a characterization of the author based on Warren Bennis and Burt Nanus, *Leaders: Strategies for Taking Charge*, 2nd ed. (London: Harper Business, 1997).

today. Particularly salient are the continuing focus on downsizing, benchmarking, and quality; the persistence of hierarchical organizational structures; and the reactive stance to change. Accordingly, it might be argued that the second column, *To*, constitutes a brief checklist to the way forward for library leadership. This solution involves two key components, which may be viewed as being in conflict, but which with effective management can make a very powerful combination: transformational leadership and dispersed leadership.

New leadership, a leadership theory that originated with the work of James McGregor Burns, distinguished between transformational and transactional leaders.[4] The new or transformational leader is an inspirational visionary who builds a shared sense of purpose and mission and creates a culture in which everyone is aligned with the organization's goals and is skilled and empowered to achieve them. Such transformational leaders are charismatic individuals who inspire and motivate others to perform beyond their contract. The transformational leader treats relationships with followers in terms of motivation and commitment, influencing and inspiring followers to give more than compliance toward improvement of organizational performance; they encourage commitment, initiative, flexibility, and high performance. In contrast, transactional leaders enact their relationships with followers in terms of an exchange, giving the followers what they want in return for what the leader desires, on the basis of prescribed tasks to pursue established goals. For example, James Castiglione suggests that the transactional library administrator is assignment- and task-oriented and expects employee compliance.[5] Transformational library administrators, on the other hand, inspire, motivate, and facilitate for the purpose of strategic renewal. They do this by empowering staff to question old assumptions. They also encourage staff to construct a compelling vision of future possibilities for themselves and their stakeholders. Although it could be argued that transformational leaders are useful throughout an organization, much of the consideration of this theory has related to senior managers and directors.

Dispersed leadership theory argues for the development of leadership capacity throughout the organization. It has its foundation in the belief that leadership is best exercised by those who have the interest, knowledge, skills, and motivation to perform specific leadership functions and roles. For instance, in an academic library the best person to lead on the development of the e-resource collection would be the e-resources librarian, and in a public library the best person to lead on the development of the digital presence of local studies collections would be the local studies librarian. This stance does not only mean that people in these roles have the appropriate skills and expertise and take responsibility for developing that expertise, but that they also are accepted by others as providing a lead on matters in their area of expertise, and indeed are relied upon and expected to do so. In addition to locating decision making and leadership closer to the expertise, dispersed leadership also provides an opportunity for the leadership development of future top managers and leaders. Accordingly, throughout this chapter, the term *leader* refers to leaders at all levels in the organization, although senior managers may sometimes be able to take actions that have wider impact that those in more junior, or, of particular relevance in the current climate, less permanent or secure posts.

The development of leadership capacity throughout the organization makes particular demands on senior leaders, and this has led to the concept of a super leader. A super leader develops leadership capacity in others, empowering them, reducing their dependence on formal leaders and stimulating their motivation, commitment, and creativity. It would seem that this might be particularly apt in uncertain times, when experienced and older staff may be leaving the organization. Hence, activities such as coaching and mentoring might be of particular value.

Another aspect of the Bennis and Nanus model, which has not received as much attention as it deserves, is the reference to the leader as change agent and to the role of the leader in balancing risks. While it is preferable to think in terms of innovation, rather than change management, this allusion to risk in this important model is prescient. In the current environment there is a persistent sense of risk and an acknowledgment that things are unlikely to stay as they are. Hence, managing risk is one aspect of leadership that library leaders need to embrace, and they specifically need to develop their competence in identifying opportunities and evaluating and mitigating risks. Successful entrepreneurship is grounded in taking the right risks.

Contingency Leadership Theories

While early theories of leadership sought to understand the traits that good leaders exhibit or the style and behavior that they should adopt, context and contingency theories of leadership propose that the most appropriate leadership behavior or style is dependent on the context. Hence, in the current context, characterized by cuts and uncertainties, in which UK libraries find themselves, it might be argued that different leadership behaviors are required from those that were appropriate in more stable and predictable times. This thought, was, in fact, the point of departure for this chapter. When I was invited to write a chapter on leadership in libraries in the UK, the one unifying characteristic of leadership seemed to be the current context in which libraries are operating.

Contingency theories offer some insights into the key contextual factors that might influence optimum leadership behavior, and this general stance of linking behavior to context is useful. However, on closer inspection many of the traditional theories are only of indirect value for our current purpose, because their consideration of the scope of context is limited. For example, the widely mentioned situational leadership theory proposed by Paul Hersey and Kenneth Blanchard describes leadership behavior in terms of the relationship between the leader and the follower, based on the balance between two types of leadership behavior: task behavior and supportive behavior.[6] Admittedly, follower readiness, which is a central concept in their model, may be affected by disruptions in the organizational setting, since it depends on followers' ability, their willingness, and their security in completing the task. Another widely used contingency theory, Robert Tannenbaum and Warren H. Schmidt's continuum of leadership, proposes different leadership styles on the basis of forces in the manager (e.g., personality and beliefs), forces among subordinates (e.g., need for independence and tolerance of ambiguity), and forces in the situation (e.g., organizational norms, effectiveness of team working, nature of the problem, type of organization, and time pressure).[7] In common with situational leadership theory, the focus is on managers and their staff, rather than on the wider context. The dimensions of forces in the situation draw in elements of the organizational context, such as organizational norms, location of working groups, and time pressures—several of which may be impacted on by the changes arising from cuts. In this sense they give guidance that can assist the leader in evaluating the forces in the situation. Tannenbaum and Schmidt suggest that successful leaders are aware of these forces, and have the ability to adapt their behavior accordingly and appropriately. Certainly, it is more important than ever for library leaders to be familiar with the context in which they are working, so that they can be proactive, rather than reactive.

Other contingency theories that may offer some useful insights include Daniel Goleman's leadership styles and models based on the stage of development of the organization. Goleman, for example, proposes six leadership styles and suggests when they might be of use. These include coercive, authoritative, affiliative, democratic, pacesetting, and coaching.[8] Arguably, the most important of these in *cutting* situations is the affiliative style, recommended for healing rifts and wounds, and to motivate people under stress. Key competencies required for this style are empathy, relationship building, and communication. The democratic style can be used to build consensus and buy-in in the context of difficult and unpalatable decisions; this require competencies in collaboration and team building. Pacesetting, to get fast results in forming a motivated and competent team, might be perceived as appropriate, on the basis of outside threats, but this style could be counterproductive if the team feels neither motivated nor competent; these precursors to success must be developed first. From the theories that argue that leadership style depends on the stage of the organization's development, maybe the concept of the *lemon squeezer* is most salient.[9] The lemon squeezer is a leadership style that is deemed appropriate should an organization go into decline; in order to revitalize the organization the lemon squeezer needs to be tough and innovative in cutting costs, improving productivity, and managing staffing levels.

Overall, then, while contingency theories of leadership offer some useful frameworks for the different styles that leaders might adopt, they have little specifically to say on situations of downsizing and decline, and how the organization can stabilize at a steady state, and along the way identify new opportunities for the future.

Another consequence of the contingency perspective is the acknowledgment that the different contexts in which specific library leaders find themselves might require different leadership styles. For example, the director of a national library, such as the British Library, is expected to develop and evolve a vision for the role of the library in a national and international marketplace. Leadership therefore occurs in national and international settings. Visioning, power, politics, and reputation management are key leadership behaviors. On the other hand, the leader of an electronic resources team in an academic library, while also needing to manage the politics and power issues around resources and to develop a credible vision for developing the service, is required to focus on leading the team to ensure reliable and effective service delivery. There is a much greater focus on developing the team. So, while the next section of this chapter proposes some key behaviors to support libraries through the current, and quite possibly ongoing crisis, the relevance and application of these behaviors vary from one context to another.

KEY LEADERSHIP BEHAVIORS IN TIMES OF AUSTERITY

The current wave of public sector austerity that is affecting the foundations of the complex edifices of public sector organizations, administrations, and services in many developed countries in the second decade of this century drives the debate about the future of libraries. Alongside this, many pundits are taking various stances in the debate on the likely impact that the rapid recent adoption of eBooks will have on the demand for library services, for both leisure reading and education.

On the basis of the old adage that *all publicity is good publicity*, one of the upsides of the current circumstances is that all types of people, including authors, educators, publishers, and digital visionaries, are talking about libraries. The downside is that the future for libraries is uncertain, both in terms of the services that will be continue to be valued by communities and the resources that will be available to support these services. Accordingly, this section proposes that certain leadership behaviors will become more important for library leaders over the next few years. The first three of these focus on the leader's role in setting the context for building effective relationships in teams and between the leader and the led, and most important, cultivating and developing the confidence and competencies of staff. These include discussion of building team relationships, cultivating follower relationships, and dealing with emotions and emotional intelligence. The next three behaviors are more strategic and focus specifically on leading through innovation, developing staff and leaders, and leading through reputation and influence.

Building Team Relationships

Leadership is concerned with influencing people to do things that leaders want them to do. It is therefore, indisputably, and in every situation concerned with relationships. One of the most difficult things about leadership through cuts is that existing working relationships are disturbed or under threat. Colleagues may be required to compete with each other for a job. They may be oversensitive about being seen to do something wrong, for fear of being the one to be shown the door. If workloads have increased, team members may be passing the work to someone else. Everyone is stressed by the uncertainty, and levels of sickness absence will increase, with knock-on consequences for the workload of the remaining staff. Everyone is unsure as to whether they have a future in that organization, and if they do, for how long (is the current round of cuts the last?), and in what role. In all this, managers, particularly middle managers, are often in jobs that are the most vulnerable, yet they are called upon to keep the ship afloat and deliver if possible even better service with fewer staff, while managing staff sickness absences, vacancies, and staff on temporary and part-time contracts. In such an environment, there is plenty of scope for conflict and relationship rifts, in even the most supportive and effective team. In such a context, leaders need to focus on people, building their confidence in a future, encouraging them to take as much responsibility for their own futures as is realistic, and managing to create a context in which relationships can be rebuilt. This must be done in full acknowledgment that this may only be a short-term situation, and the cycle of rebuilding people and relationships may need to be revisited in a year or even in a few months. In this process, leadership may be less about empathy and more about establishing tough ground rules that perpetuate and communicate as far as possible a sense of fairness and transparency as a basis for an atmosphere in which good working (even if not good social) relationships can be established and maintained. To achieve this, the ground rules need to be explicit and applied scrupulously but tempered with humanity. Typical ground rules might include the following:

• No one is guaranteed a job; this means that performance management processes must be applied, and used scrupulously to manage absences and poor performance.

- Everyone is judged on their contribution; this means that opportunities and privileges, such as some flexibility in working hours and sought-after development opportunities, are granted in accordance with the contribution that the individual makes.

- Everyone is clear what their job is, and what is not their job; too often in change situations people end up doing their old job and their new one, or being unclear as to the boundaries between their job and other people's jobs. At times a manager may have little option to ask or even pressure people to do additional work, but this must be acknowledged as such, and not expected on an ongoing basis.

- Everyone has a voice, but those who are most listened to on a topic are those with the most expertise and knowledge on that subject.

- Everyone is respected for their contribution, receives appropriate communication, and is expected to be flexible and supportive in working with other members of the team.

Cultivating Followership Relationships

A specific type of relationship that needs to be cultivated is that between the leader and the follower. First and foremost, leadership only occurs when someone else follows. Second, if all team members are following the same leader, then relationships and effectiveness will be better. There is often too much focus on leadership and too little on followership, and even less acknowledgment that leaders must also be followers. For example, most leaders have to respond to the agendas set by other leaders, either those in a more senior position in a hierarchy to them, or in a distributed leadership model in which they lead in some areas and someone else leads on another area. Further, in organizations that are being reshaped, leaders cannot assume that their leadership or senior position is permanent. Authentic leadership theory suggests that leaders need to be at ease with interdependence.[10] Accordingly, it is important for leaders to understand and manage the leadership–followership relationship.

Various authors make proposals regarding the leadership–followership relationship. For example, James M. Kouzes and Barry Z. Posner suggest that the desirable characteristics of superior leaders from a follower's perspective are honesty, competency, and being forward-thinking (visionary) and inspiring,[11] whereas Robert Goffee and Gareth Jones argue that followers are seeking emotional rewards from their leaders in terms of significance (to feel valued), community (to feel part of something), and excitement (to feel challenged).[12] The theory of transformational leadership also comments on the relationship between leaders and followers, suggesting that transformational leaders are characterized as charismatic individuals who inspire and motivate others to perform beyond their contract, by focusing on motivation, commitment, and influencing and inspiring followers.[13] Library leaders need to reflect and act on such suggestions, and continue to develop both their leadership behaviors to cultivate followership, and their followership behaviors in support of those leaders, who they identify as worth supporting. In a more fluid environment, with roles changing, a strong network of relationships, with considerable give-and-take is essential to getting the job done, achieving innovation and change, and personal survival.

Dealing with Emotions and Emotional Intelligence

The last two sections have focused on relationships; relationships involve people and people have powerful emotions about the social situations in which they find themselves. In situations of change and uncertain futures, where things *may* continue, but certainly not as they are, emotions are more at play in the workplace than in more stable environments in which more things can be taken for granted. Leaders often influence by recognizing their followers' emotional states, attempting to evoke emotions in followers, and seeking to manage followers' emotional states.[14] Some argue that team members who are able to perceive accurately and understand and appraise others' emotions are better able to respond flexibly to changes in their social environment and to build supportive networks.[15] Emotional intelligence (EI), or the ability to identify, integrate, understand, and manage our own and other people's feelings, is being increasingly recognized as important for managers and leaders. If leaders understand how people respond or, even better, are likely to respond in a given situation, there is potential for influencing their emotions to create more positive outcomes for both the individual and the organization. Goleman, Richard Boyatzis and Annie McKee, and Robert Kerr et al., for instance, suggest that emotional intelligence is associated with leadership effectiveness and can give leaders an edge in senior and leadership roles, where conventional intelligence and capabilities are assumed.[16] Increased EI can create faster, deeper, and more sustained change, and thereby impact on personal and organizational effectiveness. Goleman proposes the five dimensions of EI: self-awareness, regulated feelings, motivation, empathy, and social skills (see Table 5.2). Most importantly, he suggests that leaders need to be able to manage their own emotions before they can be effective in managing the emotions of others. Given that in times of austerity and change, leaders will often experience the same uncertainty and pressure to perform, adapt, and build new alliances; however, this is not easy to do. It is important to recognize that managing emotions and feeling is not about suppressing them or pretending they do not exist, nor is it always about sympathy and empathy. It is about leaders being aware and acknowledging and responding

Table 5.2   Goleman's Five Dimensions of Emotional Intelligence*

DIMENSION	DEFINITION
Self-awareness	The ability to recognize and understand your needs, emotions, and drives as well as the effect that you have on others
Regulated feelings	The ability to control your disruptive moods and impulses: the propensity to suspend judgment, to think before acting
Motivation	A passion to work for reasons beyond status and money; a propensity to pursue goals with energy and persistence
Empathy	The ability to recognize and understand the emotional makeup of others; skill in dealing with the emotional responses of others
Social skills	Effectiveness in managing relationships and building networks; ability to find common ground, to build rapport

*Adapted by permission of *Harvard Business Review*. From "Leadership That Gets Results," by Daniel Goleman, 78, no. 2 (March/April). Copyright © 2000 by the Harvard Business School Publishing Corporation; all rights reserved.

to both their own emotions and those of others and channeling them to be more productive for the individual, team, and organization. For example, anger can be very destructive, but it can be channeled into the drive to make things better. Being sensitive to others and their emotions, especially when those emotions are negative (e.g., fear and dislike), can challenge the confidence of leaders and make them feel insecure. However, at the same time sensitivity allows them to read and predict the emotions of others, and properly harnessed is a powerful leadership asset.

Julian Barling, Frank Slater, and E. Kevin Kelloway suggest that individuals with high emotional intelligence might be more likely to use transformational leadership behaviors, and therefore succeed in changing and tough environments. As a result,

- Leaders who know and can manage their own emotions and who display self-control and delay of gratification could serve as role models for their followers. This would, in turn, enhance follower's trust in and respect for their leaders, allowing leaders to exercise greater influence over followers.

- By understanding others' emotions, leaders with high emotional intelligence would be able to reconsider the extent to which followers' expectations could be raised, and thereby be in a good position to exercise inspirational motivation.

- Emphasis on empathy and the ability to manage relationships is a basis for leaders with high emotional intelligence to exercise consideration for individuals.[17]

Leading through Innovation, Not Change

Central to transformational leadership is the notion of inspiration. Yet, in times of insecurity and uncertainty, inspiring people becomes an uphill struggle. With cuts looming on the horizon and/or lingering as an all-too-recent memory, inspiring people to go the extra mile or to get excited and interested by things happening in their workplace becomes more difficult. Since inspiration is pivotal to successful leadership, leaders need to work out how to inspire when the odds are stacked against them. Effectively managed innovation, either in services or processes, will probably not only be necessary (how else do you achieve more with less?) but it provides an opportunity to energize the team and to look forward rather than backward. If, for example, a library service is reeling from declining user registrations due to the increasing adoption of eBooks, change is no doubt on the agenda, but the rhetoric of innovation and creativity can be so much more engaging than the language of change management. Staff see change management as something that they have done to them. Properly managed innovation can be an opportunity for participation, ingenuity, teamwork and achievement. Innovation is a way of reasserting control of a situation. Another downside of the change management approach is its association with Kurt Lewin's model of freeze-change-refreeze, and the implication that change is a one-time activity (until the next time).[18] Innovation, on the other hand, can be seen as a way of life if the leader can create an innovation-oriented team or organizational culture.

There has been much discussion as to the characteristics of an innovation-oriented culture, but for certain an innovative organization can be identified by its outcomes. And, the other thing that is certain is that experience of innovation is an essential ingredient for being innovative; being innovative is something that an organization learns from experience. Innovations may be incremental (small step-wise improvements in current processes or services) or radical (often associated with new projects and different ways of doing things). At this time, library leaders may more often be called to lead through radical innovations than in the past, sometimes needing to lead through a paradigm of innovation, innovation that changes the nature of the business that the organization is in. Fiona Patterson and Maura Kerrin, who focused on the role of innovation in the UK in recovery, list the 10 top factors that contribute to effective innovation:

1. Managers provide practical support for new ideas and their application.
2. There is a we are in it together attitude.
3. They strive for a reputation for being innovative.
4. The general management style is participative and collaborative.
5. The organizational goals are directly aligned with innovation.
6. Management practices actively enhance innovation.
7. There is a no blame culture—mistakes are talked about freely so that other people can learn from them.
8. Resources and facilities are readily available for use in testing out new ideas.
9. Personal development objectives explicitly related to innovation are set.
10. Job assignments ensure that there is enough time and scope for trying out new ideas.[19]

Some would argue that the roles of leader and innovator are tightly coupled, and that leaders continually need to monitor and engage in potential improvements, developments, and enhancements in all aspects of the organization. On the other hand, in common with the other leadership behaviors suggested in this chapter, leading through cuts by innovation is not easy, and a leader may need to exercise considerable persistence and persuasion to succeed. Kathryn Deiss, writing in more settled times, acknowledges that the mature nature of most library organizations makes it more difficult to take risks, experiment, accommodate creativity, and generate innovation, but maybe the current climate provides the opportunity to shed at least some of the constraints that have traditionally reined in creativity and innovation in libraries.[20] Interestingly, James G. Neal, writing in 2010, suggested that libraries are becoming more entrepreneurial and are more actively engaging in innovation, business planning, competitiveness, risk taking and management, and partnerships.[21]

Making Time to Develop Staff and Leaders

Training, mentoring, and coaching are all abandoned in times of cuts; they may be perceived as too time-consuming when there are more pressing short-term agendas, or the lack of availability of financial and other resources to support such activities may be a barrier. Yet, at times of change, the onus is on people to learn and adapt. They may be required to take on another role, do more tasks in the same time, learn a new system, understand a new and changing context (which possibly nobody in the context fully understands), or develop new skills to equip them for the next job when their current role is terminated. There is an even greater need for leaders, managers, and staff to learn and develop and have the skill, knowledge, and attitudes that make them flexible, and capable of not only working as part of the team, but also taking the initiative.

Time and other resources to support staff development may be at a premium, but those staff members who are still working are even more important than they were previously to the successful delivery of, and innovation in relation to, the service. Furthermore, changing agendas and staff bases offer opportunities to learn, build new relationships, and, most important, challenge and change embedded but past-their-sell-by-date customs, practices, values, and cultures. It is likely that staff will find themselves learning by doing. It is in the leader's interest to be aware of and manage this learning process, to ensure that it produces positive, rather than negative, outcomes for the members of the staff, the team, and the organization.

A key concept that is worth revisiting in these times is that of action learning. If things are always changing, then there is much to be learned from reflecting on experiences. Experiential learning and action learning are based on David A. Kolb's learning cycle, which has the following four stages:

1. Plan (plan an experiment to do something new)
2. Do (implement, trying doing something new, or innovate)
3. Think (reflect critically on the experience of the innovation)
4. Conclusion (develop theories and integrate observations emerging from the reflection to learn and inform the next innovation or learning cycle).[22]

Experiential learning can be promoted by many of the characteristics of an innovative culture, including the availability of time and space to do something new and to reflect on the experience, as well as a structured developmental appraisal process. Individual learning can also be promoted by managers giving priority to coaching and mentoring their staff by spending time listening to them, supporting them, and giving prompt and positive feedback.[23] Individual learning will be all the more effective if it is contextualized within a culture of organizational learning.[24]

Adopting a strong commitment to staff development, including leadership development, may seem like professional suicide; if the staff are too good, someone may decide that a particular job can be done more cheaply. Further, the position of successful leaders in an organization can become even more precarious, due to organizational jealousies regarding their success and the opportunities that this might generate, especially when things elsewhere are tight. Leaders need to acknowledge this and to be prepared, to be proactive, to develop their own skills, and to take care of their own futures consciously, as much as those of their staff. As Lois Burton and Deborah Dalley suggest, "The work is from the inside out—develop yourself and you develop your world."[25]

Leading through Reputation and Influence

Finally, an important role of leadership is associated with promoting the library to a multitude of internal and external stakeholders that might see themselves as having a stake in the library and its future. These might include organizations and individuals that see themselves as allocating funding for the library, are in competition with the library for scarce public sector funding, have a responsibility for building the reputation of the place or university with which the library is associated, as well as users and library staff. One of the challenges is that each stakeholder group has a different image of the library and values different aspects of its role or services. The first step in building the reputation of a library is being clear as to the identity of the library, that is knowing what the library stands for, what it is, what benefits it can deliver to its community, and why those benefits are important. Further, the identity (often, these days, captured and communicated through the library's brand and associated brand communications) needs to differentiate the identity of the library from its myriad of competitors, including competitors for the library's funding, as well as those for the attention and patronage of its potential users.

A number of commentators recognize that one of the challenges for libraries at the present time is the search for a sustainable identity. For example, Jens Thorhauge suggests that libraries "do not have a clear cut vision for the new library,"[26] and, as David Hood and Kay Henderson suggest, "you can't brand a library that doesn't know what it wants to be."[27] These issues have consequences for building visibility, marketing communication, and reputation. In addition, libraries often face a challenge in communicating a clear and unique brand identity. Typically their brand is a subbrand of their parent organization (be that a university or a local authority), and to aggravate the situation, their digital presence is controlled by the parent organization.[28] Further, in some instances, the parent organization itself (e.g., a university) may be struggling to achieve successful management of its brand.[29] Nevertheless, there are examples of successful rebranding exercises based on a refreshed identity.[30] Jonathan Schroeder and Miriam Salzer-Morling point out that leadership is pivotal to success. Leaders need to act as brand champions, encourage staff buy-in, and embed key messages in service delivery.[31]

While brand development and communication are pivotal to engaging a wide range of stakeholders, influencing, and more widely partnering are also important in building reputation. Burton and Dalley argue for the importance of authenticity and congruence to successful influencing, which are important both within the library and beyond. They suggest that successful influencing behaviors for leaders include the following:

1. "Understanding who you are and what you stand for
2. Congruence and authenticity (the link between our identity and values and the behaviour we exhibit generates trust)
3. Empathy with others
4. Communication capability (questioning, listening, feedback)
5. Intent (most successful influencers are those who operate from values such as truth, trust and integrity)
6. Ease with uncertainty
7. Ease with interdependence."[32]

Importantly, these behaviors reflect various themes that have been already picked up earlier in this chapter as being important for library leaders. The list also includes another important behavior, ease with interdependence, which acts as a platform for networking and partnering.

While there is a long-standing recognition of the need for library leaders to act as advocates beyond their own libraries,[33] the need to do this in the current climate is even more pressing. On the other hand, building partnerships is also riskier than in previous times, since the future of many of the potential partners may be less than clear, and a range of factors can intervene to disrupt an organization's commitment to a project. However, working with partners in other organizations on joint projects allows the library to not only capitalize on external assets and resources to support innovation, but also build mutual understandings and strengthen reputations.

CONCLUDING THOUGHTS

Traditional leadership theories have an implicit underlying assumption that good leaders, certainly at the strategic level, succeed in achieving organizational growth. Some might argue that leadership is easier in a growth situation because there are more opportunities for capturing new users, investment in innovation (new buildings, new services), and appointing new staff. Leadership with contracting budgets, as well as a more competitive and dynamic environment, can seem daunting. This chapter explored traditional leadership theories and used them to identity leadership behaviors and styles for survival and reinvention. Bennis and Nanus's model and contingency theories of leadership suggest the following concepts that seem particularly prescient for 21st-century library leaders in challenging times: transformational leadership, dispersed leadership, leaders as risk managers, and the contingent nature of leadership. The next section, the core of the chapter, proposed six dimensions of leadership behavior in austerity. These fall into two groups. The first three dimensions focus on the leader's role in relationships and people: building team relationships, cultivating followership relationships, and dealing with emotions and emotional intelligence. The second three dimensions focus on more strategic behaviors: leading through innovation, not change; making the time to develop staff and leaders; and leading through reputation and influence. The six dimensions have relevance in the challenging and changing environment for libraries and their leaders. Of course, in keeping with the contingency approach, different dimensions will be more or less relevant to the different circumstances in which library leaders find themselves.

It will take a very special kind of leader to transform and redefine library service with tight resources and on shifting sands. The challenge of leadership has never been greater, and success and rewards are less certain, but communities still need libraries in this digital age, and libraries need leaders.

NOTES

1. Sue Roberts and Jennifer Rowley, *Leadership: The Challenge for the Information Profession* (London: Facet, 2008).

2. Steve O'Connor, "The Heretical Library Manager for the Future," *Library Management* 28, nos. 1–2 (2007): 69.

3. Warren Bennis and Burt Nanus, *Leaders: Strategies for Taking Charge*, 2nd ed. (London: Harper Business, 1997).

4. James MacGregor Burns, *Leadership* (New York: Harper and Row, 1978).

5. James Castiglione, "Organizational Learning and Transformational Leadership in the Library Environment," *Library Management* 27, nos. 4–5 (2006): 289–99.

6. Paul Hersey and Kenneth Blanchard, *Management of Organizational Behavior: Utilizing Human Resources* (Englewood Cliffs, NJ: Prentice-Hall, 1969).

7. Robert Tannenbaum and Warren H Schmidt, "How to Choose a Leadership Pattern," *Harvard Business Review* (May/June 1973), http://www.elcamino.edu/faculty/bcarr/documents/How%20to%20choose%20a%20leadership%20pattern.pdf (accessed May 29, 2012).

8. Daniel Goleman, "Leadership That Gets Results," *Harvard Business Review* 78, no. 2 (2000): 78–90.

9. Christopher Clarke and Simon Pratt, "Leadership's Four-Part Progress," *Management Today* (March 1985): 84–86.

10. Fred Luthans and Bruce J. Avolio, "Authentic Leadership: A Positive Development Approach," in *Positive Organizational Scholarship: Foundations of a New Discipline*, edited

by Kim S. Cameron, Jane E. Dutton, and Robert E. Quinn (San Francisco: Barrett-Koehler, 2003), 241–61.

11. James M. Kouzes and Barry Z. Posner, *Credibility: How Leaders Gain and Lose It, Why People Demand It* (San Francisco: Jossey-Bass, 2003).

12. Robert Goffee and Gareth Jones, "Followership: It's Personal Too," *Harvard Business Review* 79, no. 11 (2001): 148.

13. Burns, *Leadership*; Castiglione, "Organizational Learning and Transformational Leadership."

14. Ronald Humphrey, "The Many Faces of Emotional Leadership," *Leadership Quarterly* 13, no. 5 (2002): 493–504.

15. John D. Mayer, David R. Caruso, and Peter Salovey, "Emotional Intelligence as Zeitgeist, as Personality, and as a Mental Ability," in *The Handbook of Emotional Intelligence: Theory, Development, Assessment, and Application at Home School and in the Workplace*, edited by Reuven Bar-On and James D. A. Parker (New York: Jossey-Bass, 2000), 92–117.

16. See Daniel Goleman, Richard Boyatzis, and Annie McKee, *Primal Leadership: Realizing the Power of Emotional Intelligence* (Boston: Harvard Business School Press, 2002); Robert Kerr, John Garvin, Norma Heaton, and Emily Boyle, "Emotional Intelligence and Leadership Effectiveness," *Leadership & Organization Development Journal* 27, no. 4 (2006): 265–79.

17. Julian Barling, Frank Slater, and E. Kevin Kelloway, "Transformational Leadership and Emotional Intelligence: An Exploratory Study," *Leadership & Organization Development Journal* 21, no. 3 (2000): 157–61.

18. Kurt Lewin, *Field Theory in Social Science* (New York: Harper & Row, 1951).

19. Fiona Patterson and Maura Kerrin, *Innovation for the Recovery: Enhancing Innovative Working Practices* (London: Chartered Management Institute, 2009), https://www.managers.org.uk/sites/default/files/user28/Innovation_for_the_Recovery_Dec_2009_0.pdf (accessed May 21, 2012).

20. Kathryn J. Deiss, "Innovation and Strategy: Risk and Choice in Shaping User-Centered Libraries," *Library Trends* 53, no. 1 (2004): 17–32.

21. James G. Neal, "Advancing from Kumbaya to Radical Collaboration: Redefining the Future Research Library," *Journal of Library Administration* 51, no. 1 (2010): 66–76.

22. David A. Kolb, *Experiential Learning: Experience as the Source of Learning and Development* (London: Prentice-Hall, 1984).

23. Eric Parsloe and Monika Wray, *Coaching and Mentoring: Practical Methods to Improve Learning* (London: Kogan Page, 2000).

24. Chris Argyris and Donald A. Schon, eds., *Organizational Culture II: Theory, Method and Practice* (Cambridge, MA: Addison-Wesley, 1996).

25. Lois Burton and Deborah Dalley, *Beyond Influencing*, Leadership Seminar, unpublished (Manchester, UK, 2007).

26. Jens Thorhauge, "Branding the Library," *Scandinavian Public Library Quarterly* 40, no. 4 (2007): 3.

27. David Hood and Kay Henderson, "Branding in the United Kingdom Public Library Service," *New Library World* 106, nos. 1–2 (2005): 17.

28. Lucy Smith and Jennifer Rowley, "Digitisation of Local Heritage: Local Studies Collections and Digitisation in Public Libraries," *Journal of Librarianship and Information Science* 44, no. 1 (2012), doi:10.1177/0961000611434760, http://lis.sagepub.com/content/early/2012/02/23/0961000611434760.full.pdf+html/ (accessed October 17, 2012).

29. Chris Chapleo, "What Defines 'Successful' University Brands?" *International Journal of Public Sector Management* 23, no. 2 (2010): 169–83.

30. Subnum Hariff and Jennifer Rowley, "Branding of Public Libraries," *Library Management* 32, no. 4 (2011): 346–60.

31. Jonathan Schroeder and Miriam Salzer-Morling, eds., *Brand Culture* (Abingdon, Oxon, UK: Routledge, 2006).

32. Burton and Dalley, *Beyond Influencing.*

33. See, for instance, Alan Bundy, "A Window of Opportunity: Libraries and Higher Education," *Library Management* 24, nos. 8–9 (2003): 393–400.

6

THE DANISH LIBRARY LEADERSHIP SURVEYS, 2001–2007

Carl Gustav Johannsen

This chapter deals with the origins and development of library management in Denmark or, to be more precise, the growing attention and awareness among public library directors and managers of leadership issues. One could claim that the interest of professional library managers in these issues dates from approximately 2000. The most obvious reason was a change in Danish library law to allow persons with a professional background in other areas than librarianship to assume leadership positions in Danish public libraries. Until then, librarians had had a monopoly on leadership positions in public libraries. A similar monopoly did not exist in other types of libraries such as academic libraries where people with different academic backgrounds and sometimes nonacademic backgrounds could become directors. Indeed, academic library directors with a background in librarianship were a clear minority. Thus, an obvious conclusion is that competition from other professions such as business schools was the primary motivation for Danish public library leaders to become interested in professional leadership issues and theories. To support this assumption we can review the library leadership surveys of 2001 and the significant growth in participation by library directors and middle managers in leadership courses. Indeed, many directors obtained master's degrees in management and organization theory during the following years. One purpose was to demonstrate that library leaders could match other public leaders both in terms of professional attitudes and knowledge and use of modern management tools.

Although the expected massive competition from other professionals did not take place, interest in leadership issues among library professionals apparently continued to grow. Therefore, the abovementioned simplistic and mono-causal explanation needs to be nuanced. It is the purpose of this chapter to examine those complex developments preceding the first library leadership surveys in 2001 by focusing on a number of changes that had taken place years before 2000, underscoring the importance of management and leadership in public libraries. Among those developments, the role of public library business information services in the 1980s and 1990s and the emergence of concepts such as information management and knowledge management should be addressed. Furthermore, the idea of an early emergence of a specific Scandinavian style of leadership will be addressed and questioned. The following five questions will be covered:

1. What characterizes the development and the growth of interest in management and leadership in the Danish public library sector and profession?
2. What was the role of new public management (NPM) in creating an interest in management and leadership?
3. What patterns and trends characterized Danish public library leaders' attitudes and practices according to the three Danish library leadership surveys of 2001, 2004, and 2007?
4. What theoretical interpretations have been made based on the findings of the three Danish library leadership surveys?
5. To what extent do the Danish library leadership surveys support the notion of a specific Scandinavian (Denmark, Norway, and Sweden) library management style?

The first and the second questions will be dealt with in the section on the origins of management and leadership within public librarianship. The third question will be considered in the section on the emergence of library leader and leadership surveys in 2001. The fourth question will be discussed in the section on interpretations and theoretical perspectives, and the last question will be covered in the section about a common Scandinavian library management style.

THE ORIGINS OF MANAGEMENT AND LEADERSHIP IN THE DANISH LIBRARY PROFESSION

Considering the history of Danish public libraries, the idea of getting inspired by and using management principles derived from private sector industry and businesses in libraries is not a product of the last 20 or 30 years. In fact, libraries have a long history for the rationalization of processes, cooperation, and use of new technologies.[1] Nevertheless, until about 1980, public libraries were relatively unaffected by the ongoing trends in leadership and management gaining prominence in the Danish private sector. Then NPM ideas slowly began to penetrate both the Danish public sector, in general, and the Danish public libraries. NPM is a common name for a public sector reform movement that, since the 1980s, has influenced public sector policies and practice in the western world. The NPM framework has been variously denominated as "post-bureaucratic," "managerialism," "market-based public administration," and "entrepreneurial government."[2] A common feature of all NPM efforts is to shape the public sector in the form of the private section by introducing management and the marketplace within government and public service institutions. The ultimate goal seems to be to replace administrative, hierarchical, and professional cultures with commercial market cultures. The radicalism of how the NPM framework has been implemented differs widely from country to country. Among the hardcore NPM countries are the United Kingdom, the United States, Australia, and New Zealand, whereas the Scandinavian countries are among the softer applicants of NPM. The key elements of NPM in most countries include the following elements: customer and market orientation, competition and user choice, outsourcing and privatization, contract administration and performance review, and focus on leadership and management processes.[3]

The library law of 2000 transformed the role and materials of the public libraries and set a new standard for what a library actually is, focusing on the extended hybrid multimedia library.[4] As a result, several NPM traits, including increased flexibility on interlending activities, emerged as did the use of incentives as a management tool and removal of the hitherto monopoly of individuals educated as librarians to assume positions as public library directors.[5] In Denmark, considerable variations as to how NPM was implemented were apparent between public and academic libraries. Thus, the use of contracts between a library and a government agency as a management tool was common in the academic and research library sector, but was rare among public libraries. The same was true for job titles where many chief librarians in Danish academic and research libraries changed their title to director. However, in many other respects the development in the different library sectors was the same.

The introduction in Scandinavia of concepts such as information management and information resource management, together with an emphasis on library and information management in private companies, sharpened interest in management and leadership issues.[6] Although one might question the impact on public library discussion of developments taking place in special and company libraries, the idea of profiting from information resources, certainly, also played a significant role in public libraries, for example, through the introduction of fee-based services in Danish public libraries.[7]

THE EMERGENCE OF LIBRARY LEADERS AND LEADERSHIP SURVEYS IN 2001

The first Scandinavian library leadership survey, conducted in Denmark in 2001, was financed by the Danish library association. The motivation behind the survey was a growing interest in management and leadership issues, and anxiety about the new situation where public library leaders had to compete with applicants with other professional backgrounds. In that context, it was considered important to demonstrate that Danish library leaders matched the competencies of other public sector leaders. Therefore, it was important that the survey was comparable to other similar surveys. Methodologically, it was natural that the library leadership survey borrowed inspiration from another regular leadership survey.[8]

The library survey was only concerned with attitudes and practices as seen from the leaders' point of view. There were no efforts to check or control the validity of the delivered answers. From a methodological point of view, leadership surveys such as this one share a common weakness: they are based on the opinions and statements of the leaders; the information they supplied, such as that on human resource (HR) issues, was not cross-checked by asking their staff, peers, or local politicians about the truthfulness of their leaders' statements. However, to cross-check information from more than 200 respondents would not be possible without considerable loss of reliability or excessive costs.

The first library survey was based on a questionnaire sent to 562 academic and public library leaders representing 265 different libraries, and it produced a response rate of 73 percent. The next survey, conducted in 2004, covered only public library leaders and had a response rate of 80 percent. That survey was followed by a similar one in 2007, and the results of these surveys were presented in three publications,[9] which primarily covered the results whereas interpretations and statistical analyses were presented in a number of journal articles and the like.[10]

The topics covered by the surveys included the leaders' perceived challenges and preferences; their knowledge about different management tools; their opinions about management fashions, stakeholders, leadership styles; their job satisfaction, priorities and competences; and their future educational needs. Among the background variables were, for instance, gender, age, seniority, size and type of library, and leadership position.

The 2001 survey contained about 275 questions, whereas the number of questions in 2004 was reduced to 185. The 2007 survey included 200 questions; it was a web-based questionnaire sent to 546 Danish academic and public library leaders. The response rate was the lowest—58 percent.

According to the 2001 survey, two-thirds of the respondents were women, and the average age was 51. About 50 percent of the Danish leaders indicated that they worked in libraries with 16 or more employees. The 2007 data indicated that the demographic characteristics about age and gender had not been changed since 2001. However, structural changes and merging processes in 2007, drastically reducing the number of municipalities, meant that many leaders had changed their positions recently.

As to the leaders' perception of challenges, an increased focus on external and environmental factors was remarkable in terms of increasing the visibility and legitimacy of the library and creating adequate networks. This trend also affects preferences as to leadership roles where roles emphasizing network building seemed to be strengthened. As to leadership styles, the soft approaches were still prioritized in 2007. However, it is interesting to note that an increased appreciation of harder methods was visible in the 2007 survey.

Somewhat predictably, there were certain correlations that were presented in the publications between some of the background variables and certain perceptions and preferences. Thus, in 2001, male leaders focused more on information technology and the Internet than did their female colleagues. Further, leaders of larger units were more knowledgeable about and familiar with the use of different management tools and more eager to engage in development projects and to involve external stakeholders than leaders of smaller units. On the other hand, unexpected patterns were revealed. The 20 challenges mentioned in the questionnaire as mass media hot topics (e.g., recruitment of multiethnic staff, outsourcing, and fee-based library services), surprisingly, achieved low scores. The 2001 survey results also indicated that some techniques and tools (e.g., projects and project management) were not as popular among library leaders as was believed. As to stakeholders, the 2001 survey revealed that concepts such as competition and competitors made sense to probe in libraries. Another remarkable result was that trade unions were expected to be less important in the future (by 43 percent of the respondents).

Different leadership styles and associated tools and techniques were perceived as relevant by library leaders. Here, in particular, the female leaders indicated that they preferred soft values and tools such as attitudes, dialogue, cooperation, respect, and motivation at the expense of using rules, direct orders, and control. The same types of preferences were visible concerning desired qualifications and skills where open-mindedness, the ability to motivate and to inspire employees and to create organizational change, and innovation were among the competences most sought after.

Since the 2004 survey covered only public libraries (whereas the 2001 and 2007 surveys also included research libraries), this difference should be recognized when tracing trends and developments from 2001 to 2004 and 2007. However, some changes could be observed. One was the increased use of yearly appraisal dialogues between leaders and individual staff members. Another change was with regard to the challenges, where more leaders now indicated that they were under increased pressure because of demands created by the new 2000 Danish library law. The 2004 survey also examined the relationship between leadership and democracy. A majority of leaders indicated that they appreciated that the staff were involved in both strategic and operational decision-making processes. A significant change from 2001 to 2004 could be observed regarding qualification. Here, professional skills within library and information science seemed to become less important than leadership skills and abilities to handle the external stakeholders and environment of the library. The 2004 survey in many respects revealed significant differences in perceptions and attitudes within less than three years. HR and strategic management gained in importance, whereas the importance of administration and administrative skills had diminished. Further, the recognition of management tools and skills increased significantly in the minds of the Danish public library leaders. Another interesting, and somewhat surprising, observation regards the perceived level of stress among public library leaders, where one could expect more stress, considering the increased challenges. However, the survey indicated that the 2004 leaders were more self-confident in their jobs with an increased ability to prioritize compared to earlier.

INTERPRETATIONS AND THEORETICAL PERSPECTIVES

This section, which covers the fourth question regarding the interpretations and theoretical perspectives of the three Danish library leadership surveys, is based on journal articles published between 2003 and 2005[11] and three survey publications.[12] An interesting and current theoretical perspective dealt with library leadership being positioned between new public management and value-based management.[13] A key concept here was cross-pressure, referring to a situation according to which public institutions, including libraries, operate in an environment characterized by conflicting and competing forces. In this chapter, these forces are the state, the civil society, and the marketplace. The individual library, and especially its leader, has to respond to pressures from each of the three forces, which together shape a situation characterized by cross-pressures. The analysis here tries to identify the competing forces by comparing the library leaders' degree of knowledge concerning various management tools based on data from the 2001 Danish leadership survey. Recognizing the obvious methodological problems concerning distinguishing between two different ideological positions, it is concluded that the knowledge level of library leaders concerning NPM-oriented tools is higher than the level concerning value-based management (VBM) tools. Examples of NPM tools include annual plans and accounts, user surveys, strategic planning, and performance-related salary system, whereas examples of VBM tools are workplace assessments, knowledge management, and ethical accounting. The main conclusion is that there is a paradox problem with a discourse "consisting of soft values that appears to be asynchronous with the actual performance."[14]

Another theoretical aspect of leadership concerned the relationship between leadership preferences among library leaders and other public and private sector

leaders.[15] Here, survey results from 2001 questioned whether different management styles (hard or soft) are mutually exclusive and competing concepts or represent complementary models that present managerial challenges for library leaders.
In this respect, Danish library leaders seem to differ somewhat from their private
sector colleagues. The 2001 survey indicates that library leaders are firm in their
belief in soft leadership styles. Thus, between 70 and 87 percent perceive that their
own leadership style is characterized by dialogue and cooperation, motivation, mutual respect, attitudes, and values. In contrast, from 41 to 69 percent of the library
leaders claim that they totally abstain from using rules and regulations, commands
and supervision, and control as management instruments. Their private sector colleagues are similarly firm in their belief in soft management principles. However,
only between 27 and 33 percent maintain that they totally refrain from using the
harder management tools. This pattern certainly raises the question whether the
one-sided preferences of library leaders represent an adequate answer to the challenges of the future.

Finally, one article deals with a single, but important, aspect of library leadership, that is, the international orientation among librarians and library directors.[16]
This study, which compares results from the 2001 leadership survey with a survey of participants in the 2002 International Federation of Library Associations
(IFLA) conference in Glasgow,[17] applies advanced statistical cluster analysis methods to construct two library director clusters labeled as internationally oriented and
nationally oriented managers. The two clusters are then correlated with relevant
other variables, especially the perception of issues such as cross-organizational cooperation and user orientation role internalization. One result is that internationally oriented managers tend to value professional management roles much more
than nationally oriented managers who see leadership as a primus inter pares relationship. Both groups, however, seem to value the softer management styles most.
Moreover, the study examines how Danish library leaders correspond to Geert
Hofstede's concepts of cultural particularities of different nationalities. Danish library leaders, in most respects, conform to what Hofstede considers the particular cultural characteristics of people from Denmark and the other Scandinavian
countries. The concepts applied here include his four dimensions: low versus high
power distance, collectivism versus individualism, masculinity versus femininity,
and weak versus strong uncertainty avoidance.

DOES A COMMON SCANDINAVIAN LIBRARY
MANAGEMENT STYLE EXIST?

The question whether a specific Scandinavian (Denmark, Norway, and Sweden)
management culture and style has not, until recently and apart from the abovementioned article from 2003, played a significant role in Denmark since the original
purpose of the leadership survey was primarily to give librarians as leaders increased
credibility and legitimacy facing competition from other professions; the intention
was certainly not to identify a particularly Scandinavian management style. However, according to both Hofstede's rankings and those of other researchers, there
seems to be a fit between the traits identified by Jette Schramm-Nielsen, Peter
Lawrence, and Karl H. Sivesind,[18] and Tor Grenness.[19] Cooperation and value
orientation appear in low power distance and high individualism, with managers being oriented toward staff; low masculinity can be translated as being more

process-oriented, and low uncertainty avoidance could be equaled by inclusiveness when managers want and need staff to take responsibility for situations and issues themselves (see Chapter 1). (This topic is examined in more detail in the next chapter.)

CONCLUDING THOUGHTS

While the immediate reason for or cause of library leaders' emerging interest in and motivation to achieve formal managerial qualifications was changes in the library law in 2000, other long-term developments have played a role. For instance, there is the emerging interest in the late 1980s in information management among special librarians. NPM also seemed to have played a significant role in creating an interest in a professional approach to leadership within the library sector. At least, NPM has had a remarkable impact on the 2000 library law. However, this chapter also emphasizes that, especially in the public libraries, there are recognized traditions of utilizing private sector rationalization and scientific management.

As to the patterns and trends that characterized Danish public library leaders' attitudes and practices according to the three Danish library leadership surveys, there were changes in characteristic traits over the years. In particular, attitudes among library leaders about the application of soft and hard management styles seemed to be relatively stable and consistent characteristics of library leaders compared to, for example, leaders from the private sector. Library leaders shared private sector leaders' preferences as to the use of soft leadership instruments. However, whereas private sector leaders were open to the use of the harder management tools, most library leaders preferred to abstain from the use of such tools.

One theoretical concern has been to investigate the extent to which modern library leadership has been influenced by NPM or by alternative management principles such as value-based management. The character of different external pressures such as the state, the civil society, and the market has influenced current debates within the library sector. Analyses prepared based on data from the three leadership surveys have not presented definitive answers, but have indicated the existence of balances and paradoxes associated with values, practices, and applications of different types of tools.

Finally, the question about the extent to which the Danish library leadership surveys support the notion of a specific Scandinavian (Denmark, Norway, and Sweden) library management style has been answered by identifying some similarities between identified traits and Hofstede's description of cultural characteristics of the Scandinavian countries. However, the question should be handled with caution since the data of the leadership survey have not been collected or constructed with Hofstede's concepts, research questions, and theoretical framework in mind.

NOTES

1. Anders Ørom, "Folkebiblioteket i Samfundet: Et rids af 100 års Historie" (The public library in the society—A history of 100 years), in *Det Stærke Folkebibliotek—100 år med Danmarks Biblioteksforening* (The strong public library—100 years with the Danish Library Association), edited by Martin Dyrbye, Jørgen Svane-Mikkelsen, Leif Lørring, and Anders Ørom (Copenhagen: Danmarks Biblioteksforening og Danmarks Biblioteksskole, 2005), 9–37.

2. Lawrence E. Lynn, Jr., "A Critical Analysis of the New Public Management," *International Public Management Journal* 1, no. 1 (1998): 107–23.

3. Carl Gustav Johannsen and Niels Ole Pors, "Between New Public Management and Ethics: Library Management under Cross-Pressure," in *New Frontiers in Public Library Research*, edited by Carl J Gustav Johannsen and Leif Kajberg (Lanham, MD: Scarecrow Press, 2005), 111–25.

4. Jens Thorhauge, *Danish Library Policy: A Selection of Recent Articles and Papers* (Copenhagen: Danish National Library Authority, 2002), http://www.bs.dk/publikationer/english/library_policy/pdf/dlp.pdf (accessed May 19, 2012).

5. Carl Gustav Johannsen and Niels Ole Pors, *Udfordringer og forandringer* (Challenges and change) (Copenhagen: The Danish Library Association, 2002).

6. Carl Gustav Johannsen, *Firmabiblioteker I Danmark 1945–2007* (Special libraries in Denmark 1945–2007) (Copenhagen: Dansk Bibliotekshistorisk Selskab, 2009).

7. Carl Gustav Johannsen, "Money Makes the World Go Around: Fee-Based Services in Danish Public Libraries, 2000–2003," *New Library World* 105, nos. 1–2 (2004): 21–32.

8. *Det Danske Ledelsesbarometer: Dansk Ledelse anno 2000* (The Danish Leadership Barometer: Danish Leadership 2000) (Copenhagen: Århus, Handelshøjskolen i Århus & Ledernes Hovedorganisation, 2000).

9. Carl Gustav Johannsen and Niels Ole Pors, *Ledere og ledelse i danske biblioteker—Bibliotekarforbundets lederundersøgelse 2001* (Leaders and leadership in Danish public libraries—the leadership survey of the Union of Danish Librarians 2001) (Frederiksberg: Bibliotekarforbundet, 2001); Niels Ole Pors, *Ledere og ledelse i danske folkebiblioteker—Bibliotekarforbundets lederundersøgelse 2004* (Leaders and leadership in Danish public libraries—the leadership survey of the Union of Danish Librarians 2004) (Frederiksberg: Bibliotekarforbundet, 2004); Niels Ole Pors, *Ledere og ledelse i danske biblioteker—Bibliotekarforbundets lederundersøgelse 2007* (Leaders and leadership in Danish libraries—the leadership survey of the Union of Danish Librarians 2007) (Frederiksberg: Bibliotekarforbundet, 2007).

10. Carl Gustav Johannsen and Niels Ole Pors, "Library Managers and Management 2001: A New Danish Survey," *New Review of Information and Library Research* 7 (2001): 186–200; Niels Ole Pors and Carl Gustav Johannsen, "Library Directors under Cross-Pressure between New Public Management and Value-Based Management," *Library Management* 24, nos. 1–2 (2003): 51–60; Niels Ole Pors and Carl Gustav Johannsen, "Attitudes towards Internalization in the Library Sector: The Case of Danish Librarians and Library Managers," *New Library World* 104, no. 7 (2003): 278–85.

11. Johannsen and Pors, "Library Managers and Management 2001;" Niels Ole Pors and Carl G. Johannsen, "Job Satisfaction and Motivational Strategies among Library Directors," *New Library World* 103, no. 6 (2002): 199–209; Pors and Johannsen, "Library Directors under Cross-Pressure;" Pors and Johannsen, "Attitudes towards Internalization;" Johannsen and Pors, "Between New Public Management and Ethics."

12. Johannsen and Pors, *Ledere og ledelse i danske biblioteker*; Pors, *Ledere og ledelse i danske folkebiblioteker*; Pors, *Ledere og ledelse i danske biblioteker.*

13. Pors and Johannsen, "Library Directors under Cross-Pressure."

14. Pors and Johannsen, "Library Directors under Cross-Pressure."

15. Johannsen and Pors, "Between New Public Management and Ethics."

16. Pors and Johannsen, "Attitudes towards Internalization."

17. Niels Ole Pors, "Perceptions of the Quality of the IFLA Conference in Glasgow," *IFLA Journal* 28, nos. 5–6 (2002): 328–35.

18. Jette Schramm-Nielsen, Peter Lawrence, and Karl H Sivesind, *Management in Scandinavia: Culture, Context and Change* (Cheltenham, UK: Edward Elgar, 2004).

19. Tor Grenness, "Scandinavian Managers on Scandinavian Management," *International Journal of Value-Based Management* 16 (2003): 9–21.

7

SIMILARITIES AND DISSIMILARITIES AMONG SCANDINAVIAN LIBRARY LEADERS AND MANAGERS

Ane Landøy and Angela Zetterlund

In Scandinavian literature few research studies have exclusively focused on the concept of leadership in a library context, even though the management of libraries has been regarded as a distinct arena for professional practice for a long time. This chapter takes a first step to conceptualize leadership in libraries from a Scandinavian point of view and reflects on the content and patterns related to empirical findings. This chapter, as a result, explores the following questions:

- What is the demographic composition of Scandinavian library leaders?
- To what extent are these leaders oriented toward interaction and processes in their organizations?
- To what degree do they adhere to professional norms and values from library and information science?
- To what extent are they involved in the political, ideological, and democratic context of their organizations?

Looking at the research on library leadership in Scandinavia, most of the relevant work was presented in the previous chapter with an emphasis on studies of Danish leaders. These studies are good starting points for exploring the concept of Scandinavian library leadership and can be used both in a comparative way and as empirical evidence of library leadership patterns.

There are some obvious theoretical perspectives on library leadership, but no robust models cover the concept in a broader sense as does the literature in disciplines such as in business administration and political science. Some pioneering work must be done to get a more complete picture of library leadership, gathering data to describe the patterns in several countries in this region, and connecting more explicitly to the theoretical body of knowledge in library and information science (LIS).

Research and theories on management and leadership generally, especially from the business research literature, point to a certain Scandinavian management style, which, to a high degree, is oriented toward consensus, participation, and co-operation. Tor Grenness states that even though Scandinavian management as an issue and concept has been around since the early 1980s, there is doubt about what it is, and whether there is a common management style applicable to Denmark, Norway, and Sweden.[1] He argues, based on earlier literature and his own research on middle managers, that there is such a concept and that it contains the following aspects: consensus, participation, and cooperation between staff and managers, both as a general approach and as a decision-making strategy. Managers are more interpersonally oriented and keep the role of the other people in mind, and they engage in vision management or value-based management. It would be interesting to see how library managers from Denmark, Sweden, and Norway address the image of Scandinavian management. Following the previous chapter, it would seem that some of the individual factors that can be identified as part of a Scandinavian management style are consensus, inclusion, value orientation, reasonableness, and persuasive inclination.

METHODOLOGY

Leadership and management are fields of interest for many disciplines in the social sciences and humanities, and the concepts gain from being illuminated in a multidisciplinary way. The possible methodological strategies and methodologies are many. This chapter draws mainly on survey data. Empirical findings from Sweden are based on a web survey conducted between December 2011 and January 2012, and the findings from Norway are based on a web survey conducted in September and October 2011.

Both surveys are based on the Danish questionnaire used in both traditional and web-based surveys by Niels Ole Pors and Carl G. Johannsen between 2001and 2007,[2] but with some questions being added, deleted, or changed. In this study we concentrate on a set of variables based on the following concepts in library leadership:

- Challenges for the future
- Decision making at the workplace
- Stakeholders (relation to external groups) (users)
- Leadership tools
- Further education.

Some of the statements that examine Scandinavian library leaders cover different aspects of leadership and the actual work situation, and respondents were asked to indicate the extent to which they agree with the statements on a five-point scale (1 = disagree, 2 = agree a little, 3 = agree, 4 = quite agree, and 5 = totally agree). Other questions explore the perceived significance of knowledge and issues, and also use a five-point scale with 3 as the neutral point. For all of these, there is a 6 or a 0, to indicate do not know or not applicable, but those numbers are excluded in the calculation of means.

FRAME FOR ANALYZING LIBRARY LEADERS

There are many ways to put library management and leadership in perspective, and it is not possible to give a complete review over the whole spectra in this chapter.

The first thing to establish is the complex political and social context related to libraries. Catarina Ericsson and Angela Zetterlund, who analyzed Swedish systems, suggest that it is possible to differentiate between different social levels and types of regulations.[3] They also identified two different directions or cardinal points: central/local and public/private. These cardinal points provide a basis for generating a tool for mapping the library community.

Table 7.1   The Main Characteristics of Different Types of Libraries (Academic, Public, Joint, and Other Types)

	ACADEMIC LIBRARY	PUBLIC LIBRARY	JOINT LIBRARY, OTHERS
Purpose	Educational and knowledge development	Cultural, educational, and lifelong learning	Multifunctional, digital interfaces
Type of regulation	Regulations from state policy and public authority. Library law	Regulation from municipal regulations and political policies at local and regional level. Library law	Different parts of rules. Joint agreements and informal practices
Target groups	Students, researchers, and society, specialized users	Citizens, special groups, unspecialized users. Lifelong learning and social mobilization	Both advanced and wider groups of users. Digital users and distance users.
Professional identity	Related to form and content of scientific communication and information seeking and retrieval. Service-oriented.	Related to societal role of libraries. Paternalistic or participatory.	Several identities or split identity
Administrative reach	National, regional, and local	Municipal, local, and regional	Crossing institutional borders, networking and digitized arenas
Political sphere	Educational and research policy	Municipal, local cultural politics	Multipolitical

The institutional complexity of a library system is often related to the fact that libraries address different areas of political and administrative control. An important distinction is the division between the academic libraries and the public libraries, where there are differences in purpose, regulations, target groups for their services, and more (see Table 7.1).

Many researchers studying the concept of joint libraries have made it clear that there are differences and sometimes different sets of values between libraries in academic and educational settings and libraries directed to needs and demands in local public society.[4] Different sets of values produce conflicts and barriers in processes of change and development at the organizational level, where goal-setting agencies and the funder prescribe coordination and sharing of resources.

In the research literature, there is often a dichotomy between two distinct and different theoretical traditions or schools: the classical, instrumental, and rational school and the mere symbolic, interactive, and socially oriented institutional school. In an instrumental rational perspective, management theories emphasize formal functions and processes such as strategic planning and performance measurement, and they represent an analytical approach to organizational activities. In an institutional perspective, the focus builds on the pillars of rules for practice, conceptual frames, and norms and values related to institutional interpretations of organizational activities in society. This is called a kind of logic of appropriateness that makes sense of organizational behavior and self-images. The institutional logic of libraries builds on certain social practices and rules, both formal and informal, for action and problem solving in the library. A core activity is developing rules for how to organize and give access to collections, service delivery, and systems of planning and decision making in these matters. Values and norms in the library are bound to the position of the organization in the social and political system, where there might be tensions between its role as an educator and research facilitator and as an instrument for cultural politics. Institutional structures are not static, but they must be regarded as conservative and something that creates stability and sustainable conditions for library leaders and staff. To change and develop institutional organizations, it is important to affect organizational work at three levels: conceptual, rules for practices, and norms and values. Regarding library leadership in the light of institutional theory we are especially interested in

- tools and conceptual frames for library leadership and management;
- routines and practices in the everyday life of the library leaders; and
- professional and ideological values and norms in library leadership.

In the study of Danish leadership Geert Hofstede has conducted important work on national cultures as an analytical tool.[5] According to him, the Scandinavian countries (Denmark, Norway, and Sweden) have the scores expressed in Table 7.2.

Because the rankings are in a close cluster, it would make sense to see the Scandinavian countries as a single group with more or less the same characteristics: low power distance, high individualism, low masculinity, and low uncertainty avoidance (see Chapter 1). The point where some differences could be expected is uncertainty avoidance, where Norway ranks higher than Sweden and Denmark, signifying that the Norwegians would thrive and manage less well in chaos and uncertainty than would Swedes and Danes. Overall, however, Hofstede's rankings

Table 7.2   Scandinavian Countries' Ranking on Hofstede's Dimensions*·**

	DENMARK	NORWAY	SWEDEN
Power distance	51	47/48	47/48
Individualism	9	13	10/11
Masculinity vs. femininity	50	52	53
Uncertainty avoidance	51	38	49/50

* Ranking from 1 (highest) to 53 (lowest).

**The data in this table were gathered from different tables in Geert Hofstede, *Culture and Organisations: Software of the Mind* (London: McGraw-Hill, 1991).

fit well with the traits identified by Jette Schramm-Nielsen, Peter Lawrence, and Karl H. Sivesind,[6] as well as Grenness,[7] in that consensus, cooperation, and value orientation are found in low power distance and high individualism, with managers being oriented toward staff; low masculinity can be translated as being more process-oriented, and low uncertainty avoidance could be equaled with inclusiveness when managers want and need staff to take responsibility for situations and issues themselves.

Is this management style recognizable in Scandinavian library leadership and management? Danish researchers Niels Ole Pors and Carl Gustav Johannsen have examined this and other questions among Danish library leaders from 2001.[8] Their findings support Hofstede's suggestions: "In sum, it seems as if Danish librarians, in most respects, conform to what Hofstede considers the particular cultural characteristics of people from Denmark and the other Scandinavian countries."[9]

In the Danish surveys several variables may apply to the library leaders. However, there are no direct questions about "How inclusive are you?" or even "How important do you think inclusiveness to be in your role as a leader?" Moreover, it can be difficult to distinguish between variables that measure consensus orientation and persuasive inclination, and consensus orientation and inclusion.

SOME DEMOGRAPHIC DATA ABOUT SCANDINAVIAN LIBRARY LEADERS

Study samples consist of 214 library leaders from Sweden and 244 from Norway, while the Danish sample from 2007 consists of 314 library leaders. The library leaders who responded to the surveys (2001, 2004, and 2007) mainly work in public and academic libraries. In the Norwegian sample, the academic libraries are limited to university and university college libraries. "Others" in the Norwegian sample refers to county libraries. A majority of the responding library leaders work in public libraries in all three countries (see Table 7.3).

Most of the library leaders have positions in public libraries, which are the main part of the library sector in the Scandinavian countries. The Norwegian public libraries are the smallest (121 of 153 have fewer than 11 employees), while the academic libraries can be seen to be more medium-sized (51 of 77 have more than 11 staff members). As Table 7.4 reflects, the majority of the library leaders work

Table 7.3   Number of Respondents by Library Type

Public	74	63	65
Academic	26	32	28
Other	0	5	7
Total	314	244	214

Table 7.4   Leaders in Libraries (Grouped by Number of Staff in Percentages)

NUMBER OF STAFF IN LIBRARY	DENMARK	NORWAY	SWEDEN
Up to 25	24	80	0
26–50 (Sweden: 50 or fewer)	26	6	79
51–100	30	14	8
101 or more	20	0	11
N=	287	243	214

in rather small organizations or divisions and just a small group of respondents (10–20 percent) are responsible for units with more than 100 individuals. One of the findings from these studies is the huge difference between the sizes of the libraries where these Scandinavian library leaders work. The mean number of staff in Norwegian libraries is 24.2 full-time equivalents, while the mean size for Sweden is 38.4. Looking closer at the distribution, approximately half of Norwegian library leaders work in libraries with 5 or fewer staff, and 80 percent in libraries with fewer than 25 staff. Only 24 percent of the Danish library leaders work in libraries with fewer than 25 staff.

The library profession in the western world is generally seen as a female profession, and this hold true also for the samples as the survey data show that the proportion of female respondents in Denmark is 68 percent, in Norway, 84 percent, and in Sweden 75 percent. Looking at the gender distribution, it is interesting to see the high number of male leaders in Norway, and especially within the public libraries. The proportions are somewhat different in Sweden and Denmark, but the trend is clear. There are few reflections in literature on library leadership from a gender perspective, although it would be fruitful to have such research.

When analyzing the answers from the leaders about gender and type of libraries, there are more male leaders working in academic libraries and a higher number of female leaders in the public library context (see Table 7.5). This might correspond to the traditional pattern of gender stereotypes where male occupations are focused on science and higher education and female occupations are more directed to social context and everyday life.

Table 7.5 Gender and Type of Library (in Percentages)

	DENMARK		NORWAY		SWEDEN	
	Public	Academic	Public	Academic	Public	Academic
Male	30	38	10	20	22	34
Female	70	62	90	80	78	66

It is also interesting to see how gender structure corresponds to position in power structure in the libraries. In Norway, the distribution is almost equal within the three main leader responsibility levels, whereas in Denmark there are more male directors and more female team/group leaders, and in Sweden it is opposite: more female directors and more male branch and team/group leaders. Looking further at the demographics, leaders in all three countries are around 50 years old with the Norwegian library leaders a little younger. On the other hand, the mean time in the current leader job is higher among the Norwegian respondents. The expression of "mean time in current leader position" covers leaders being in the job from less than one year to 40 years. A total of 38 percent of the Norwegian leaders have had leader jobs in the library before taking this one, and the mean overall work experience from libraries is 19 years. This gives an image of library leaders being recruited from the ranks and not aiming for a leader job right out of school.

JOB SATISFACTION, INTERACTION, AND PROCESSES

Library leaders are very satisfied with their job situation. Although there are some variations in the degree of satisfaction they experience (see Table 7.6), Scandinavian leaders have a low degree of dissatisfaction with their job situation. In other words, they express a very high degree of job satisfaction. This tendency is clear in some other variables too, and we are not really sure about the reasons for this. Public libraries, in particular, have been facing economic restraints and challenges during the last two decades, but they have also been the focus of some political initiatives related to adult learning and democratization of information technology. Perhaps this perceived focus on libraries as important for the citizens is a factor when it comes to the satisfaction.

A large percentage of library leaders (at least 72 percent), when asked if they would apply to their job again if possible, give positive answers that confirm their appreciation of their leadership position and job situation.

One aspect of leadership in Scandinavia is the priority assigned to processes and interaction in management. From the survey data, library leaders seem to be dedicated to internal collaboration, creating contacts, and maintaining good relations in the organization (see Table 7.7). Library work is complex, and leaders must be involved in communication and translations on many technical and service delivering activities. At a university library, for example, libraries link to all scientific disciplines at the university while they provide service to all educational levels from preparation summer schools to advanced expertise research. Institutional logic must be both stable enough to carry this complexity and differentiation, and dynamic enough to be able to adopt and influence other institutional structures.

Table 7.6   Library Leaders' Overall Satisfaction

	DENMARK	NORWAY	SWEDEN
Very satisfied	35	49	23
Quite satisfied	41	39	56
Medium satisfied	20	10	17
A little satisfied	3	3	2
Dissatisfied	2	0	0.5
Mean (on a 5-point scale)	4.0	4.3	4.0
$N =$	299	178	214

Table 7.7   Extent of Agreement with Statements about Interaction (Mean)

	DENMARK	NORWAY	SWEDEN
Leader creates contacts and network	4.7	4.7	3.1
Leadership in close collaboration with staff	4.1	4.2	4.2
Significance of the leader as coordinator, integrator, and conveyor	3.8	4.1	3.7
I use too little time in informing and communicating	2.7	2.4	2.9
Important competence for the future: Human knowledge and empathy	4.4	4.4	4.1
Important competence for the future: Ability to handle conflicts	3.7	3.4	3.7
Good relations between different groups of staff	3.9	4.1	3.8
$N=$	280	244	214

Leadership that involves interaction is preferred. Following this, the next section explores whether library leaders are focused on processes rather than hierarchical structure.

PROCESSES AND STRUCTURES

Process-oriented leadership means having an emphasis on delivery, problem solving, and relation to the user segments. Library activities and strategies are often described in terms of information systems modeling the chain of activities and

Table 7.8   Extent of Agreement with Statements about Processes (Mean)

	DENMARK	NORWAY	SWEDEN
Strategic decisions are delegated	3.3	2.9	3.1
Staff have large influence on decisions	3.4	3.8	3.6
Significance of the leader as problem solver	3.5	4.0	3.6
Management of teams, groups, and projects	3.5	3.6	4.0
Ability to communicate, motivate, inspire	4.7	4.7	4.6
Friendly atmosphere	4.0	4.4	4.0
Often participate in meetings with short notice	2.9	2.3	3.2
Open-door policy for staff	4.5	4.7	4.2
N=	280	244	214

functions in information processes. However, from a leadership perspective, the person is not directly responsible for specific solutions in accomplishing professional tasks; rather, the person makes the rules and settings for relevant process to work effectively for the staff involved. We analyzed how the leaders responded to questions of how involved the staff were on decisions, the leader as problem solver, and the importance of the leader in process-oriented activities such as teamwork and projects (see Table 7.8).

There is a high level of process orientation in library leadership concerning social aspects such as "an open door policy for staff," "ability to communicate," and "friendly atmosphere," even if there are some small variations among the countries; leaders in Norway have a little lower values on "participate in meetings with short notice" and have more time to engage in planning. However, when it comes to formal decision making and delegation, the values are average, and the data from Norway suggest the values are under average; this might indicate that some bureaucratic structures relate to power distribution in the libraries.

NORMS AND VALUES

It is obvious from literature that library leaders in Scandinavia are both restricted and strengthened from their own professional and institutional heritage. Rules, conceptual frames, and ideological values embedded in institutional identity were supposed to set the logic of management. From an analysis of the responses to questions about forms of leadership, expectations of leadership roles in the future, the priorities between tasks and tools, how the leaders experienced relations at the workplace, in what way there were informal leaders, and their willingness to delegate, this section presents some of the results (see Table 7.9).

Table 7.9   Extent to Which Library Leaders Focus on Norms and Values of the Profession*

	DENMARK	NORWAY	SWEDEN
Leadership mainly through attitudes, values, etc.	88.0	79.7	87.4
Theoretical competences in LIS	–	55.5	35.5
Leader must have librarian professional qualifications	25.0	55.0	33.2
Competent professional	40.0	75.0	32.2
Strategic decision are delegated	49.0	46.4	31.3
Staff large influence on decisions	45.0	68.3	51.8
Knowledge of value-based management	55.0	20.7	31.3
Informal leaders among staff	76.0	31.7	39.7
Significance of leader as specialist and expert	27.0	49.4	21.8
N=	135	184	214

*Expressed as a percentage of country sample.

There is a strong emphasis on values and norms, but there is no clear evidence for the claim that leaders must have librarian professional qualifications. This pattern is most obvious in the Swedish and Danish data. Swedish leaders are less oriented to staff delegation in making decisions and, more likely, there are informal leaders. Previous studies concluded that professional norms are of importance, but are not the only factor influencing organizational life and decision making in libraries.[10] In a way, library leaders are a kind of middle managers, and studies of this kind of leadership in general provide a set of activities and attitudes conceptualized as pragmatic and conveying progressive learning.[11]

Regarding the leader as specialist and professional expert, in Denmark, leaders from both library types considered the significance of the leader as a specialist and professional expert rather low—less than 20 percent considered it an important role. The same picture emerged from Sweden. The situation concerning this was different in Norway, where 40–60 percent of the leaders, depending on library type, found it important that the library leaders possess professional expertise.

There is variation between both countries and types of library, where Sweden seems to be less oriented at the professional expert role of the leader. Norwegian leaders give this a higher ranking, and Danish library leaders do not find this significant. The differences between academic and public libraries are smaller than we expected; the main differences are between the countries, and it is interesting that this dimension seem to be of higher importance among the public library leaders

Table 7.10   Extent of Agreement with Statement about Importance of Staff Management and Staff Development (in Percentages)

	VERY HIGH	HIGH	MEDIUM	LESS	NOT
Denmark					
Academic	23	57	13	8	0
Public	37	42	15	5	1
Norway					
Academic	52.5	28.8	6.8	10.2	1.7
Public	52.6	21.6	8.2	14.4	3.1
Sweden					
Academic	61.0	33.9	3.4	1.7	
Public	48.9	42.3	8.8	0.0	

Table 7.11   Extent of Agreement with Statement about Leadership Being Conducted through Rules, Order, and Control*

	VERY HIGH	HIGH	MEDIUM	LESS	NOT
Denmark					
Academic	11	2	37	26	25
Public	2	4	11	44	39
Norway					
Academic	0.0	8.1	22.6	29.0	40.3
Public	0.0	6.7	16.3	27.9	49.0
Sweden					
Academic	0.0	5.1	27.1	47.5	18.6
Public	0.7	2.2	27.0	48.2	19.7

*Percentages by country and type of library.

than among those in academic libraries. An explanation might be that there is a higher degree of diversification in academic libraries and more professional staff with a high degree of expertise, working with collections and user in ways that require higher-level knowledge, whereas public library staff must be more of generalists and act more thematic than do the staff in academic libraries.

We next examined the extent to which library leaders regard staff management and staff development as an important task. Staff management is rated "very high" and "high" importance in Denmark, Norway, and Sweden, especially

Table 7.12   Extent of Agreement with Statements about Challenges (Mean)

	DENMARK	NORWAY	SWEDEN
User orientation	4.5	–	4.36
User interaction and library 2.0	4.0	4.27	3.92
Technology	4.5	4.83	4.32
Cooperation with others (libraries)	4.2	4.57	4.17
N=	282	219	214

among Swedish leaders; hardly anyone regards this task as not important at all (see Table 7.10). This supports the assumption that there is a professional and internal focus in Scandinavian library leadership. Looking at the statements on the importance of leadership conducted through rules, order, and control, the opposite pattern emerges (see Table 7.11), which supports the theoretical assumption that professional norms function as a substitute for unclear or vague regulations of operation.

It is interesting to see the extent to which institutional norms are reflected in how library leaders estimate the importance of future challenges. Perhaps a subjective professional scheme of preferences guides in making priorities in these matters unless there are considerations based on other issues.

The professional aspects are estimated high in all countries, and the connections within the library system and the user community are regarded as very important (see Table 7.12). To be oriented to internal professional logic is a barrier to adoption to important changes in society, especially looking at technological aspects, where libraries are important, but yet comprise just one actor among a lot of powerful others in a global arena. There is a problem, however, and this is an important aspect for public libraries to consider if their leaders focus too much on direct users and thereby might lose significant perspectives of potential users. In this respect, library leadership is interrelated to both technical and social development in society and the choices that leaders make, whether leaders want to get involved or avoid something that has consequences for the further development of the library sector.

EXTERNAL INTEGRATION AND OUTREACH

When it comes to public libraries the connection to the social political dimensions of librarianship is evident and its role in democratic civil society is one of the reasons that this type of library have emerged all over the world. Public libraries have an identity related to both information and cultural distribution, and it is an ideological issue about how we prioritize selection and accessibility. Academic libraries are normally described in a more technical and professional way, but there are strong connections between decisions made in them and the broader educational and research arenas (i.e., political systems). The politics of science and higher

Table 7.13   Extent of Agreement on Estimates of Stakeholders (Mean)*

	DENMARK	NORWAY	SWEDEN
Library in close contact with principal	3.9	3.4	3.6
Library active in educating users	4.0	3.2	3.8
Library is respected by principal	4.3	3.8	4.0
Library is often in the media	3.5	2.7	3.2
Solving tasks in network with other organizations	3.8	3.2	3.8
The legitimacy in the principal organization will be more important in the near future	4.0	4.5	3.5
Commercial actors have larger influence	N/A	N/A	2.7
Other groups: writer's union and labor union	N/A	N/A	2.4
N=	282	219	214

*The scale covers 1–5, with 5 being totally agree.

education can be investigated much more in library and information science and are crucial in the creation of a sustainable knowledge society. Our study recognizes this important relationship and explores how library leaders are involved with, and are influenced by, a wider political, ideological, and democratic context.

From the survey questions about the relationship to stakeholders (see Table 7.13), it is clear that there are lower estimations of the relationship to different stakeholders than to internal structure. Thus, the sociopolitical dimension is evident, but is less influential than the professional dimension. The most important stakeholder is the one who funds the library, called the principal. The legitimacy of the library concerning this stakeholder is more important than, for example, users or organizations other than libraries. The Swedish data show how leaders in libraries view commercial actors as well as organized groups of social interests, and these relations are estimated as low or under average. It seems as if library leaders neither are concerned with the broader political spectra nor interested in conditions in the private sector.

There are important differences between types of libraries in all the countries. Close contact with the principal is far more important in academic libraries than in public libraries. In Denmark the gap between the two types are smaller. It is difficult to explain this, but the stronger position of a library law and a less decentralized political and administrative system in Denmark might be one reason. The Swedish political administrative system is decentralized, and the library community has been built upon informal and professional networks rather than strategic national policy. Efforts in these directions have been stronger, but still regulations at a national level are weak.

One important stakeholder is the user, and it is interesting to know whether connections to the user community vary between different types of libraries. Overall, academic libraries are much more involved in different forms of user education than are public libraries. However, there are marked differences between the countries. A total of 74 percent of the public libraries in Denmark state that they are involved in user education; similar percentages for Norway and Sweden are 24 and 57. This might be due to a focus in academic libraries on a specific target group, students and research staff, while the public libraries are connected to a wider group of social interests. The low percentage for Norwegian public libraries can probably be explained by the dominance of small organizations.

Regarding how library directors estimate the respect they get from their main funding stakeholders, there are marked differences between academic and public libraries. For the statement that academic libraries are respected, the percentage in Denmark that agrees is 97. For Norway and Sweden the percentages are 85 and 80. In the same sequence, the percentages for the public libraries are 83, 59, and 61.

A common feature for all three countries is that the public libraries, to a smaller extent, agree to the statement that the library is respected by the principal. This may be due to the fact that municipalities have a wide range of responsibilities than academic institutions, and that the public libraries can more easily feel neglected.

A different picture emerges looking at the statement that "the library is often in media," where academic library leaders agree less than their counterparts in public libraries. Public libraries can also represent a larger public interest than do academic libraries. In Denmark 68 percent of the public library leaders agree with the statement in contrast to 46 percent of the Norwegian public library directors and 44 percent of the Swedish public library directors.

A conclusion is that political contexts are relevant and library leaders are engaged in political processes. An important question is how do library leaders have a responsibility to take action in external processes and be influential in societal movements. As representatives for public sector authorities they act on and defend what is important to their societal and economic role. Academic libraries are connected to a smaller group of the population, but people with occupations high in the social power structure. Public libraries are wider and more widespread in their obligations to a larger group of citizens, almost everyone is included, but they are generally related to interest groups with less influence (e.g., children, the elderly, and blue-collar workers). This can be one explanation about why the political agenda varies between the types of library, but this also raises normative questions about what role library leaders should have in public debates and decision-making processes where the political agenda is designed. There are some differences between the countries, and one explanation for this could be that the focus on leadership in libraries has been more pervasive in the Danish library community than it has been in the other two countries.

CONCLUDING THOUGHTS

The majority of library leaders work in rather small organizations or divisions, and just a small group of respondents (10–20 percent) is responsible for units with more than 100 individuals. Library leadership is typically a female environment, but more male leaders work in academic libraries and a higher amount of female leaders work in public libraries. Library leaders tend to be female, middle-aged (mean age around 50), quite experienced (mean working time in this job 6–8 years), and highly educated. Typically they would have a bachelor's degree in library and information science, but have taken some subject courses. The library leaders are very satisfied with their job situation. The overall satisfaction is at least 4 (on a five-point scale).

One aspect of leadership in Scandinavia is the priority to processes and interaction in management. Library leaders are dedicated to internal collaboration, creating contacts, and maintaining good relations in the organization. There is also a high level of process orientation in library leadership concerning the social aspects such as "open door policy for staff," "ability to communicate," and "friendly atmosphere," even if there are some small variations among the countries.

We asked if Scandinavian library leaders are influenced by professional norms and values from library and information science. Survey data support the assumption that there is a professional and internal focus in Scandinavian library leadership. When it comes to priorities among assorted professional issues, the professional aspects are estimated high above the average in all countries that the connections within the library system and the user community are regarded as very important. When it comes to the degree Scandinavian library leaders are involved in the political, ideological, and democratic context of their organizations, there are differences among the library types and among the countries. There are lower estimations of the relationship to different stakeholders than to internal structure, which suggests that the sociopolitical dimension is evident, but less influential than the professional dimension. The most important stakeholder is the principal, and the legitimacy of this stakeholder is more important than users or other organizations outside library. Further, academic libraries are more dependent on their users as important stakeholders than are their colleagues in the public libraries.

Altogether this study reveals interesting patterns in library leadership in the Scandinavian countries and a strong connection to a general professional structure of librarianship. The research, though, is too fragmented to build or verify any robust theory and requires more research with both empirical and theoretical foci.

NOTES

1. Tor Grenness, "Scandinavian Managers on Scandinavian Management," *International Journal of Value-Based Management* 16, no. 1 (2003): 9–21.

2. For coverage of these surveys, see the previous chapter.

3. Catarina Eriksson and Angela Zetterlund, "Den Svenska Biblioteksgeografin," *Svensk biblioteksforskning/Swedish Library Research* 17, no. 1 (2008): 39–63.

4. Cecilia Gärdén, Anette Eliasson, Eva-Maria Flöög, Christina Persson and Angela Zetterlund, *Folkbibliotek och Vuxnas Lärande: Förutsättningar, Dilemman och Möjligheter i Utvecklingsprojekt* (Borås, Sweden: Valfrid, 2006); Angela Zetterlund and Cecilia Gärdén, "Why Public Libraries Have Problems Sharing a Vision of Joint Use Libraries: Experiences from a Program concerning Adult Learners," in *Proceedings of Joint Use Libraries: An International Conference. Manchester UK* (Blackwood, South Australia: Auslib Press, 2007), 36–45; Joacim Hansson, "Just Collaboration or Really Something Else? On Joint Libraries and Normative Institutional Change with Two Examples from Sweden," *Library Trends* 54, no. 4 (2006): 549–68; Joacim Hansson, *Libraries and Identity: The Role of Institutional Self-image and Identity in the Emergence of New Types of Libraries* (Oxford, UK: Chandos, 2010).

5. Geert Hofstede, *Cultures and Organizations* (New York: McGraw-Hill, 2010).

6. Jette Schramm-Nielsen, Peter Lawrence, and Karl H. Sivesind, *Management in Scandinavia: Culture, Context and Change* (Cheltenham, UK: Edward Elgar, 2004).

7. Grenness, "Scandinavian Managers on Scandinavian Management."

8. Niels Ole Pors and Carl Gustav Johannsen, "Attitudes towards Internationalization in the Library Sector: The Case of Danish Librarians and Library Managers," *New Library World* 104, no. 7 (2003): 278–85.

9. Ragnar Audunson, "Folkebibliotekenes Rolle i en Digital Framtid: Publikums, Politikernes og Bibliotekarenes Bilder," in *Det Siviliserte Informationssamfunn: Folkebibliotekernes Role vid Ingangen til en Digital Tid*, edited by Ragnar Andreas Audunson and Niels Windfeld Lund (Oslo, Norway: Fagbokforlaget, 2001), 206–24; Ragnar Audunson, *Change Processes in Public Libraries: A Comparative Project within an Institutional Perspective* (Oslo, Norway: Högskolen i Oslo, 1996); Ragnar Audunson, "Between Professional Fields Norms and Environmental Change Impetus: A Comparative Study of Change Processes in Public Libraries," *Library & Information Science Research* 21, no. 4 (1999): 523–52.

10. Audunson, "Between Professional Fields Norms and Environmental Change Impetus."

11. Robert Wenglén, *Från dum till klok? En studie av mellanchefers lärande* (Lund, Sweden: Business Press, 2005).

Part III

THEMES

8

DRIVING FORCES

Niels Ole Pors and Peter Hernon

This chapter, which reflects a plurality of issues, is not primarily concerned with the so-called driving forces per se, but with leadership and leadership issues in relation to those driving forces. The authors believe that libraries just like other public organizations must possess a high degree of legitimacy and that stakeholders expect them, like other organizations, to do a job and perform tasks that are necessary and of value to others and to society as a whole; libraries therefore must often emphasize economic efficiency as well. Harvesting legitimacy must be an overriding concern for library managerial leaders, and a prerequisite to this is their ability to read both the organization and its relationship to the environment. Closely connected to legitimacy is the identity of the organization. Identity, which concerns how the organization perceives itself, is associated with and part of the organizational culture. Leadership also plays a significant role in relation to identity.

SOME DRIVING FORCES

It is impossible to cover all driving forces of change in this chapter, but some of the most important are addressed. For a single institution, driving forces can be either internal or external. Examples of an internal driving force include restructuring of an organization or appointing a new director or assigned leader. Examples of external forces are changes in external financing, developments associated with information technologies, legislation, and changes in general norms and values in the society (see Table 8.1).

Instead of discussing a multitude of both specific and general developments and changes that influence libraries, it is useful to categorize driving forces. However, before doing so, this chapter examines some of the global megatrends that will likely influence libraries during the next decade. Many countries have not totally

Portions of this chapter are based on the following: Pors, Niels Ole, and Carl Gustav Johannsen. "Library Directors under Cross-Pressure between New Public Management and Value-Based Management," *Library Management* 24, nos. 1–2 (2003): 51–60.

Table 8.1   Some Driving Forces

INTERNAL DRIVING FORCES	EXTERNAL DRIVING FORCES
• New staff members	• Globalization
• New technology	• Educational level
• Requirements for effectiveness, efficiency, and accountability	• Demographic shifts and changes • New needs in the market
• New products and services	• Competing services and products
• New leaders and managers	• Technological development
• Adoption of recipes and internalization of new ideas concerning work processes, services, and the like	• Legislation • New trends in values and norms in the society

recovered from the economic recession that started in 2007, and governments around the world strive to overcome it. The financial crisis has had dire consequences for both academic and public libraries as many institutions have seen a decline (or no improvement) in public funding, and many employees, including those in libraries, have been made redundant. At the same time organizations and institutions have struggled to deliver services in a more cost-effective manner and reduce many forms of organizational slack. The crisis and the consciousness about the fragility of the economy will probably last for some years. Globalization will probably be a cause for rapid innovations both in relation to products and services, including service delivery systems. One of the reasons that crisis consciousness will last is globalization. Globalization also affects libraries because economies outside Western Europe and the United States will be able to produce technology, services, and goods at a lower price and probably also of at least an equal quality.

The development of information technologies (IT) has probably been the most influential driving force behind the rapid restructuring of libraries worldwide. There are reasons to believe that the development and change rate of IT will continue at an even faster rate than during the last 30 years, and one of the things libraries have to confront is the augmented reality about their service roles that is much more advanced and embedded than we see in the so-called second life that some libraries have adopted. Some libraries have confronted this reality successfully, and others have not.

On the whole, libraries have been rather good at adopting technologies and turning them into effective and efficient tools to improve their effectiveness and reduce operating costs. During the last couple of years much of the debate concerning IT has centered on social media and social communication through tools like Facebook and similar services, and, as a result, libraries and other public institutions face new challenges. One of the questions has been to what degree should libraries have a presence in social media, and another question is whether and how they ought to use the media to communicate with users and potential users. These are not questions that can be answered in a simple way as social media are perceived and used in different ways depending on the particular national culture.

Changes in learning will continue for two main reasons; one is related to the increase in speed of technological development and the other is simply that people on average will live longer and probably stay longer as part of the workforce. The latter reason could indicate that the number of students seeking higher education degrees and the number of people participating in continuing professional development will dramatically increase. Academic libraries will have to serve a much more diversified group of learners and accommodate more learning styles. Teaching will continue to change simply because of the presence of new information technology. Universities and their libraries have to cope with the diversity of information technology services and tools people use as part of their daily lives. Smart phones, tablets, and other gesture-based tools (and new generations of them and whatever replaces them) will probably be at the center of learning. University libraries also have to understand and learn to use cloud computing and the immediate access most people have to a vast amount of information. This will mandate that they redefine some of the more traditional tasks they perform and make them suitable for the ever-changing technology. Public libraries face the same type of challenges with changed demographics, and they will have ample opportunities to support lifelong learning and institution-independent pursuit of various interests. Demographic changes are extremely important. Most European countries have low birth rates, indicating an aging population. Before the financial crisis hit the western world, many countries decided to take measures to increase the size of the workforce by increasing the age of retirement, creating other incentives to keep older members of the workforce in the labor market for a longer time. For many countries, the demographic change will probably mean that welfare states have to restructure and minimize their expenses for services and experiment with other forms of financing services and welfare benefits. Teaching, learning, and information delivery will probably be an area with tough competition, and traditional institutions such as universities and libraries have to prove the quality and efficiency of their services, and they have to market their services much better than they are able to today.

The increasing need to confront and cope with the driving forces of change has also had an impact on organizational structures, and much research indicates that the building of change readiness and change capabilities of an organization is correlated with flatter structures, empowerment, and sharing of responsibilities at the workplace. Knowledge work becomes more important; this implies that the average level of both formal and informal qualifications in the workplace has increased. Simply put, there are more well-educated people who foster ideas and solutions, and tools of communication become more effective and widespread. At the same time, there is a much more transient workforce that changes jobs more often than before, and there is a quicker flow of new ideas into organizations. Additionally, there is a new trend in which leaders in many countries are hired on contracts for a limited period of time, and much of their salary structure is based on negotiated performance. This is also a driving force of change, and it makes it extremely important to address as part of the recruitment process. A more transient workforce is the result of the presence of a higher degree of individualism, and, to some extent, the loyalty of employees has shifted slightly from the organization to a kind of self-realization that implies more frequent job changes and moves. For any organization, this means more change and cost to integrate new employees and a more turbulent internal environment.

A RATIONALISTIC VIEW OF MANAGING CHANGE PROCESSES

From a European perspective, John P. Kotter, a frequent writer on the topic of leadership, is a typical American proponent for change processes and leadership in relation to change. He has formulated a clear and instructive model for the implementation of organizational change. His model, which includes eight steps, is based on a top-down approach:

1. Establish a sense of necessity
2. Create a leading coalition
3. Develop vision and strategy
4. Communicate the vision of change
5. Improve staff's competencies
6. Generate quick successes
7. Consolidate results and continue the change process
8. Change work processes.[1]

The model contains three phases. The first is to destroy or radically change the existing situation. This phase relates to steps 1 to 4. Phase two concerns change methods, and the last phase integrates the change into the organizational culture.

Implementing the change process begins with the establishment of a sense of necessity; this means convincing the whole organization about the necessity of the change. This step can be achieved in several ways depending on the existing situation; however, Kotter suggests that the contours of a coming crisis could be an effective instrument. Other means could be to set up demanding goals and objectives and to reduce unnecessary slack in the organization. Further, it will also help to get employees to generate a dialogue with customers about any dissatisfaction and let external feedback spread throughout the organization. It can come across as a bit manipulative, but it is important to be aware that many institutions and organizations are complacent and very inward-looking. Sometimes it is necessary to shake them up. Even if the change process suggested by Kotter is a top-down process, there is need to establish a coalition of central players and actors and to include staff members who are influential in more than one department, area of work processes, and teams. Further, it is important that appointed members of the coalition have a reputation for expertise and trustworthiness. It is necessary to develop trust among the members of the coalition and this trust can be developed through joint and common activities. The most important of these is to develop joint goals in relation to the strategy and the vision. Further, it is important that the goals be rational, sensible, and emotionally appealing. The vision must appeal to long-sighted interests, be realistic, and point to achievable objectives.

Both internal and external communication are key elements in the recipe. Kotter states that it is extremely important constantly to discuss, talk about, and communicate the central elements in the vision and the strategy.[2] Too often, the key words in a vision, a set of values, and a strategy are only communicated on special occasions; however, as Kotter states, it is the responsibility of leaders and managers to talk about these all the time. This responsibility rests on an assumption that key words and the symbols they represent can change attitudes and behavioral patterns. Further, change processes need to incorporate thinking and actions related to the competencies that the staff will need in the future, and managerial leaders need to take steps to help them gain those competencies. As leaders engage in the change process they need to demonstrate successes. It is, of course, important to change the existing organizational structure if the change process requires it.

This short outline probably does not give enough credit to the analysis of how to lead change, but the main point in this context is that Kotter sees change management as a process based on rationality, an instrumental relationship between goals and means, and he looks at the organizational culture as a kind of variable that leadership can change.[3] One could also argue that Kotter and the tradition he represents present a kind of ideal or the contours of a change process that can work as a kind of benchmark. It is a benchmark because of the rationality of the model and the fact that the organization responds to changes in the environment. This is a situation known as external adaptation.

However, many change processes occur in other circumstances due to the specific configurations of the driving forces. The most common is probably that changes take place in an incremental manner, indicating small and often nearly invisible changes that at some point in time will shape a strategy, which as a matter of fact is a kind of postrationalization of the existing development.

ANALYSES OF THE CONTEXT

There are many models and standards for analyzing the environment and changes in the environment. One of the most used and misused tools is the so-called SWOT (strengths, weaknesses, opportunities, and threats) analysis. Strengths and weaknesses relate to the internal situation in the organization, whereas opportunities and threats refer to the situation or to factors in the environment. SWOT analysis is a simple model that organizations often engage in at meetings involving staff, but it must be used in a cautious manner. It is not easy to assess the strengths and the weaknesses internal to an organization, and the interpretation of opportunities and threats in the environment also seems to be difficult because it often depends on whether a particular issue is viewed as a threat or as an opportunity.

The SWOT analysis can be employed as a tool for example in relation to projects, and it is probably useful to combine it with either the PEST or SEPTEMBER analyses. They are much more oriented to broader macrotrends in society and are part of an environmental scanning conducted in a systematic manner. PEST is another formula for analyzing developments and important trends in the environment. PEST indicates that one should analyze the political, economic, sociological, and technological situation and trends. SEPTEMBER, a more expanded version of PEST, denotes an analysis of society, economics, politics, technology, education, the marketplace, business, ethics, and finally regulation.

These models, found in nearly every introductory textbook on organizational theory, to a certain degree underestimate the institutional configuration in the environment. The institutional configuration is concerned with dominant norms, values, attitudes, and perceptions in the value system of society. These models, however, are useful tools to analyze macrotrends in the society and force the organization to focus on the possible impact of trends on the library. For example, if a national government decides that citizens as a whole need to have upgraded access to IT, this would be beneficial to public libraries because some of them may be able to play a central role in the implementation of such policies. If a government announces a policy to reduce taxes, it will concern all types of libraries because public spending will decrease. Another example could concern technology and eBooks. It is not easy for libraries to cope with the eBook situation as it would pose problems for the whole library system and for the single library, and it involves a plethora of problems concerned with contracts with the publishers, a download policy, and internal resource allocation, just to name a few of the many problems facing libraries. The last example concerns the demographic change in Europe. Most European countries have, for many years, had a rather low birth rate, resulting in an aging population. Another important shift is that the population becomes more multicultural because of immigration. Public libraries must ask themselves how to prioritize services to the elderly and how to prioritize them for people with different cultural backgrounds.

Change in the institutional configuration is subject to interpretation. It is a common psychological mechanism that people tend to look at the environment for those traits that confirm their beliefs, and they tend to overlook traits and issues that challenge at least long-held beliefs.

The interpretation of the environment can be incorrect due to several factors. An organization could have epistemic blind spots, meaning that warning signals, signs, and triggers in the environment are misinterpreted because they do not conform to the mental programming existing in the organization. Another mistake is that an organization more or less explicitly decides to take a risk or has a structure that hinders the cross-organizational flow of information. Coupling these factors with an unclear decision-making structure can result in decisions or failures to decide that can have dire consequences.

Acknowledging libraries and their services does not involve life-and-death issues, meaning that the misinterpretation of traits in the environment does not cause catastrophic consequences. Misinterpretations can still contribute to wasting resources or dissatisfying users or potential users. However, the kinds of deficiencies outlined above are interesting for libraries, and they are something about which library leadership ought to be concerned.

There might be a misinterpretation or an oversight of warning signals. An example can illustrate a possible warning signal. Many studies have indicated that many students and university teachers extensively use electronic services, but many of them do not realize they are using library resources.

Some examples related to library situations highlight the impediments resulting from epistemic blind spots, risk denials, or structural barriers. The most striking example of an epistemic blind spot is probably the attack on the World Trade Center in New York City. Different authorities had all the information required to detect the coming attack, but nobody could really believe that the United States would be attacked on its own ground. It was outside the range of possibilities embedded in the collective frame of reference. It was an epistemic blind spot. Elements of epistemic blind spots exist in all organizations and in the norms and values in professions. An example could be libraries developing web tutorials as a base for information literacy teaching and activities. There are examples of tutorials that are constructed, for example, according to pedagogical and information-seeking models developed by Carol C. Kuhlthau, and the intention is that students during their interaction with the tutorial go through the steps laid out in the tutorial; as a result, they become informed students.[4] Students, in fact, do not use the tutorials this way. They use them only as a reference tool or as an instrument to produce the right kind of references.

Risk denials are another way to cope with turbulence in the environment. An example could be that there is talk and preliminary discussions about the merging of two universities. Two university libraries are in the process of buying new, and different, library systems. They continue with the acquisition process denying the possible consequences and implications of the coming merger process. The acquisition of a new library system involves data transfer, competence development, changes in the websites, and many other activities that are rather costly.

Climatic changes such as flooding and other phenomena can also serve as an example. A situation could be the following: if a library is situated near a coast or a harbor, precautions ought to be taken in relation to the risk for flooding, but management could choose to deny the risk and hope that the climate will behave itself in the future.

Structural impediments are often the result of the organizational structure, which is not limited to bureaucratic and silo organizations. There is a risk in relation to flatter and matrix organizations. A classic example is at a larger university library there was a department for cataloging and another for classification, each with its own manager. This arrangement often resulted in huge delays from acquisition to shelving owing to the lack of cooperation between the departments. Newer examples related to matrix structures are unclear decision procedures, resulting in frustration among staff members who think they serve several masters not knowing the boundaries of their portfolio. This causes a situation in which responsibilities are unclear for both staff and managers.

It is part of leadership to challenge the organization and force it to look deeply into the relationship between organizational beliefs and issues in the environment that challenge these beliefs. In a scientific sense, one should look for falsification instead of verification of one's own beliefs. One can further recommend other leadership activities in connection with the problems mentioned above. The question leaders must ask themselves and their organizations is how managers and staff members can avoid group thinking resulting in epistemic blind spots. A leader must work out strategies suitable to force processes of falsification in relation to strongly held beliefs. It is possible that different kinds of evidence-based approaches can facilitate these processes.

There are straightforward countermeasures that can be applied to avoid the consequences of an erroneous interpretation of situations or of the environment, and they are suited to detect and interpret signals in a more appropriate manner. In most cases it would be appropriate to be more conscientious in seeking information more broadly and to adopt measures to avoid a too confirmative approach to the information. This could also be amended by using other interpretative frames and wildcards. A wildcard is a method to think the unthinkable. A good example: if people in the 1980s had asked themselves, What would happen if the Berlin Wall collapsed as a consequence of the possible downfall of the communist system? This question was more or less unthinkable, but there were several signals in the environment that pointed in that direction. The wildcard is sometimes used as an element in scenario planning, and it might be referred to as thinking out of the box.

It is also important to establish, if possible, a climate in the organization that reduces pressures to conform to dominant thinking together with efforts to bring members of the organization in contact with the environment and important stakeholders to avoid the tendency for group thinking. Performance measurement, satisfaction surveys, and other instruments are important in this context, but it is probably much more effective to engage employees in conversation with less than satisfied stakeholders.

Structural problems, to a certain degree, can be counterattacked through an open and honest flow of communication and information. It is especially important to foster a climate for cross-departmental knowledge sharing and a culture that is able to respond to signals. This sounds easy but in practice it is really difficult, especially in organizations with hierarchical and bureaucratic structures. It is nearly impossible to be against the concept of knowledge sharing, but it is not easy to implement a system that fosters knowledge sharing. A manager's point of view could be that much of the sharing takes too much time and effort away from accomplishing core tasks. Another obstacle could be that minutes from meetings have to be approved by the next meeting before the minutes go into the intranet or are distributed in other ways. This delay of communication can be a foundation for talk, rumors, and other forms of misinterpretation of both intentions and content. Technical solutions (e.g., open offices) do not work in all cases, and it is also expensive to restructure a building.

Path dependency is often overlooked in the literature concerning organizational change, but as a strategic instrument it is extremely important. Path dependency, which is the result of decisions, can be explained in a simple way. In every decision process, there exists a multitude of ways to choose from. A strategic analysis will often favor a few of the possibilities, and one of them is chosen. Another way to say this is that other possibilities are deselected. It narrows the next steps to be taken, and every new decision is built, more or less, on the previous action, as well as the room for future actions, unless there is a radical shift in strategy and probably an influx of new funding.

LEADERSHIP AND MANAGEMENT

Leadership and management involve checks and balances. Both capabilities are important in an organization. The administration has, among many other things, to keep the budget in order to secure the smooth, effective, and efficient operation of processes. Management is also about assuring that operations run according to regulations, guidelines, and standards. Figure 8.1 shows the possible result of an imbalance between leadership and management.

One could argue that an outstanding leader also needs management capabilities, and, for us, the ideal term is managerial leadership. A library with a weak administration and a strong leadership has the risk of becoming an organization that is out of control, or if both leadership and administration are weak the situation could be

	Management or administrative processes	
	Weak	**Strong**
Strong leadership	Out of control	Development and innovation
Weak leadership	Chaotic situation	Too much control

Figure 8.1: Imbalance between Leadership and Management

chaotic, or it could also be one of total complacency and self-satisfaction, without room for change and development. A weak leadership and a strong administration could turn the organization into a culture focusing too much on processes and a no-error culture thwarting innovation.

Public institutions including libraries operate in an environment characterized by conflicting, competing, and ill-defined factors. We can characterize these factors as the state, the civil society, and the market. Each of these puts pressure on the public institution and defines freedom of action. The library has to respond to and accept pressures from each of these factors. Following is a brief description of the kind of forces and pressures that are embedded in the three factors. Basic to the concept of the state is the notion of a social contract between the public institutions and the citizens, which emphasizes democracy, control, efficiency, and equal treatment of all citizens. The notion of civil society has more do with attitudes, feelings, values, and symbols. The concept of belonging is central in defining civil society, in the same way as it is central to defining the culture of an institution. Values and norms related to belonging are important factors that help keep a society together, and the marketplace is a quid pro quo in regard to money serving as a mediator.

An example explains some of the elements of cross-pressure. It is evident that bureaucracy and bureaucratic procedures are important in relation to the state. Bureaucratic procedures are a means of obtaining an impartial, professional, and equal treatment of the citizens in their interaction with public institutions. Rules, guidelines, and legal documents form the bureaucratic procedures, and they tend to make institutional changes difficult. The intrinsic values of public bureaucracy, to a certain degree, explain why decentralization of the state apparatus nearly always produces centralization or the establishment of a new body of control.

The discourse on leadership often emphasizes values and the need to control elements. There is also a discussion about quality, service delivery, rationalization, and related concepts. The single institution is a mix of the pushes and pulls of the three factors. The cross-pressure that emerges from the interaction between the three factors has consequences for the organizational structure, for the strategy, and for the leadership.

There is a general consensus that leadership in the coming years will become even more important than it is today and that it will be more difficult. The context of leadership is extremely important, and it calls for strategic capabilities. Leaders need to possess strategic capabilities. The important strategic capabilities are about being able to analyze and sense the context and the environment and to understand some of the complex driving forces that shape organizations and the way we think about tasks, objectives, and strategies. Another important leadership capability is the ability to formulate aspirational and inspirational visions in cooperation with employees. To get staff and stakeholders to understand this indicates the need for effective communicative skills that will generate an impact on others and the ability to foster collaboration and networking both inside the organization and with stakeholders outside the organization.

The strategy must be put to work, and the prerequisite for this is the ability to empower employees to be able to work with intrinsic motivational strategies, and to create a culture that is based on the general principles of the learning organization. The strategic sensing ought to foster a culture that welcomes innovation and entrepreneurial approaches at the same time as the procedures and processes run smoothly, effectively, and efficiently.

INNOVATION AND ENTREPRENEURSHIP

Factors that foster innovation are a well-educated, highly motivated staff that is willing to engage in risk-taking and to look at services and operations differently, and a decentralized decision-making system, including flat structures. It is also an advantage to possess a low degree of bureaucracy and to have relatively small differences in salaries. Perhaps the most important ingredient is a director who wants to change the library dramatically and have the staff assume new roles and services, reset the vision to redefine the library as a virtual resource, one not limited by time and space, and not dependent on buildings for the housing, use, and servicing of information. Furthermore, for such a director, the library competes in the information marketplace for new business and for corporate, foundation, and government investment. As more managerial leaders in libraries leverage their digital content, reshape the organizational culture, build the physical and expertise infrastructure, and set new directions, they may be willing to view themselves as *entrepreneurs*.[5] James G. Neal introduces this concept, connects it to innovation, and applies it to the future of academic libraries, as he asks, "Are there opportunities for the academic library to be an aggressive partner in … new learning communities, and to export resources, services, and expertise into new markets?"[6] As libraries venture into new markets, he connects what they are doing to "entrepreneurial business initiatives," and he sees them as producing

> new income to benefit library collections and services, to learn through these activities, and to apply these lessons to library programs. The objectives also aim to secure expanded visibility in the national library and information technology communities, and to increase credibility in the University, where the tradition for such activities in the academic divisions is established.[7]

Maria T. H. Carpenter takes the overview that Neal provides and examines the perceptions of library directors engaged in entrepreneurial activities. She has them comment on the definition of entrepreneurial leadership as "the ability to envision and create a scenario or possible challenges that are enacted by followers and backed by stakeholders." Further, she identifies the attributes associated with such leadership, the activities that define the entrepreneurial activities in which their libraries engage, the opportunities they see for such activities, and the support they provide for activities in which they engage. The participants see "their roles in entrepreneurial activities primarily as cheerleader and conveyor of vision, opportunity seeker, and master strategist."[8]

It seems likely that with severe fiscal constraints on a number of institutions, as those constraints are passed on to libraries, more directors will explore entrepreneurial opportunities as a remedy to offset, to some extent, the loss of money allocated to operate them and achieve the vision set for their broader organization. As the participants in the Carpenter study explained, they are entrepreneurial for three reasons: to improve financial management conditions, foster innovation, and build prestige.[9]

CONCLUDING THOUGHTS

Academic libraries are in the process of reengineering their workforces, engaging the communities they serve, refining digital collections and services, creating tools for data curation across disciplines, publishing digital scholarship and research, integrating technology with teaching and learning, and coping with fiscal stringencies. Such a climate creates opportunities to connect driving forces to factors such as organizational agility, values, and trust; organization innovativeness; stewardship of the public's trust; and entrepreneurial leadership. As more libraries engage in entrepreneurial leadership, their leaders will be inclined to take more risks (not be averse to risk), favor change and innovation to obtain competitive advantage, and complete aggressively with other libraries, museums, and firms wanting to do the same thing. Clearly, the image of what a library is will continue to change and evolve.

NOTES

1. John P. Kotter, *Leading Change* (Boston: Harvard Business School Press, 1996).

2. Kotter, *Leading Change.*

3. Kotter, *Leading Change.*

4. Carol C. Kuhlthau, *Seeking Meaning: A Process Approach to Library and Information Services*, 2nd ed. (Westport, CT: Libraries Unlimited, 2004).

5. It merits mention that there is a new peer-reviewed, open-access journal, the *Journal of Library Innovation*, which publishes articles dealing with, among other things, "creative collaboration between libraries, or between libraries and other types of institutions, resulting in demonstrable improvements in service to users;" "explorations of the future of libraries"; "pilot testing unconventional ideas and services;" "redefining the roles of library staff to better serve users;" and "developing processes that encourage organizational innovation" (see, http://www.libraryinnovation.org/about/editorialPolicies#focusAndScope, accessed May 21, 2012).

6. James G. Neal, "The Entrepreneurial Imperative Advancing from Incremetal to Radical Change in the Academic Library," *portal: Libraries and the Academy* 1, no. 1 (2001): 6.

7. Neal, "Entrepreneurial Imperative," 11.

8. Maria T.H. Carpenter, "Cheerleader, Opportunity Seeker, and Master Strategist: ARL Directors as Entrepreneurial Leaders," *College & Research Libraries* 73, no. 1 (2012): 29, 22.

9. Carpenter, "Cheerleader, Opportunity Seeker, and Master Strategist," 23.

9

CULTURE, ORGANIZATIONAL RECIPES,
AND LEADERSHIP IN LIBRARIES

Niels Ole Pors

A leader or manager in libraries today faces many challenges that are related to cultural issues. For example, libraries are increasingly working with other institutions and organizations, and the amalgamations or mergers of organizations are not readily apparent to everyone. These mergers may be difficult to manage because the cultures of the organizations are different, and they have to be reconciled in some ways during the process of merging. In addition, leaders sometimes move from one institution to another, be it in the same country or to another country, and these moves might be frustrating because the cultural codes often differ from country to country and from institution to institution. In addition, leaders and managers often have to implement what we can call *management tools* (see Chapter 1). Sometimes the process is easy, and at other times it is complicated by the structures and the value system existing in the organization. Leaders have to consider different professional groups that have complex and conflicting value systems.

These possibilities only serve to emphasize that the culture is an organizational fact with which library leaders have to contend. Culture exists at several levels. There is a national culture but there is also a culture or a value system connected to professions. Individual institutions or organizations have organizational cultures, probably with subcultures embedded within them, and these different layers of cultures color their daily working life and are extremely important, especially in relation to change processes. It can be argued that culture is an important fact of life in organizations.

Culture, however, is not just a fact of life of organizations. It is also a topic that interests researchers. There exists an extensive literature on organizational culture,

Portions of this chapter are based on the following: Pors, Niels Ole. "Globalization, Culture, and Social Capital: Library Professionals on the Move," *Library Management* 28, no. 5 (2007): 181–90; Pors, Niels Ole, Pat Dixon, and Heather Robson. "The Employment of Quality Measures in Libraries: Cultural Differences, Institutional Imperatives, and Managerial Profiles," *Performance Measurement and Metrics* 5, no. 1 (2004): 20–27.

and it is not surprising that the literature presents different theories, approaches, philosophies, definitions, and mode of applications.

The purpose of this chapter is to discuss cultural issues in libraries in relation to issues concerning the adoption of management tools, both at national and organizational levels. The concept of organizational recipes is especially relevant in this context.

ORGANIZATIONAL RECIPES

Much management information comes in forms of recipes. A recipe, a broad concept that can take many forms, is a kind of management tool that can be implemented in organizations. Examples of recipes are total quality management, the balanced scorecard, business process engineering, and lean processes as well as more limited practices (measurement instruments such as LibQUAL+™, http://www.libqual. org/home, and Counting Opinions' LibPAS™, http://www.countingopinions. com/). A recipe or a standard that becomes a trend has the following characteristics: it may originate in an academic setting, and it is created in cooperation with libraries or businesses. Prestigious firms and companies use it, and the recipe incorporates the promise to solve serious problems in the companies and in the institutions that want to work with management tools. Recipes are marketed, and they are frameworks for actions; most of all, they have interpretable meaning so that institutions can adopt and change them according to the national and organizational cultures. They are connected to stories of success, and the story behind the recipe takes the form of a drama. In time, successful recipes disclose trends and can be applied across boundaries and cultures. Some recipes, such as the balanced scorecard, have a rather long life span, whereas others, such as business process reengineering, have a shorter life span. This does not mean that they are not used. Instead, they are incorporated in the organizational operations, and people stop talking about them. Finally, all recipes have both content and symbolic aspects. It is, of course, extremely interesting to see which recipes dominate in a profession's discourse and which ones a given profession does not include in its arsenal of recipes.[1]

The process of adopting recipes in a single organization can take many forms.[2] Some recipes are adopted because of institutional requirements, whereas others are adopted because they fit into the normative structure of the profession and an individual institution. Adoption can happen as a mimetic process; a recipe is adopted because other organizations use it and because it appears to work.

The complex process of origination, social authorizing, diffusion, translation, and adoption of recipes has been studied in the context of both national and organizational culture. Several studies have indicated that the national culture influences the selection of acceptable recipes, the emphasis that is placed on different elements in the recipe, and the way the recipe is integrated into the management system.[3] Organizational recipes can be considered a means of reducing the perceived complexity of the environment.

The issues concerning organizational recipes raise questions that are of interest for the leadership. One issue is the possible relationship between national culture and recipes. Another is the organizational culture and recipes, especially the question about the adoption and interpretation process and the actual use or nonuse of the organizational recipe. Finally, there are questions about leaders' awareness of cultural issues and their insight in the forces and factors that promote and implement organizational recipes.

NATIONAL CULTURES AND INFORMATION IN THE FORM OF RECIPES

One of the most influential researchers in the area of cross-cultural studies is the Dutch sociologist Geert Hofstede. His huge body of research on different aspects of culture has had an enormous importance for cross-cultural studies, and it is also interesting and important in relation to different aspects of leadership. His work emphasizes cultural differences and points to the fact that no universal model for good leadership exists. Leadership is bound in a context that is rather specific.[4] It is impossible to give his work all the credit it deserves in this short introduction, but a few of the more important aspects of it will be covered. His analyses of the mental programming in different nations are detailed, and his analyses cover this mental programming in relation to different types of workplaces, social groupings, and issues concerning educational levels. It is another way to state that a presentation of his work only can illustrate some of the major tendencies. Hofstede's main interest in his research is the relationship between a more or less shared set of values and its consequences for behavioral patterns. He further defines culture as "the collective programming of the mind which distinguishes the member of one group or category of people from another." His theories have changed and become more refined and detailed from the first research to later writings. His earlier writings operated with four dimensions of a national culture. This has later been expanded to five. In this introduction we will only cover the four dimensions that categorize and classify the value systems and the related behavioral traits. The four dimensions are the degree of power distance in society, individualism versus collectivism, the degree of masculinity in society, and the need for avoidance of uncertainty (see Chapters 1 and 14).

Countries with a low power distance tend to favor values like equality, democratic structures, decentralization, and involvement of employees and citizens at all levels. This is in contrast with countries that emphasize values like hierarchy, centralization, and top-down processes. In relation to behavior these values express themselves in the way people interact and in the formality of this interaction. The second dimension concerns the question about individualism versus collectivism and this dimension emphasizes the importance of the group in relation to the individual. A collectivist culture will tend to appreciate loyalty in relation to the group, the organization, or the clan, whereas the individual culture to a much higher degree emphasizes the persons as individuals with values and responsibilities based on the individuals' achievements.

If we turn to the third dimension concerning masculine versus feminine values and behavior it is about the softness or hardness of approaches to life, values, and interpersonal relationships. In an organizational context it is about preferences for results versus preferences for a more process-oriented approach. It is the balance and specific configuration of the two preferences that are interesting in an organizational context. The dimension also indicates how people communicate and how they perceive different societal issues. Without doubt, this dimension is closely connected to how societies are structured.

The fourth dimension concerns weak and strong uncertainty avoidance. The position in relation to uncertainty is both a psychological and a cultural trait. It is in many ways a measure of how people and organizations cope with change and muddy situations with an unknown outcome. One way to reduce uncertainty in an organizational setting is, for example, to run the organization with rules and with decision-making processes that are carefully conducted, for example, through extensive preparation and valuation of alternatives.

Hofstede's theory has many similarities to a model by Fons Trompenaars and Charles Hampden-Turner.[5] They identified seven cultural dimensions: universalism versus particularism, communitarianism versus individualism, neutral versus emotional, diffuse versus specific cultures, the human–time relationship, the human–nature relationship, and achievement versus ascription. These dimensions are more or less the same as the ones used by Hofstede, and it is fair to state that the models to identify the essential aspects of national culture do not differ very much. Both perspectives are based on a belief that culture consists of values and preferred behavior related to the values.

Shalom H. Schwartz is behind what is probably some of the most comprehensive research in cross-cultural studies as he has investigated over 60,000 people worldwide. In the research he operates with 10 different value types and their influence on preferred behavior.[6]

Brian P. Mathews, Akiko Ueno, Tauno Kekäle, Mikko Repka, Zulema Lopes Pereira, and Graça Silva did a comparative study of European quality management practices.[7] This study is important in relation to leadership. They explore Hofstede's concepts and investigate how different aspects of culture can contribute to an explanation of the selection, employment, and use of different quality instruments or management tools. They conclude that the theoretical models based on Hofstede's research are useful as means to answer the question as they document a certain predictive power. Edgar H. Schein considers quality tools as artifacts that have to be seen in the context of organizational values.[8] It means that an organization tends to choose artifacts conforming to its values and to reject artifacts seen as alien or a threat to the culture of the organization. Tauno Kekäle and Jouni Kekäle, who investigate the spread and diffusion of the total quality management concept or recipe in different countries, found that the theories of national cultures partly explain why different countries emphasize different aspects of the recipe.[9] Both studies inspired a comparative study of British and Danish library directors and managers.[10] Some of the most important results from this comparative study follow in the next paragraphs.

The comparative study of British and Danish library leaders and managers was conducted using surveys, and it covers a wide range of issues including, for instance, the perception of challenges, priorities, leadership styles, cooperation, staff-related issues, job satisfaction, and perceptions of job content.

An inductive analysis indicates surprisingly different attitudes to some issues. It is, for example, striking that Danish library directors express a much higher job satisfaction than their British colleagues do, and it is obvious that they find the job less stressful than the British directors do. The Danish leaders perceive their leadership style and their interaction with staff as based on respect, interaction, trust, and other soft values and behaviors to a much higher degree than do the British directors. The Danish directors and managers perceive that they possess a higher degree of freedom on the job and in relation to decision-making processes.

Other intriguing patterns emerge in the data. One of them is that, among Danish managers, there is a correlation between the amount of use of management tools and job satisfaction. This is not the case in the United Kingdom (UK). There is a correlation between the level of knowledge of management tools or organizational recipes and job satisfaction in Denmark, but the same pattern is not found among the UK managers. Further, the knowledge and use of management tools are much more pervasive in the UK than in Denmark. These differences cannot be explained by classic background or demographic factors such as age, gender, position, type of organization, and salary level.

The comparative study focused on the masculine–feminine dimension as it was the single dimension where UK and Denmark really differed. In this terminology, Denmark appeared as a much softer or more feminine country than the UK. The difference in relation to the other cultural dimensions is much less. One of the main questions in the research was to investigate if a difference could be found in the use of management tools. It is, of course, difficult to classify a management tool or an organizational recipe as either hard or soft. However, in the research, the different management tools were classified.

The questionnaire contains questions about how the library directors perceived their own knowledge about different management tools. They stated their perceived knowledge in relation to 21 different management tools and approaches. Statistical significant differences between leaders from UK and Denmark exist in relation to 18 out of 21 tools. The results correlated in relation to the masculine versus feminine dimension as the leaders and managers from the UK possess much more perceived knowledge about so-called harder tools than their Danish colleagues, who possess more knowledge about the human-oriented tools and recipes.

The ranking of the tools or organizational recipes differs between the two groups and the main difference is that the Danish leaders and directors tend to have a rather comprehensive knowledge about softer tools that are very staff-oriented. Examples of these tools are tools concerned with intellectual capital, competency plans for staff members, ethical accountancy, and value-based management. The British directors score high on tools directed toward organizational efficiency, economy, customer orientation, and strategies.

The research clearly indicated that other issues are connected or related to the masculine–feminine dimension. It was apparent that the higher degree of job satisfaction among Danish directors is correlated with a factor like the feeling of job security. Job satisfaction is also strongly correlated with factors such as the perception of freedom in the job and the ability to make decisions without interference from other stakeholders. These types of correlations led the researcher to conclude that one of the main differences between the leadership situations in libraries in the two countries is the degree of institutional imperatives. An institutional imperative is simply the fact that British libraries have less freedom in relation to the selection and use of different organizational recipes. This is probably a result of a situation in which the assessment culture is much more pervasive in the UK than it is in Denmark, thereby reducing the director's freedom and decision-making power in important areas. The higher degree of job satisfaction among Danish library directors can be explained by the perception of the higher degree of freedom in the job and in decision-making processes. At the time of the investigation, Denmark simply had a less hierarchical structure, which implies a higher degree of autonomy in the organizations. This finding fits well with the theoretical analysis based on cross-cultural concepts.

The research indicated that factors in the national culture is a fruitful perspective analyzing leadership situations in different countries, and it also indicated that leadership and management problems cannot be discussed meaningfully without context.

It is evident that culture consists of many factors shared by nations and by social groups, and these factors comprise guidelines for behavior and the interpretation of the environment and for the interpretation of human interrelationships. At the very least, the concept of culture consists of both values and norms, including basic assumptions that affect behavior. Together they manifest themselves in human institutions.

In relation to Hofstede's dimensions, there are similarities and dissimilarities between the UK and Denmark. The ranking of the nations are the following: in terms of power distance, the UK ranks 43 and Denmark 51. On the dimension of individualism the UK ranks 3 and Denmark 9. The ranking on the masculine–female dimension is 10 for the UK and 50 for Denmark. And, finally, the ranking on the insecurity scale is 47 for the UK and 51 for Denmark.

Both countries have a relaxed attitude to authorities, power structures, and changes in both the workplace and society. The societies are also individual-based. However, there is a marked difference in the dimension concerning masculinity. Denmark is a much more feminine country than the UK, and there is a preference for softer values.

A conjecture is that the institutional imperatives are stronger in the UK. This follows the nature of the culture of assessment in Britain. Assessment tools and strategic managerial approaches are more embedded in the culture of organizations. The findings confirm the relevance of the tentative model, and the differences in discourse and in the employment of tools may be related to differences in national culture. The manager's position in relation to the cross-pressure between institutional imperatives and freedom of decisions and actions also plays a role, at least in relation to such factors as the sense of job security, workload, and well-being at the job. These factors, of course, are also part of the organizational culture. This culture is important as a zone of acceptance, in relation to which tools and managerial approaches are conceivable and legitimate in a given institution.

The employment of management tools is closely connected with the discourse in society concerning factors such as accountability, effectiveness, value for money, empowerment, change, flexibility, incentives, motivation, and evaluation. Employment, however, is tentatively modified by the basic values of a given profession. These basic values are based on commonly shared assumptions, which constitute at least a part of the ethos of a given profession. Common assumptions, in a way, are the essence of the culture of a given group. It is important to emphasize that commonly shared assumptions can drive the choices of values and artifacts. On the other hand, value decisions and artifacts together can either strengthen or reformulate the basic assumptions. Basic assumptions are not static, but they change more or less conspicuously.

The analyses indicate that some of the ambiguities can be explained. One key ambiguity relates to the correlation in Denmark between employment of a management tool and job satisfaction. In contrast to the UK, there are few requirements for the employment and reporting of management tools. This implied that leaders usually decide on the employment of a tool or a management concept on a voluntary basis. One could argue that this is one way to promote the organization and give it a kind of symbolic expression, which indicates that the library through the employment of the recipe is in the forefront of the development. This contrasts with the situation in the UK where organizations and institutions, to a much higher degree, are forced to employ certain management tools and report them, thereby reducing the room for independent decision making. This is what could be called an *institutional imperative*.

It is interesting to see that the use of cross-cultural studies such as those by Hofstede appears to be limited in the literature of library and information science, in contrast to studies of fields such as knowledge management, where studies use national cultures as one factor in analyses of knowledge management strategies and implementation.[11] However, Gillian Oliver has conducted studies of information culture in organizations and its possible relationships with national cultures.[12] The study comparing Danish and British library directors and managers focuses on the dimension named masculinity. Oliver focus on the power distance dimension and the dimension concerned with uncertainty avoidance and correlates the dimension with Henry Mintzberg's classification of organizational structures.[13] The results of these correlations are an identification of four types of organizations:

1. Full bureaucracy or a pyramid model characterized by a high power distance and a strong need to avoid uncertainty
2. Implicit structure or a market model characterized by a low power distance and a low need to avoid uncertainty
3. Workflow bureaucracy or a model of the well-oiled machine with a low power distance and a strong need to avoid uncertainty
4. Personnel bureaucracy or the family model with a wide power difference and a low need to avoid uncertainty

Oliver studies three universities situated in Hong Kong, Australia, and Germany. She is aware that it is impossible to generalize from three case studies. The research design, however, provides rich insight into the possible interactions among different levels of cultures. Her illuminating study indicates that national cultures defined through the lenses of Hofstede's concepts affect national legislation and the whole framework concerning organizational structures and the embedded management of information and the values that are connected to types of information and behavior in relation to, for example, information sharing. She concludes that

> both Germany and Australia are active in developing and promoting international standards in the information management domain, whereas Hong Kong does not have a national standards body … . Although the three universities were engaged in similar functions, approaches and attitudes often resulted in quite different systems being implemented to achieve the same ends. Differences in the relative values accorded to information as evidence and information as knowledge were distinguishing features of the three information cultures.[14]

The main point is that her case studies provide the reader with arguments for the necessity and fruitfulness of combining analyses of national cultures with organizational cultures in the research oriented toward information.

Oliver has continued her work and has written a book, *Organisational Culture for Information Managers*, which expands the analyses mentioned above. In the book she works systematically with the interaction of the different cultural layers in relation to questions of interest for information management and information managers.[15]

ORGANIZATIONAL CULTURES AND THE ADOPTION AND INTERPRETATION OF RECIPES

The previous section points out that national cultures influence which types of recipes and management tools tend to dominate in a given country or at least which aspects of a given tool will be emphasized. However, the single institution still has a wide choice of recipes to focus on. The organizational culture is an important mediating factor in this context. Many different theories and models of organizational culture exist. Common to nearly all of the theories and definitions are the focus. There is a widespread agreement that organizational culture encompasses several layers such as deeply held assumptions and norms that are taken for granted. The culture also consists of values and beliefs systems. Following Schein,[16] the culture consists of observable artifacts such as architecture, communication modes and patterns, organizational diagrams, and narratives. This classification of organizational culture available in different versions can be found in many textbooks, and it is one of the backbones of the many typologies of organizational culture that exists in the scholarly literature. An example of this follows: Kim S. Cameron and Robert E. Quinn, who have worked with a useful typology of organizational culture,[17] look at organizations with either an internal or external focus and organizations with an orientation or preference for change or stability. The combination of the two types of orientation produces four distinct different cultural outcomes. The outcomes in terms of cultural orientation are the following:

1. External orientation and preference for change results in a kind of *adhocracy* and open system characterized by innovation, entrepreneurship, and the culture, which emphasizes values such as dynamic and risk-oriented behavior.
2. External orientation and preference for stability results in a market culture that values rationality, rational models, fulfillment of goals, production and task-oriented, completion, and results.
3. Internal orientation and preference for change results in a kind of clan structure with family-like traits, and the values are concerned with human relations, personal interaction, caring, loyalty, cohesion, equality, and group orientation.
4. Internal orientation and preference for stability in a hierarchical culture values processes, rules, procedures, efficiency, formalization and structure, and standards.

All orientations exist in a single organization at the same time, however. For this reason the orientation of the single organization is a specific configuration of patterns in the orientations.

This typology is also useful to classify dominant traits and structures on organizations, but it is important to emphasize that it is just a classifying instrument and no organization fits only one part of the typology. The dominant organizational feature consists of the structure of the organization, for example, whether it is hierarchical, organized as a matrix, or team-based. The leadership style points to both styles and preferred roles of leaders and managers. A feature such as staff points to issues such as demographic factors, educational level, gender, communication patterns, and attitudes. The glue in the organization keeps things together. It can be either tasks or personal relations, and it relates to a value system. In many ways it is a feature that is hard to define, but something most members in the organization know as tacit knowledge. Strategic goals, which can be clear or fuzzier, can be directed toward products or tasks, or they can be more internal. Criteria for success can differ. Are they oriented toward the market, the customers, the processes, or innovations? It is also important to consider whether the criteria for success are supported by reward systems and the structure of incentives. These features represent operationalization of different aspects of the organizational culture, and they are useful as an analytical tool.

Recipes and organizational cultures are interesting because there will probably be a kind of fit between the adoption of recipes and the dominant culture. Management information comes to the libraries in forms of recipes and standards, and it is often disseminated through formal activities such as workshops, staff courses, reading, and networking as well as by participating in educational activities such as leadership courses and graduate programs.[18]

The approaches described above have been studied in a large-scale investigation of culture, leadership, and change processes in Danish public libraries.[19] The original study concerns library managers and directors in those public libraries. That study scrutinized 24 library directors by means of personal interviews and by interviews with staff members. In total, nearly 100 persons participated in interviews. The 24 directors studied shared some common organizational features such as size and location. The organizations were small- to middle-sized, and they were located in smaller towns or suburban areas. In summary, they reflect the typical Danish public library.

The interviews were conducted as broad thematic interviews covering the following issues and topics:

- Change and change processes in the library, with questions concerning process implementation, task prioritizing, organizational structure, technology, staff policies, and perceptions of the environment
- Knowledge-sharing procedures with questions concerning leadership development, strategic development of competencies, knowledge-sharing initiatives, staff development policies, the relationship between different groups employed, artifacts and stories in the organization, projects, and customer orientation
- Organizational culture with questions concerning values and norms, the interpretation of strategies and objectives, patterns of cooperation, and leadership and management styles
- Leadership and management, with questions concerning the interpretation of cross-pressures, perception of management styles and personality, reading, networking and integration with stakeholders, and the perceptions of benefits of participation in seminars, courses, and educational programs.

Each interview with the director lasted between 1.5 and 2 hours, and corresponding interviews with two to five staff members were conducted as a group interview for the same length of time. The interview guides for the two types of interview were nearly identical. Together all the interviews took approximately 100 hours, and they formed a rich picture of the relationship between leadership and organizational culture.

The organizational cultures differ depending on traditions, staff composition, and patterns of cooperation. In nearly all of the libraries the staff expressed a need for change and innovation, but the emphasis on such issues as staff versus users or objectives greatly differed. Different configurations of organizational cultural orientations emerged in the libraries. It is fair to emphasize that many of the directors and staff members interviewed perceive themselves and their libraries as innovative and risk-oriented, but a deeper analysis indicates that, to a high degree, innovation in the public libraries originated largely in technological developments. Anyway, it is a difficult distinction to make if the establishment and implementation of, for example, an Internet-based library service is an innovation, or if it is simply the adoption of a technological possibility existing outside the library. At the heart of the distinction is whether one would distinguish between service development and innovation. Many of the libraries, however, resisted some technological developments. A good example is the discussion on filtering software. Most of the public libraries have resisted implementing this kind of software, emphasizing that such software violates values associated with free access to information. Those interviewed further stated that conversations with people misusing Internet access together with a kind of personal supervision and control should be pursued. The arguments can be seen as ideological in relation to the interpretation of the norms of the profession. The arguments are based on a perception that filtering software does not do what it is supposed to do. These arguments continue independently of experiments and research that demonstrate that some of the filtering software actually does exactly what it sets out to do. There appears to be a certain blindness for information not conforming to the discourse of the profession.

In this context, all of the libraries had one dominant organizational feature in common, namely their ability to adopt and translate technological developments and to introduce them into the library setting. The openness in considering and applying technological developments is one of the main factors behind the advanced level that public libraries in Denmark have on the information technological level.

Some of the configurations of cultural orientations relate to the combination of an internal or external focus of the organization or one could say a people-oriented or a task-oriented orientation. In this context, it is interesting to note that the orientation toward running of processes smoothly, the process orientation in the typology of organizational culture, was not perceived as an orientation by either directors or staff, but it is interesting because one phenomenon that characterizes public libraries in Denmark is their effectiveness, efficiency, and smoothly running processes. At the same time, there is a long tradition that budgets are balanced and everything in relation to stakeholders is orderly and outside the boundaries of critique. This is probably a result of a long tradition of cost-effectiveness and joint solutions. It is something that is taken for granted, and behavior conforms to that on a nearly subconscious level. One can argue that the process orientation is dominant but hidden, is a part of the situation, and shapes the organizational rules in a way that makes it possible not to reflect on them. This process orientation, in many ways, shapes the attitudes of both leaders and staff in a user-friendly and cooperative manner. An example is the speed in providing interlibrary loan service and the knowledge sharing that exists across regions and types of libraries. This orientation is so ingrained in the culture, however, that it is nearly impossible to discuss.

Another example concerns the automated self-service system. When the interviews were conducted, many libraries had self-service automats; those without these facilities tended to be in the process of implementing them. Self-service automats are not a recipe in a traditional sense; they are a technological innovation that becomes a standard and that contains both technical and symbolic aspects. The attitudes of staff toward these automats vary between *very positive* and *very negative* especially depending on the professional status of those interviewed and the context in which the machines were introduced in their library. In some libraries the self-service automats were introduced because of a political decision in the municipality, and if the imposed decision was followed with requirements to eliminate staff positions, the situation evoked a negative overall attitude, especially among library assistants. In most cases, library assistants are the victims of redundancies as a consequence of the technological introduction. Most of the respondents believe that self-service automats dehumanize the library because the personal contact with the users declines. In these libraries it was often the case that the introduction of the machines was done half-heartedly, meaning that only a limited number of automats were installed with the implication that real savings were unobtainable because the issue (circulation) desk was manned nearly as before. At the other end of the spectrum, libraries embraced the introduction of the technology. They often applied for funding on their own initiative and succeeded in redirecting staff to other and more demanding tasks. In these libraries, there is a positive attitude toward the self-service technology. This is probably owing to the context. The introduction is based on the organization's own decision and is not associated with an economic downsizing.

CONCLUDING THOUGHTS

One important element in leadership is the ability to read an organization, its internal and external factors that influence the life and the possibilities of the organization. The cultural orientation of an organization, to a certain degree, determines what is possible to achieve, for example, in change processes. Organizational cultures are probably not just an organizational variable that can easily be manipulated or changed. It is a complex configuration of assumptions, beliefs and values, artifacts, discourses, and behavior, and every leader ought to consider if he or she is caught in this configuration or which parts of it are more or less changeable. A leader must be able to read the organization and evaluate the importance of the different parts. This is a central leadership role to consider as the organization seeks better internal integration and challenges value systems that conflicts with the organization's strategies.

Another important leadership responsibility is to read the environment and the important trends in society. Leadership involves adapting the organization to the changes in society or at least adaption to dominant themes and issues in the field of interest. Organizational recipes provide an example of such adaptation. It is important to interpret dominant cultural traits and act accordingly, and to judge the fit or the possible mismatch between these trends and the organizational culture. A leader ought to decide if it is the symbolic or the cognitive aspects of change processes that need to be emphasized in given situations. Furthermore, the leader ought to ascertain which types of recipes best fit the organization.

NOTES

1. Kjell Arne Røvik, *Moderne Organisasjoner: Trender i Organisasjonstenkningen ved Tusenårsskiftet* (Bergen, Norway: Fagbokforlaget, 1998).

2. Paul J. DiMaggio and Walter W. Powell, "The Iron Cage Revisited: Institutional Iso-morphism and Collective Rationality in Organizational Fields," in *The New Institutionalism in Organizational Analysis*, edited by Walter W. Powell and Paul J. DiMaggio (Chicago: University of Chicago Press, 1991), 63–82.

3. Tauno Kekäle and Jouni Kekäle, "A Mismatch of Cultures: A Pitfall of Implementing a Total Quality Approach," *International Journal of Quality and Reliability Management* 12, no. 9 (1995): 210–20; Michelle L. Kaarst-Brown, Scott Nicholson, Gisela M. Von Dran, and Jeffrey M. Stanton, "Organizational Cultures of Libraries as a Strategic Resource," *Library Trends* 53, no. 1 (2004): 33–54; Niels Ole Pors, "Management Tools, Organisational Culture, and Leadership: An Explorative Study," *Performance Measurement and Metrics* 9, no. 2 (2008): 138–52.

4. Geert Hofstede, *Culture's Consequences: International Differences in Work-Related Values* (Newbury Park, CA: Sage, 1980); Geert Hofstede, *Culture and Organisations: Software of the Mind* (London: McGraw-Hill, 1991).

5. Fons Trompenaars and Charles Hampden-Turner, *Riding the Waves of Culture: Understanding Cultural Diversity in Business* (London: McGraw-Hill, 1997).

6. Shalom H. Schwartz, "Beyond Individualism/Collectivism: New Dimensions of Values," in *Individualism and Collectivism: Theory Application and Methods*, edited by Uichol Kim, Harry C. Triandis, Cigdem Kagitcibasi, Sang-Chin Choi, and Gene Yoon (Newbury Park, CA: Sage, 1994), 85–121.

7. Brian P. Mathews, Akiko Ueno, Tauno Kekäle, Mikko Repka, Zulema Lopes Pereira, and Graça Silva, "European Quality Management Practices: The Impact of National Culture," *International Journal of Quality and Reliability Management* 18, no. 7 (2001): 692–707.

8. Edgar H. Schein, *Organizational Culture and Leadership* (San Francisco: Jossey-Bass, 1992).

9. Kekäle and Kekäle, "Mismatch of Cultures."

10. Niels Ole Pors, Pat Dixon, and Heather Robson, "The Employment of Quality Measures in Libraries: Cultural Differences, Institutional Imperatives and Managerial Profiles," *Performance Measurement and Metrics* 5, no. 1 (2004): 20–28; Niels Ole Pors, "Globalisation, Culture and Social Capital: Library Professionals on the Move," *Library Management* 28, nos. 4–5 (2007): 181—90.

11. Jihong Chen, Peter Y. T. Sun, and Robert J. McQueen, "The Impact of National Cultures on Structured Knowledge Transfers," *Journal of Knowledge Management* 14, no. 2 (2010): 228–42; Rémy Magnier-Watanabe and Dai Senoo, "Shaping Knowledge Management: Organization and National Culture," *Journal of Knowledge Management* 14, no. 2 (2010): 214–27.

12. Gillian Oliver, "Information Culture: Exploration of Differing Values and Attitudes to Information in Organisations," *Journal of Documentation* 64, no. 3 (2008): 363–85.

13. Henry Mintzberg, *Structure in Fives: Designing Effective Organizations* (Englewood Cliffs, NJ: Prentice Hall, 1983).

14. Oliver, "Information Culture," 380.

15. Gillian Oliver, *Organisational Culture for Information Managers* (Oxford, UK: Chandos, 2011).

16. Schein, *Organizational Culture and Leadership.*

17. Kim S. Cameron and Robert E. Quinn, *Diagnosing and Changing Organizational Culture: Based on the Competing Values Framework* (Reading, MA: Addison-Wesley, 1999; New York: Wiley & Sons, 2006).

18. John D. Politis, "The Relationship of Various Leadership Types to Knowledge Management," *Leadership and Organization Development Journal* 22, no. 8 (2001): 354–64;

John D. Politis, "Transformational and Transactional Leadership Enabling Knowledge Acquisition of Self-managed Teams: The Consequences for Performance," *Leadership and Organization Development Journal* 23, no. 4 (2002): 186–97.

19. Niels Ole Pors, *Mellem Identitet og Legitimitet: Forandringer, Kultur og Ledelse i Danske Folkebiblioteker* (Between identity and legitimacy: Changes, culture and leadership in Danish public libraries), Research Report (Copenhagen: Royal School of Library and Information Science, 2005).

10

PERSONALITY AND LEADERSHIP

Niels Ole Pors

During the last couple of years, interest in leadership and management, including within library and information science (LIS), has greatly increased.[1] This interest is due, in part, to the fundamental changes that took place overall in the public sector. Many of these changes are related to requirements concerning accountability, user orientation, outsourcing, quality, information technology, and staff-related issues. The topic is complex because it relates to turbulence of the work environment, change processes, and the vast amount of information with which leaders need to deal.

These are good reasons to discuss and analyze different aspects of leadership. One aspect of leadership in libraries that has started to evolve in the research is the study of personality, including topics such as emotional intelligence. There are several important reasons for this. One of them is that organizational structures change and different forms of team-based work are introduced. It raises questions concerning the best composition of members of a team. People have preferences about whom they work with and certain roles they assume. One can analyze the most important task-oriented and social roles of a team and try to put together a team in which the different kinds of roles are covered. Some research indicates that a careful team composition makes a difference in team success.[2]

The same arguments can be put forth when one looks at the composition of a team of leaders. They perform different tasks and have different roles and preferences. It has become increasingly frequent that part of the recruitment process of new leaders in some countries includes some kind of testing of personality, preferences, or style. This is just a part of the recruitment process, and it is important that the tests be conducted in a professional manner and with a validated instrument.

Portions of this chapter are based on the following: Pors, Niels Ole. "Leadership and Service Provision in Public Libraries," in *Qualitative and Quantitative Methods in Libraries: Theory and Applications*, edited by Anthi Katsirikou and Christos H Skiadas. Proceedings of the International Conference on QQML 2009. Chania, Crete, Greece, May 26–29, 2009. World Scientific Books, 2010. ISBN: 978-981-4299-69-5. pp. 37–47.

Personality is also important because leaders, managers, and staff interact. Staff members tend to expend much energy talking about leaders and their perceived personality or peculiarities. The personality in this type of gossip-oriented talk is often inferred from perceived behavior and can easily take the form of stereotypes that can affect interactions in a negative way.

Personality is also an important element, for example, in relation to how newly recruited staff members seek information about the organizational culture and how it works. It is also important to know about personality dimensions for staff working with educational tasks as research clearly indicates that personality type influences information-seeking behavior and learning styles. The concept of personality should be of interest to library directors as they practice leadership, and it is also evident that personality is a concept of importance for researchers studying leadership.

With all of the challenges currently facing libraries, including the impact of the economic recession and its aftermath for collections, services, and staff, there is need for studies that examine leadership and the personality traits of library directors. One can argue that there is a relationship between the directors' personality and preferences and the direction and change processes in libraries. This topic is the focus of this chapter.[3]

PERSONALITY

Although the research about leadership personalities in LIS is limited, there appears to be a growing interest in it. For example, Peter Hernon, Joan Giesecke, and Camila A. Alire explore emotional intelligence, a dimension of personality.[4] Other studies look at the relationship between job positions and career choice in the profession in relation to personality.[5] Information-seeking behavior, learning styles, and personality have also become a focus area in some research.[6] Anne Goulding, Beth Bromham, Stuart Hannabuss, and Duncan Cramer compare the personality traits of LIS and other students in the United Kingdom. They conclude that there is a gap among educators, students, and employers about the qualities needed for success.[7]

Most theories of personality build on the assumption that personality dimensions are relatively stable and, to a certain degree, are predictive, in a broad sense, of behavior. In reality, one can argue that, in a general sense, researchers using tests assume a hypothesis about possible behavior based on the test results. One of the implications of this is that a test ought to be followed up by an interview or another form of debriefing.

There are several measurement instruments and theories that come into play investigating personality. Probably the most widespread instrument is the Myers-Briggs Type Indicator (MBTI) based primarily on the psychological theories developed by Stephen P. Robbins and Timothy A. Judge.[8] This test consists of approximately 100 questions, and the analysis of the answers is used to classify respondents into types. It is used often and is relatively well validated. Its typology is based on a theory that classifies people according to four dimensions, which are:

1. Extrovert (E) versus introvert (I)
2. Sensing (S) versus intuitive (N)
3. Thinking (T) versus feeling (F)
4. Judging (J) versus perceiving (P)

Extroverts are more sociable, outgoing, and expressive than introverts. Sensing people tend to be more practical, detail-oriented, and often have a preference for routines, systems, and orders, in contrast to intuitive people, who tend to be more creative and have a more holistic view of situations. Thinking people tend to base their decisions on logic and rational decisions, whereas feeling people rely more on their feelings and personal convictions. Judging people tend to prefer control and structure much more than perceptive people, who tend to be more flexible and spontaneous.

Based on these dichotomies there are 16 different personality types. It is important to state that the result of the measurement is dichotomies, which means that a person is classified either as an extrovert or as an introvert, and in reality many people will be placed as both. It is fair to state that the analysis produces results that only must be interpreted as global tendencies. A person who is classified as ESTJ is an extrovert, sensing, thinking, and judging, while someone classified, for example, as an INTJ is introverted and has a tendency to stubbornness, critical analysis, and independency. In actuality, the characterization of the personality types is more complex.

The MBTI gives a rather broad picture of the person taking the test, but the broad categories mean that the test can be viewed as dubious if it is used to place people in certain job types. Most of the measurement instruments based on the trait theory elicit the same type of information as the MBTI. In this context, the Revised NEO Personality Inventory (NEO PI-R) and the NEO-PI-3, an updated version of the NEO PI-R, are used. Both are the standard questionnaire of the five-factor model, a concise measure of the five major domains of personality (neuroticism, extraversion, openness, agreeableness, and conscientiousness), and the six facets that define each domain are used.[9] Besides allowing for both a general and a detailed description of personality, the test takes into consideration the characteristics of the specific test person in focus. Specific norms for groups of people and profiles have been developed from research to help validate the test result.

The NEO-PI-R and the NEO-PI-3 measure five broad personality factors based on 30 traits or facets. Each factor is a summary and an average of six facets. Each of the five factors and their associated six facets are measured through 48 statements, implying that all 30 facets are measured through 240 statements. The result of the 240 statements is distributed into low and high scores on the five factors and the 30 facets, hence demonstrating a personality profile. Each factor in the test summarizes six traits or facets that also are measured by the test.

The measurement instrument exists in two forms. There is the long form, described above, and a shorter form that consists of 60 questions covering the five factors. Either of these forms comprises the measurement instrument that is most often used in large-scale studies. It is probably fair to state that this instrument gives the same type of information as the MBTI. Jannica Heinström is an example of a researcher who used the NEO-PI-R.[10]

Table 10.1, which illustrates the relationship between the long and the short version of the text, depicts the relationship between factors and facets or traits. Each factor is the result of the scores on six facets. Each facet is measured through eight items, be it statements or questions.

Obviously, the long form produces much more detailed information than does the short form. The long form is in this respect much more applicable for studying recruitment to different types of jobs or associated tasks. In reality, the relationship between the short and long form is much like the relationship between a quantitative and a qualitative analysis. It is a question about the depth and breadth of the

Table 10.1   Factors and Facets

NEUROTICISM	EXTROVERSION	OPENNESS	AGREEABLENESS	CONSCIENTIOUSNESS
Anxiety	Warmth	Fantasy	Trust	Competence
Temper	Gregariousness	Aesthetics	Straightforwardness	Order
Pessimism	Assertiveness	Feelings	Altruism	Dutifulness
Social fear	Activity	Actions	Compliance	Achievement striving
Impulsiveness	Excitement seeking	Ideas	Modesty	Self-discipline
Nervous	Positive emotions	Values	Tender mindedness	Deliberation

analysis, and the results of the long form come from a rather complicated analysis including interviews. If we look at two facets in the factor called *openness*, we can easily imagine that the same score on that factor is a result, for example, of very different scores in the facets called *actions* and *ideas*. A high score on actions indicates a person who is open to change through actions, and a high score on ideas suggests a person with a high degree of intellectual curiosity. These facets do not necessarily correlate, and they will probably result in different forms of behavior.

It is extremely important to emphasize that personality testing involves a hypothesis about behavior and that a personality test employing the long version ought to be followed up by a debriefing, exploring that hypothesis with the respondents. The long form was used in a Danish study that will be presented later in this chapter.

Turning to the literature, this chapter does not offer an overview of the extensive literature but rather highlights some interesting studies about the relationship between personality and leadership. John H. Bradley and Frederic J. Hebert use the MBTI to analyze the performance of two teams,[11] and they provide a good introduction to the MBTI. They also give an insightful discussion of work tasks and the factors that have to be present in order to produce good team results. The factors are leadership, communication, cohesion, and heterogeneity. These factors are discussed in relation to the type indicators. The two teams are in the same work area, and they are similar in relation to all important demographic variables. The only noticeable difference between the two teams is the composition of different personality types. One of the teams has an unsatisfactory performance, whereas the other performs very well. The authors explain the difference in performance with the composition of team members and the distribution of the different types of personalities. A good team that produces well has a good diversity of skills and an effective balance of personality types. It is probably impossible, however, to put forward a typology of personalities that would constitute the most effective team because the exact work tasks also play an important role. The authors propose that the combination of work tasks should influence the team composition also in relation to members' personality type and preferences. The example illustrates that an insight into these types of problems is an important leadership capability, and the composition of the management or leadership team must be viewed in the same manner.

Tiina M. Hautala, who investigates the relationship between personality and transformational leadership, has studied more than 400 leaders and 380 employees.[12] Using the MBTI, the investigator shows how different personalities overestimate and underestimate themselves when they compare their ratings to those of subordinates. More precisely, according to leaders' self-ratings, those with extroverted, intuitive, and perceiving preferences favor transformational leadership, whereas the ratings of subordinates indicated that leaders with sensing preferences are associated with transformational leadership.

Brian P. Niehoff uses a five-factor personality test, based on an International Personality Item Pool representation of the five-factor model of personality, to explore the relationship between personality and participation as a mentor among nearly 200 American veterinarians.[13] His findings indicate that personality factors such as extroversion, openness to change, and conscientiousness were positively correlated with participation as a mentor to younger professionals. As such, the findings point to the fact that many organizations have adopted ideas about mentoring, and it can be of managerial interest to consider a possible relationship just as it is interesting to consider in the case of team composition.

Maria Vakola, Ioannis Tsaousis, and Ioannis Nikolaou investigate nearly 140 professionals from different organizations in Athens, Greece.[14] The respondents completed a version of the five-factor personality model. In addition, their emotional intelligence and their attitudes toward organizational change were measured. This complex study emphasizes that extroversion, openness to experience, agreeableness, and conscientiousness negatively correlate with emotional stability.

This small selection of studies indicates that personality plays an important role in organizational behavior. Many of the studies employ short measurement instruments based on fewer than 100 items, which means that they focus on the personality factors and not the underlying facets.

A DANISH STUDY OF PERSONALITY AND CULTURAL ORIENTATION IN PUBLIC LIBRARIES

A study of Danish library managers and directors in public libraries used the long version of NEO-PI.[15] As discussed in the previous chapter, 24 library directors and some of their staff members were examined through personal interviews. In total, nearly 100 persons participated in extensive interviews. The 24 library systems under investigation have some common features such as size and location. Ten of the directors selected randomly agreed to participate in a personality test, but only eight of them did so and also participated in a follow-up interview. A personality study with only eight individuals cannot be generalized in any way. However, the findings contribute a rich picture. The richness emerges through a qualitative analysis especially of the facets and through the combination of interviews with the directors and representatives of their staff.

The analyses are conducted as broad thematic narratives. Table 10.2 depicts the results of the personality testing for the eight directors, named A through H. The profiles of the directors as a whole are congruent with modern expectations of leaders and managers. They tend to possess emotional stability, are extroverted and open to change, and score high on the facets of assertiveness and conscientiousness.

Table 10.2 The Distribution of Scores on Factors and Facets

	VERY LOW	LOW	MIDDLE	HIGH	VERY HIGH
Neuroticism	A, B, D	G	C, H, F, E		
Anxiety	B, D	A, C, E, G	H	F	
Temper	A, B	C, D, H	G, F	E	
Pessimism	B, D		A, C, H, G, F	E	
Social fear	A, D	B, H, G	C, F, E		
Impulsiveness	H, G	B	A, F	E	C, D
Nervous	A, B, C, D	E	G, F		H
Extroversion		G	H, F, E	B, C	A, D
Warmth	G	C, F, E	B, H	A, D	
Gregariousness		H, E, F, G	B, C,	A, D	
Assertiveness				C, D, E, G, H	A, B, F
Activity			G	B, C, H, F, E	A, D
Excitement seeking		B, H, G, F	A, C, D, E		D
Positive emotions		G	H, F, E	A, B, C, D	
Openness		B		D, G, F, H	A, C, E
Fantasy	B, H	G	F	E	A, C, D
Aesthetic	B		D	H, G, F	A, C, E
Feelings		B	H, G	C, F, E, D	A
Actions			H	B, F, E	A, C, G, D
Ideas			B, F, D	H, G	A, C, E
Values			F	B, C, H, E, G	A, D
Agreeableness		B, C, F, E	A, G	D	H
Trust		E, F, G	A, C	B	D, H

	Up to 34	35–44	45–55	56–65	66 and up
Straightforward-ness	C	B, G, F	A, E, D	H	
Altruism		B, E, G	A, C, F	D, H	
Compliance			C, E, F, G	A, B, D, H	
Modesty	B	A, D, H	C, E	D, G	
Tender mindedness		B, C, G, F	A, D, E, H		
Conscientiousness		E	C, D	H, G, F	A, B
Competence			H, E, G	B, C, F, D	A
Order	D	C, G	H, F	A, B, E	
Dutifulness	E		C, F, D	A, B, G	H
Achievement striving			G, D	C, F, E	A, B, H
Self-discipline		H, E	C, F	G	A, B, D
Deliberation		C, E	A, G, F, D	B, H	
T scores	Up to 34	35–44	45–55	56–65	66 and up

Overall, the profiles appear to differ from the traditional stereotypes of librarians as shy, introverted, a bit old-fashioned, nervous, and timid.

One of the most important things to notice in the table is the relationship between the factors and the facets or traits. It is easy to notice that directors with approximately the same factor score can have diverse and different facets or traits forming the factor. This is important because the factors can be hypothesized to predict orientation and preferences in behavior and facets, and traits can be hypothesized to predict the way and the mode of the orientation preferences on a kind of microlevel.

The library directors possess a middle to high degree of emotional stability, measured on the neuroticism scale. The deviations in the facets are more interesting than the average figure of the factors. One of them (director H) comes out with a very high score on nervousness. E has high scores on temper, pessimism, and impulsiveness, and C and D both have a very high degree of impulsiveness.

On the extroversion factor, seven directors score from middle to high, and only one scores below middle indicating that the group as a whole possesses a rather high degree of extroversion. Looking at the facets it becomes evident that director named A differs very much from, for example, director B. A scores very high on all the facets, and B is low or in the middle range on four facets and high on the facets related to actions and values. It is also striking that all directors score high on assertiveness and activity.

The openness factor is often considered an important factor in relation to change processes because the factor denotes openness to experience and willingness to change and explores new areas of experience. As shown in Table 10.2, seven directors score high on this factor. One director is distinct from the others, scoring rather low. It is director B who scores low on half of the facets. What is more interesting is probably that all directors score high on some of the more important facets related to getting things done. All score from middle to very high on actions, ideas, and values indicating openness to new ideas and a mixture of interest for new theoretical insights combined with a preference to put things into activities and action.

The agreeableness factor is also interesting. The deviation among the eight directors is rather high. The score varies from low to very high. The deviation becomes even more marked when facets are compared. The poles would be director H and director B. H scores very high on one of the facets, high on four other facets, and in the middle range on the last facet. In contrast, B scores rather low on several of the facets, but high on trust.

On the last factor, conscientiousness, seven directors score from middle to very high on this factor. Only director E scores low; she scores low or very low on order, self-discipline, dutifulness, and deliberation. This contrasts especially in relation to directors A and B, both scoring very high on this factor. The conscientiousness factor denotes, to a certain degree, a person's inner quality.

Common for all the directors is the fact that they are involved in change processes. These change processes focus on both the provision of services and on organizational development implementing more flexible and democratic structures. They all succeed in changing the libraries both internally and in relation to the users. One of the reasons that change processes have been successful overall can be attributed to the assertiveness of the directors, their overall openness to experience and change, and their general high degree of conscientiousness. The organizational culture is an important mediating factor in relation to the possibilities the director possesses for implementing change, but the style of change management varies. This can be partly explained by situational factors such as the local political climate, restrictions due to the building and economy, and the organizational culture.

In the interviews, all of the directors express positive attitudes toward continuing professional education, but their own participation in educational activities and the implementation of them in their institutions varied widely. And most of the directors acknowledge the importance of continuing professional education, but only a few of the libraries have introduced a systematic plan for the development of competences. With their staff, three directors (A, C, and E) implemented staff development as an integrated part of the management of the library. A's test indicates a person with an interest in learning new things and working with them in a conscientious manner. A also possesses a high level of ambition and is productive. C is similar to A, but C is more attracted to new ideas and probably has more difficulty following up on implementation processes. E is also similar, but the style indicates even bigger problems following up and keeping focus. All these directors have themselves participated in a huge range of master programs and other forms of leadership programs, and they have introduced a kind of strategic plan for staff development through elicitation of maps of competences among staff members and have implemented plans accordingly. A part of this problem is to what degree the development of competences happens in relation to a strategic plan or to what degree it is based on the professional and personal interests of unique staff members.

Another more general aspect of development of competences is how the directors value innovations or changes. A comparison of H and D indicates the usefulness of analyzing behavior using all the facets and not only the factors. It is evident that H's profile indicates a person oriented toward actions and change. D also possesses a high degree of impulsiveness and a middle orientation toward ideas. D is more of a doer than a thinker, and this is also the way D comes across in the interview and in interviews with the staff. Things must happen, and failures—both their own and their staff's failures—are accepted as inevitable. Some of the change processes are conducted nearly on the spot, and many traditional activities are set in motion. In some ways, the change processes run in a goal-oriented manner, but there is a high degree of acceptance of the chaotic nature of some of the processes involved. The reason is that, based on trust and one's disposition to accept new challenges, the director delegates responsibility and results. The change processes that take place in H's library are conducted in a different way. They are just as goal-oriented and strategic, but they are much slower and much more deliberate. It is evident that H places a very high value on bringing the staff along. The disposition for activity seeking is much less evident here than in relation to D. It results in a flavor of the library as somewhat more old-fashioned and somewhat slower or a bit more cautious in change processes.

Another issue is team-based management, which can be integrated in many different ways in the organization depending on the existing structure and culture. The detailed analysis of structures and how directors and staff members talked about and named the organizational structures indicated a very interesting pattern. It was found that exactly the same organizational structures could exist in different libraries, but they were named differently. Some of the libraries in fact have team and matrix structures but still view them as part of a traditional departmental structure. Other libraries have a traditional departmental structure but view it in more modern terms. The naming of the structure depends on information received and discussed with management consultants and the educational programs in which the directors or staff members participated. It also depends on how the director values more theoretical management information as a basis for the job. Some directors, for example, D, are not very interested in theoretical ideas but are much more oriented toward actions; they really do not care much about the symbolic aspects of management terms and recipes.

Some of the library directors, A, C, and G, are conscious of the fact that they introduced team-based structures, for example, in the form of matrix structures, and they work to implement them. They also spend some time naming the teams according to the objectives and the amount of delegation. They all state that management structures are a part of both competency development and a symbol directed toward the political system about the modernity of the library system in the community.

Facets and traits, such as openness to new theoretical ideas and striving for innovation, resulted in deliberations concerning both the technical and the symbolic aspects of management standards, become important. The symbolic aspect surfaces as employment of management terms and ideals. Directors more oriented toward practical activities tend to neglect the symbolic aspects of recipes, and they are also more inclined to value practical solutions based on, for example, implementing best practices without much consideration for the theoretical underpinnings. The practice in their libraries can be very innovative, but it is not based on an expressed recipe or standard. What matters for them is that it works and gets the job done.

The final example from the analysis will attend to two other cultural orientations. One of the libraries scrutinized has an explicit market orientation, and the other a much stronger focus on staff and staff well-being. We will discuss director A in relation to director D. Director A is a female director in a medium-sized library in a rather prosperous municipality not far from Copenhagen. Her profile as indicated in Table 10.2 indicates a person who conforms to the modern leadership ideal. She possesses a high degree of emotional stability, is an extrovert, is open in her interaction with staff and the environment, is imaginative and open to change, and has a well-developed conceptual approach to problems. She has high standards for herself, and her work and her activities are based on a feeling of duty. She is in many ways a very assertive and powerful leader, but these traits are balanced by openness in relation to other people, their situation, and possible conflicting interests. She is intellectually curious and accepts that the leadership role implies compromises. However, she is extremely goal-oriented, and she tends to conclude what she has decided. She has drive, and she is very open in relation to cooperation. She fits well with the culture at the library. The organizational structure changed into a matrix structure. This structure is integrated in the library, and the staff members feel that they are working in a flat and decentralized structure. She has introduced very clear and precise goals and objectives for the operations of the library. In relation to these goals, she has introduced a system of incentives for the staff. She is task-oriented, but this task orientation is balanced by an open, communicative, and delegating leadership style. This means that even staff member with other priorities respect her very much. This respect is not minimized by the fact that she has succeeded in establishing good connections to both local politicians and the administration in the municipality as demonstrated by the library taking the lead in many local projects. The library is at the forefront in the process of implementing newer organizational recipes. They are implemented fully, and the organization takes them seriously.

Director H has many similar personality traits. He is also very dutiful and goal-oriented, and he has very clear objectives for his library's future. He scores very high on agreeableness, and his whole personality is much more modest, not in any way self-promoting. However, he has very clear ideas about needed actions and has also envisioned the strategic path, but he is very aware that the staff must follow him, and he has deliberately chosen a process that is rather slow in comparison with other processes we witnessed. This coincides with the fact that the director does not seek excitement or experiments. The culture in this library is family- or clan-oriented, and a friendly atmosphere means a lot to the staff. There is a correlation between the cultural orientation in the library and the profile of the director. The library selectively adopts organizational recipes emphasizing the practical or operational aspects that have worked elsewhere.

CONCLUDING THOUGHTS

There is no doubt that the profession could benefit from more systematic analyses of the role of personality in relation to change processes. Overall, the detailed analysis of facets gives a much richer picture than the general analysis of factors, and the data from interviews and observations confirm the benefit of employing the detailed analysis. Analyses exploring both facets and factors through interviews with both directors and staff members have potential to form a richer picture of relations among leaders, organizations, and change processes. The picture is much richer than it would have been only employing a traditional analysis by factors alone. It is also important, however, to emphasize that the chapter only skims the surface for future research in information interaction in an organizational context.

The Danish study confirms the importance of situational factors such as the fit between the leadership personality and the dominant aspects of the organizational culture. A limitation of the research, however, is that the cultural dimension is implicit in most of the analyses. On the other hand, there is a certain fit between culture and leadership personality in implementing information-based change processes. The implicit formulated hypotheses about the relationship between personality traits and profiles indicate that the director's openness especially to intellectual experiences or practical innovations and changes influences the process of implementation of both structures and processes of competences. It also influences the way the recipes and standards are conceptualized in the organization. The integration of the recipes was influenced by the perseverance of the director with cultural factors as a mediating factor.

Library directors are change-oriented, and the eight directors demonstrate leadership capabilities and profiles fitting modern and change-oriented institutions. The libraries as organizations and the staff also have an orientation toward change as demonstrated through an intensive cultural project that the dominant discourse supports. This discourse is directed toward the future and emphasizes change processes in structure, services, and activities. The profession is open in relation to technological developments and innovations; it is adaptable to modern management concepts. The preferences for chance among directors and library staff interact, and together they create a culture on the move. The changes are probably faster than changes in users' perceptions of what constitutes a library.

Finally, leadership has to do with people and insight into peoples' behavioral patterns, and the background for that, including insight into oneself, is a requisite for a successful leadership. Effective leaders must know and be able to read themselves, the staff, the broader organization or institution, and the environment.

NOTES

1. Peter Hernon, Joan Giesecke, and Camila A. Alire, *Academic Librarians as Emotionally Intelligent Leaders* (Westport, CT: Libraries Unlimited, 2008); Peter Hernon, Ronald R. Powell, and Arthur P. Young, "University Library Directors in the Association of Research Libraries: The Next Generation, Part One," *College & Research Libraries* 62, no. 2 (2001): 116–45; Peter Hernon, Ronald R. Powell, and Arthur P. Young, "University Library Directors in the Association of Research Libraries: The Next Generation, Part Two," *College & Research Libraries* 63, no. 1 (2002): 73–90; Peter Hernon and Nancy Rossiter, *Making a Difference: Leadership and Academic Libraries* (Westport, CT: Libraries Unlimited, 2007).

2. John H. Bradley and Frederic J. Hebert, "The Effect of Personality Type on Team Performance," *Journal of Management Development* 16, no. 5 (1997): 337–53.

3. Lory Block, "The Leadership–Culture Connection. An Exploratory Investigation," *Leadership & Organizational Development Journal* 24, no. 6 (2003): 318–34; F. William Brown and Nancy G. Dodd, "Utilizing Organizational Culture Gap Analysis to Determine Human Resource Development Needs," *Leadership and Organization Development Journal*

19, no. 7 (1998): 374–85; Peter Lok and John Crawford, "The Relationship between Commitment and Organizational Culture, Subculture, Leadership Style and Job Satisfaction in Organizational Change and Development," *Leadership & Organizational Development Journal* 20, no. 7 (1999): 365–73.

4. Hernon, Giesecke, and Alire, *Academic Librarians as Emotionally Intelligent Leaders.*

5. Jeanine M. Williamson, Anne E. Pemberton, and John W. Lounsbury, "An Investigation of Career and Job Satisfaction in Relation to Personality Traits of Information Professionals," *Library Quarterly* 75, no. 2 (2005): 122–41; Jeanine M. Williamson, Anne E. Pemberton, and John W. Lounsbury, "Personality Traits of Individuals in Different Specialties of Librarianship," *Journal of Documentation* 64, no. 2 (2008): 273–86.

6. Jannica Heinström, *Fast Surfers, Broad Scanners and Deep Divers–Personality and Information Seeking Behaviour* (Åbo, Turkey: Åbo Academi University Press, 2002); Jannica Heinström, "Five Personality Dimensions and Their Influence on Information Behaviour," *Information Research* 9, no. 1 (2003), http://Informationr.net/ir/9–1/paper165. html (accessed November 15, 2011); Jannica Heinström, "Psychological Factors behind Incidental Information Acquisition," *Library & Information Science Research* 28, no. 4 (2006): 579–94; Jannica Heinström, "Fast Surfing, Broad Scanning, and Deep Diving: The Influence of Personality and Study Approach on Students' Information-Seeking Behavior," *Journal of Documentation* 61, no. 2 (2005): 228–47; Jannica Heinström, "Fast Surfing for Availability or Deep Diving into Quality-Motivation and Information Seeking among Middle and High School Students," *Information Research* 11, no. 4 (2006), http://Infor mationr.net/ir/11–4/paper 265.html1 (accessed November 15, 2011); Michael Tidwell and Patricia Sias, "Personality and Information Seeking: Understanding How Traits Influence Information-Seeking Behaviors," *Journal of Business Communication* 42, no. 1 (2005): 51–77; Jette Hyldegård, "Collaborative Information Behaviour—Exploring Kuhlthau's Information Search Process-Model in a Group-Based Educational Setting," *Information Processing and Management* 42, no. 1 (2006): 276–98.

7. Anne Goulding, Beth Bromham, Stuart Hannabuss, and Duncan Cramer, "Professional Characters: The Personality of the Future Information Workforce," *Education for Information* 18, no. 7 (2007): 7–31.

8. Stephen P. Robbins and Timothy A. Judge, *Organizational Behavior* (Upper Saddle River, NJ: Prentice-Hall, 2009).

9. Paul T. Costa and Robert R. Mccrae, *NEO PI-R: Professional Manual* (Odessa, Ukraine: Psychological Assessment Resources, 1992); Paul T. Costa and Robert R. Mccrae, "Stability and Change in Personality Assessment: The Revised NEO Personality Inventory in the Year 2000," *Journal of Personality Assessment* 68, no. 1 (1997): 86–94; Charles Jackson, *Understanding Psychological Testing* (London: Blackwell, 1996).

10. Heinström, "Fast Surfing for Availability or Deep Diving."

11. Bradley and Hebert, "Effect of Personality Type."

12. Tinna M. Hautala, "The Relationship between Personality and Transformational Leadership," *Journal of Management Development* 25, no. 8 (2006): 777–94.

13. Brian P. Niehoff, "Personality Predictors of Participation as a Mentor," *Group Development International* 11, no. 4 (2006): 321–33.

14. Maria Vakola, Ioannis Tsaousis, and Ioannis Nikolaou, "The Role of Emotional Intelligence and Personality Variables on Attitudes towards Organisational Change," *Journal of Managerial Psychology* 19, no. 2 (2004): 88–110.

15. Niels Ole Pors, *Mellem Identitet og Legitimitet: Ledelse, Kultur og Forandringer i Danske Biblioteker* (Between identity and legitimacy: Leadership, culture and change in Danish libraries), Research report (Copenhagen: Danmarks Biblioteksskole, 2006).

11

FOLLOWING THE LEADER

Peter Hernon

Although some of the leadership theories discussed in Chapter 1 refer to those who follow as followers, there is no universal agreement about the use of this concept. In Scandinavia, for instance, there is a preference for referring to followers as staff or employees. The reason is the impression that followers merely react and that staff would have a negative reaction to the term *followership* because they do not think of themselves this way and the term has not been widely used or adopted in this part of Europe. This chapter, therefore, focuses on those who follow leaders while simultaneously recognizing that followers might at times become leaders, especially when individuals engage in team or group work. Clearly, leadership is not confined to someone charged as team leader; in fact, this person may not be the actual leader. Such a characterization of followership recognizes that the focus is most likely internal to the organization. In the broader organization or institution, library directors, for instance, may not always be leaders; they might carry out the vision, direction, and goals set by the university president or provost or other institutional leaders. Still, in some instances, they might be part of the leadership team and serve as leaders on occasion. In other words, in the broader institution or organization, they might be both leaders and followers.

Barbara Kellerman, among others, adopts the word *followership* and offers a typology of followers. Her typology indicates that followers both influence and are influenced by leaders, and she recognizes that each type of followers will respond accordingly to how they see their situation in relationship to the organization and the leader or leaders.[1] Although she does not address the point, it is conceivable that individuals might not be permanent members of a type; might they not move from one type to another, especially with a change in leadership or as their skill set matures or advances? Brian Crossman and Joanna Crossman provide an extensive review on the literature on followership. They view the literature as falling into "four broad overlapping categories within a fluid continuum: (i) individualized or leader-centric theories; (ii) leader-centred theories which rely on follower perspectives; (iii) multiple leadership which encompasses what is often referred to as shared, distributed or collective leadership . . .[;] and (iv) the followership literature *per se*."[2]

Roy Smollan and Ken Perry refer to the last category as the "follower-centric model," and they show how employees perceive the leaders of their organizations.[3]

Regardless of the category, followership implies a relationship between subordinates and those superiors who are actually leaders, and, in critical moments, a response of the former to the latter. That response ensures that followers keep their focus on change and implementation of a strategic plan. They must be involved in developing the plan and accept it as the basis for guiding future actions. Complicating matters, the line that separates superiors and subordinates may be blurred. Still, viewing leadership in terms of superiors and subordinates is limiting in that, as already noted, subordinates might serve as both followers and leaders, especially when they work on teams.

Those who follow do so as they implement the vision that the library director, perhaps together with the senior management team, set. The premise that leaders develop the guiding vision and keep the organization focused on the accomplishment of it is central to the various chapters of this book.

Effective followership (or buy-in to and follow-through on the leadership vision) depends on staff who are motivated to make the changes specified in the library's strategic plan and to accomplish the leadership's vision. In a team context, leadership focuses on effectiveness or the degree to which the

- group's productive output (i.e., product or services) meets the standard of quantity, quality, and timeliness of the people who receive, review, and/or use that output (*results* or productivity);
- process of carrying out the work enhances the capability of members to work together interdependently in the future (*socialization*); and
- group's experience contributes to the growth and personal well-being of team members (*professional growth*).[4]

As J. Richard Hackman and Richard W. Walton explain, determining how well a team performs is much more complicated than quantifying performance metrics. Team effectiveness, which is multidimensional, includes the continued socialization of team members and their growth as individuals. Personal, social, and systems conditions within the organization must also be addressed to determine a team's effectiveness.[5]

Both socialization and professional growth should be connected to improved results or productivity, meaning the ability to work together in the accomplishment of stated goals, targets, and objectives, and thus to achieve a more effective and efficient organization. To achieve better socialization and to help the staff grow professionally, libraries engage in formal and informal activities. Formal activities might involve work to obtain an advanced degree or a series of programs or workshops aimed at a particular outcome (see Table 11.1 for examples), increased involvement in professional associations in a leadership capacity, and helping others obtain the necessary skill set and abilities. Information activities involve self-education and a network of friends and associates.

Although this chapter focuses on results or productivity, socialization, and professional growth, it should be recognized that the staff should recognize and accept a new normal, namely that the following conditions exist:

- Focus on *how*, not *what*
  - How the work of individuals fits into the larger organization
  - The value of a systematic approach to problem solving and critical thinking

- Library work occurs in a political environment
- Nature of work changes—the job evolves
- New organizational models will emerge
- Staff must be adaptable
- A new economic reality prevails

In short, there is no normal; change is part of everyday work. To get teams and individuals to produce better results, these conditions must be addressed through socialization and professional growth. The staff, together with the organization's leadership, must realize that they need to define, and not merely react to, the future. They must accept innovation and not be adverse to some risk, while constantly focusing on the image, one that is future-oriented and enables the library to maintain a brand that does not define itself solely in terms of the past.

As becomes evident, the results that leaders and managers expect the staff to accomplish, perhaps through teams or groups, cannot occur effectively without

Table 11.1 Topics for Training Programs and Workshops

Capacity building or gaps

Confidence building

Conflict resolution

Cross-training ability

Diversity in the workforce

How to run a meeting/facilitation

Instructional skills

Interactions with the media

Latest developments with:

- intellectual freedom

- scholarly communication

- technology

Learning organizations

- sharing new knowledge

Management/leadership skills

New innovations

Organizational values

Project management

Quality—exceptional customer service

attention to socialization and professional growth. As leaders focus on both categories, they should decide whether to focus their resources, develop a plan to accomplish their expectations, and measure progress in the achievement of that plan. Naturally some of the results will be accomplished in the short term and others in a longer term. The plan should focus on both fronts and pay attention to the followers and team leaders, while encouraging followers to seize appropriate moments to lead and team leaders not to feel threatened by shared leadership.

THE PLAN

When leaders develop the plan, they need to be guided by the concept of team leadership as discussed in Chapter 1. In this regard, when they form teams they first make clear the purpose of the team, ensure that the tasks assigned to it are clear, delineate the team's authority, provide stable membership over time, and monitor discreetly that team members work well together. Second, they see that the team understands the expected outcome(s); they do not specify the means by which the team accomplishes the results. Third, they pay close attention to the team's structure, which means "designing team tasks that motivate members, specifying codes of conduct, putting the right people on the team, ensuring the size of the team is appropriate and that the mix of members is balanced for the tasks assigned to the team."[6] By accomplishing these general tasks, leaders have put in place the foundation for any effective team. Still, they must provide support through a reward system, education, information, and technology that support the team's productivity; and coaching that takes the form of having someone who is able to answer questions as they arise and educate team members.

Once such questions have been addressed, the plan focuses on the timeline for completion of the assigned tasks and an evaluation component that is not confined to the results. Evaluation must address each component of the conditions that Hackman discusses.[7] Similar to any evaluation study, the goal is to ascertain and link the results to the planning process, making adjustments as necessary to accomplish the expected results.

As the library develops the plan, it is important to consider succession planning and the skill set and abilities that the staff will need for at least five years. At the same time, managers should review the literature on followership and the types of followers. One typology that Barbara Kellerman proposed covers the following categories:

- *Isolates*, people who care little for their leaders and rarely respond to them regardless of who they are. They tend to keep a low profile and want to stay out of the way and just get on with their job without interference from above.

- *Bystanders*, people who offer little support to any leader. They just observe things from the sidelines and rarely get involved in very much. They differ from isolates in that they tend not to hide from being led or managed nor do they resent it like the isolates might.

- *Participants*, people who care about the organization and do usually want to make an impact. If they agree with the leaders they actively support them, but if they think that the leaders are wrong they will actively oppose them, sometimes behind their backs.

- *Activists*, people who have strong beliefs both about the organization and its leaders. If they like what they what is going on they will engage and help create even better conditions. If they do not they will actively try to get rid of a leader.

- *Diehards*, people who are passionate about the vision and/or leader. When they consider something worthy, they become a disciple of change.[8]

As the leaders prepare to implement the plan, they need to analyze the staff and to see which types of followership exist in the organization. If they determine that the first two types exist largely in the organization or on a team, what do they do given that any typology of followership typecasts people into types and does not recognize that they might change? Some people will not fully embody a particular type and they might change, sometimes rapidly, in accordance to how they are interpreting things going on around them and the level of legitimacy they feel with the leader and the organization.

SOCIALIZATION

The theory of group socialization refers to a process by which a person becomes a member of a group. That person moves through several role transitions, including becoming a new member to a full member during the process of socialization. The individual determines the benefits of participation in the group and whether it outweighs the costs. And the group evaluates the individual to determine how dedicated he or she is to the group. Richard L. Moreland and John M. Levine identify five classes of roles; these are prospective member, new member, full member, marginal member, and ex-member.[9] If an individual places value on a group in a positive light, that person generally become more committed to the group. Individuals can, however, also be committed to groups even if they find the group unfavorable, possibly to keep their jobs.

Socialization within an organizational context, defined as "a process in which an individual acquires the attitudes, behaviors, and knowledge needed to successfully participate as . . . [a productive] organizational member,"[10] often focuses on entry into the organization as opposed to feeling part of an organization going through change that involves more than just incremental change. Socialization becomes a process that helps new hires adapt, form work relationships, and find their place in the organization. Another perspective is that it goes beyond new hires and assists in the advancement to positions of managerial leadership.

Organizational assimilation theory focuses on individuals new to the organization and how they are assimilated or become productive members.[11] This theory, which stresses that an individual's socialization is the key factor in determining that person's contribution to the organization, describes the values that people place in different work-related positions and their feelings about different organizations. It also focuses on organizational goals, values, history, and power structures.

In summary, socialization can be approached from three different perspectives: (1) entry into the organization, (2) membership on a given team, and (3) advancement to higher positions within the organization. One goal is to decrease the likelihood that people will leave the organization soon after being hired, and another goal is to make them productive members of the team. The focus is on the team and its accomplishments, and not so much on the individual per se. The analogy is a professional baseball or football team that focuses on the team and the individual's contribution to that team. The final goal is to create a management team well adapted to the organizational culture and climate.

Examples of Relevant Activities

Conflict occurs whenever people disagree over their values, motivations, perceptions, ideas, or desires. Sometimes these differences seem trivial, but when a conflict triggers strong feelings, problems result. Because of this it is important to introduce conflict resolution early in the formation of teams, and this can be accomplished through the hiring of a consultant to conduct workshops, engaging in role playing or group discussions, and the use of case studies (see the next section).[12]

Increasingly as the workforce becomes more diverse, managerial leaders need to ensure that socialization extends to racial, ethnic, and other forms of diversity. Chapters 1 and 2 discuss minority diversity and some key readings; these could guide discussion groups that individuals, within or outside of the organization, who are themselves members of diverse groups, lead. The goal is to create better understanding and a more productive workforce. At the same time, if the organization has a workforce that cuts across different generational groups, how do the teams deal with generational diversity? Such diversity might hinder productivity and lead to frustration, conflict, and poor morale.

When teams or groups cut across libraries and involve virtual teams, it is important not to forget the personal side of teamwork. Nonverbal communication cues, also known as micromessages, such as expressions and gestures, get lost, and communication barriers can exist because team members come from, for instance, different geographic areas and cultural milieus. To combat the lack of socialization and the sense of fragmentation that results, the group should create ways to make the whole team visible to each member and find ways to gain some understanding of individual members.

PROFESSIONAL GROWTH

Professional growth focuses on acquiring certain attributes associated with both management and leadership, and the skill sets and abilities related to evaluation and assessment research. Certain leadership theories and their application are important for team leaders and members to understand and be able to apply. These include emotional intelligence, adaptive leadership, team leadership, and resonant leadership (see Chapter 1). Emotional intelligence requires a realistic understanding of oneself and an ability to manage relationships with other members of the team or group. Still, by itself, emotional intelligence probably is not a strong predictor of job performance. Rather, it provides the bedrock for attributes and abilities that are. Daniel Goleman represents this idea by distinguishing between *emotional intelligence* and *emotional competence*.[13] The latter refers to the personal and social skills that lead to superior work performance, and these skills are linked to and based on emotional intelligence. Some emotional intelligence is necessary to learn the emotional competencies. For example, people who can regulate their emotions find it easier to develop their initiative or sense of achievement. Ultimately it is these social and emotional competencies that we need to identify and measure in order predict performance.

Adaptive leadership, which emerges from theories such as situational and transformational leadership, recognizes that there are basically two kinds of problems that require solution. The first are *technical problems*, where the response depends on a recognized expert and adherence to an established procedure or process. The problem is mechanical, and someone can fix it. The second are *adaptive problems*, where there are no set procedures, no recognized experts, and no adequate, already developed responses. The problem requires a solution, which necessitates an increased ability to conduct evaluation and assessment research and to relate findings to strategic planning and decision making. Unfortunately, many master's degree programs in library and information science do not require students to take courses in research, in general or focused on evaluation, to graduate, and a number of managers in the profession have never taken such a course in their undergraduate or graduate programs. Research is a difficult skill area for professions to develop upon graduation, in part because leadership institutes and continuing education programs do not cover it. Further, one course at the master's level insufficiently introduces students to the complexity of evaluation and assessment research, especially when such research involves the application of experimental designs that test how well students and others learned.

Team leadership, which relates as well to socialization, focuses on the relationship among team members and members of the group with the person designated as team leader. Everyone must understand (1) the purpose of an effective team; (2) the goals it is charged to accomplish; and (3) the knowledge, skills, and abilities that each member brings to the group. Furthermore, everyone must have sufficient knowledge about the goals and how to achieve them. Excellent communication among the members of the group is required, and leaders must provide proper guidance and communication. The theory of team leadership, as one might suspect, tends to focus more on those assigned to leadership positions than on members of the group. Still, from that literature it is possible to infer roles for group members. There are also team models, one of which is called Hill's team model, one of the better-known models; it provides the leader or a designated team member with a mental road map to diagnose problems with the team.[14]

Resonant leadership, which applies to those in positions of managerial leadership, recognizes that resonant leaders are in tune with themselves and the people with whom they work. They create a sense of resonance in the workplace, so they and their subordinates can be productive and accomplish great things. They also develop their emotional intelligence. Leaders and mangers are susceptible to the power stress that emerges from the daily management of crises, complex decision making and communication, and loneliness. Still, those working in libraries in nonmanagerial positions face pressures associated with an unknown future and change management. Thus, both managerial leaders and the staff must engage in renewal activities and be on guard against the sacrifice syndrome, a vicious cycle in which exhaustion and stress coupled with some unexpected problems or crises starts someone down a path of burnout.

Staff members need to see the value of professional development and be motivated to benefit from it. They need to regard such development as part of a coherent plan to help them be more productive in carrying out the strategic plan and to gain the skills and abilities that the organization will require over time. They treat their coworkers as colleagues and seek to learn from them. Most important, everyone realizes that professional development is a critical component to succession planning. However, that planning must be linked to succession or talent management and the ongoing examination of the organization, its needs, expertise, and personnel. The goal is to prepare for organizational change, deal with the retirement or other departure of the professional staff, focus on staff retention, and ensure continuity of how the organization functions. Furthermore, it involves a review of staff positions and sets strategic directions and priorities for the organization as it moves forward.

Examples of Relevant Activities

As libraries adjust to the economic realities that emerge from the global recession and its lingering aftermath, more than likely they will prefer activities that are less costly. More than likely, they might only fund a few staff members to attend programs and activities that are not locally based. The problem is that those staff remaining in the organization might resent those who attend such meetings and refer to these individuals as receiving preference or worse. The use of consultants is expensive and whatever consultants do must be directly related to the plan and the accomplishment of specific tasks.

Leadership

Leadership institutes and similar training programs focus on those entering or already in leadership positions. They do not focus on staff and the type of training they need to assume leadership roles on a selective basis. For this reason, libraries might encourage team members, regardless of their particular team or group, to engage in reading and discussion groups. For example, they might take one of the following works, discuss the particular theory, and its application to their charged tasks:

- Peter Northouse, *Leadership: Theory and Practice*, 6th ed. (Thousand Oaks, CA: Sage, 2013)
- *The Emotionally Intelligent Workplace: How to Select for, Measure, and Improve Emotional Intelligence in Individuals, Groups, and Organizations*, edited by Cary Cherniss and Daniel Goleman (San Francisco: Jossey-Bass, 2001); Cary Cherniss and Mitchell Adler, *Promoting Emotional Intelligence in Organizations: Making Training in Emotional Intelligence Effective* (Arlington, VA: American Society for Training & Development, 2000)
- Ronald A. Heifetz, Marty Linsky, and Alexander Grashow, *Practice of Adaptive Leadership: Tools and Tactics for Changing Your Organization and the World* [Kindle Edition] (Cambridge, MA: Cambridge Leadership; Boston: Harvard Business School Publishing, 2009); and
- Annie McKee, Frances Johnston, and Richard Massimilian, "Mindfulness, Hope and Compassion: A Leader's Road Map to Renewal," *Ivey Business Journal* (May–June 2006): 1–5.

Another useful source is *Developing Library Leaders*, which covers a number of topics relevant for staff to review as they learn about leadership and its application. In the foreword to that book, James G. Neal writes, "Across the organization, we demand a commitment to rigor, to innovation, and to assessment. We need individuals with outstanding communication, marketing, project development, and management skills. We must develop staff who are ready for political engagement, have entrepreneurial spirit, are committed to new resource development, and have an inspirational capacity."[15] This quote identifies a number of key attributes that leaders need to instill throughout the library and to stress when they hire new professional staff members.

Problem-Solving Skills

The research process, such as that associated with evaluation and assessment research, is central to problem solving. Knowledge about research, when defined as a process of inquiry that consists of certain components (reflective inquiry, procedures, data collection and analysis, reporting of findings, and relating those findings to the reflective inquiry), might be gained from coursework, reading, and studying the published literature. The best way to learn about problem solving might be to engage in formal studies under the mentorship of someone who has credibility as a researcher. Sage Publications (Thousand Oaks, CA) is the leading publisher on research, particularly relevant procedures (research designs and methodologies). Readers might also consult *Engaging in Evaluation and Assessment Research*, in particular Chapter 3 and Appendix B.[16] That appendix contains a case study, a method for teaching and learning in different courses in higher education that is widely used, for instance, by the Harvard Business School and the Harvard Graduate School of Education. It introduces the reader to leadership and describes two practical research studies for which staff members could develop the research components. Another appendix (A) reproduces a research study, which the staff might also review. They could do the same for the studies depicted throughout the book.

Other

Project management is another critical topic for team members to understand as they develop a timeline to accomplish their goals. More than likely, some members of the staff will have greater familiarity and expertise with the topic and can offer tutorials and other instruction to members of their own team as well as to other teams. It is possible that these experts might develop some case studies for others to review. Before that review is done, everyone should read "AJ's Problem-Solving Model—The Steps to Be Followed."[17]

Before an individual, team, or organization forms a plan for performance improvement, a clear picture of current performance must be established. Self-assessment allows a means for the staff to look at their own performance, form conclusions about their performance level, and act upon those conclusions to create a personal development plan. Accurate self-assessment requires introspection and realistic self-perception, and the staff must be willing to do so. Team members must also be able to reflect on their performance and determine where improvements are necessary.

Self-assessment takes many forms. In many organizations, self-evaluation is incorporated into the performance appraisal process or used to identify developmental needs. A self-evaluation can be used on its own to identify opportunities for improvement, or it can be combined with the feedback of others to create a more rounded view of performance.

A number of publicly available tools exist.[18] Some of these apply to team members and their ability to work collaboratively and others address the skill set needed for team members.[19] These instruments might best be separated from performance appraisal so that term members are more receptive to the findings. The other crucial question is, "How does the organization use the results in a positive way to improve staff performance?"

RESULTS

The goal of any organization and work-based team is to make employees more productive and to achieve the results that enable that organization to meet its mission more effectively and efficiently: Employee performance appraisal, for instance, centers on productivity, how much each employee accomplishes perhaps in accordance with the intended goals for a given year. In other words, the focus is on what employees do to accomplish the mission and part of the organization's strategic plan.

Examples of Relevant Activities

As this chapter indicates, any activities that center on socialization and professional growth are centered around one purpose, namely enhancing the productivity and results produced by teams and, it is hoped, their members outside their role as team members.[20] It is also important to welcome new employees and help them gain organizational socialization and advance their productivity. When they join already existing teams, however, how are they integrated into the collective work? In such instances, there might be lunch meetings with preexisting members and opportunities to feel a part of the group. The purpose is not to make everyone friends but to improve working relationships.

CONCLUDING THOUGHTS

Explicit in a learning organization is the ability of everyone on the staff, whether formal leaders or individuals who are not even in managerial positions, to expand their abilities, understanding, and capacity to learn, grow, and work together to achieve the vision that the leaders set in new and creative ways. A learning organization responds to change and in fact manages that change in an effective and efficient manner. The leadership assumes an exemplary role in creating and sustaining a supportive learning culture, and it is committed to the importance of learning and communicates that learning is critical to organizational success. The leadership provides the rationale or purpose, means, and opportunity for learning. A library that functions as a learning organization is most likely characterized by a flat managerial structure and customer-focused teams that are innovative and thrive in a rapidly changing environment.

Learning organizations recognize that organizational change can be an emotional experience as people cope with uncertainty and challenge themselves and others. As such, leaders must ensure that they create and maintain a culture and a climate that depend on continuous employee learning, critical thinking, problem solving, and risk-taking; allow mistakes; value employee contributions; let everyone learn from experience while engaging in experiment; and disseminate new knowledge throughout the organization for incorporation into day-to-day activities. The characterization of Hackman and Walton offers a general blueprint that organizations can use to develop strategies and plans for maintaining an environment that benefits from continuous learning.

NOTES

1. Barbara Kellerman, *Followership: How Followers Are Creating and Changing Leaders* (Boston: Harvard Business School Press, 2008).

2. Brian Crossman and Joanna Crossman, "Conceptualising Followership: A Review of the Literature," *Leadership* 7, no. 4 (2011): 484.

3. Roy Smollan and Ken Parry, "Follower Perceptions of the Emotional Intelligence of Change Leaders: A Qualitative Study," *Leadership* 7, no. 4 (2011): 435–62.

4. J. Richard Hackman and Richard W. Walton, "Leading Groups in Organizations," in *Designing Effective Work Groups*, edited by Paul S. Goodman and Associates (San Francisco: Jossey-Bass, 1986), 72–119.

5. Hackman and Walton, "Leading Groups in Organizations."

6. Elaine Martin, "Team Effectiveness and Members as Leaders," in *Making a Difference: Leadership and Academic Libraries*, edited by Peter Hernon and Nancy Rossiter (Westport, CT: Libraries Unlimited, 2007), 127.

7. J. Richard Hackman, *Leading Teams: Setting the Stage for Great Performance* (Boston; Harvard Business School Press, 2002).

8. Excerpt from Barbara Kellerman, "What Every Leader Needs to Know about Followers," *Harvard Business Review* 85, no. 12 (2007): 84–91. Reprinted by permission of *Harvard Business Review*.

9. Richard. L. Moreland and John M. Levine, "Socialization in Small Groups: Temporal Changes in Individual-Group Relations," in *Advances in Experimental Social Psychology*, edited by Leonard Berkowitz, vol. 15 (New York: Academic Press, 1982), 137–92.

10. John Van Maanen and Edgar H. Schien, "Toward a Theory of Organizational Socialization," *Research in Organizational Behavior* 1, no. 1 (1970): 209–64.

11. Fred M. Jablin, "Organizational Communication: An Assimilation Approach," in *Social Cognition and Communication*, edited by Michael E. Roloff and Charles R. Berger (Beverly Hills, CA: Sage, 1982), 255–86.

12. For some excellent teaching tips on conflict resolution, see the American Humanist Association, http://www.americanhumanist.org/What_We_Do/Education_Center/HELP/6_Peace_and_Social_Justice/6.1_A/Conflict_Resolution_Teaching_Tips (accessed May 20, 2012); and Mediate.com, http://www.mediate.com/articles/taylor.cfm (accessed May 20, 2012).

13. For relevant works of Daniel Goleman, see http://danielgoleman.info/purchase/ (accessed May 21, 2012).

14. For the Hill Model, see http://www.nwlink.com/~donclark/leader/team_leadership.html (accessed May 21, 2012).

15. Robert D. Stueart and Maureen Sullivan, *Developing Library Leaders: A How-to-Do-It Manual® for Coaching, Team Building, and Mentoring Library Staff* (New York: Neal-Schuman, 2010). For the quote from the Foreword, see page viii.

16. Peter Hernon, Robert E. Dugan, and Danuta A. Nitecki, *Engaging in Evaluation and Assessment Research* (Santa Barbara, CA: Libraries Unlimited, 2011).

17. A. J. Anderson, "AJ's Problem-Solving Model—The Steps to Be Followed," in *Shaping the Future: Advancing the Understanding of Leadership*, edited by Peter Hernon (Santa Barbara, CA: Libraries Unlimited, 2010), 118–34.

18. See, for instance, see Authenticity Consulting, LLC®, Free Management Library, http://managementhelp.org/personaldevelopment/self-assessments.htm (accessed May

21, 2012). One of these tools involves a SWOT (Strengths, Weaknesses/Limitations, Opportunities, and Threats) analysis of one's strengths and weaknesses, http://www.quint careers.com/SWOT_Analysis.html (Quintessential Careers™) (accessed May 21, 2012).

19. For instance, there is the "Employee Self-Assessment Instrument: Core Competencies" (Environment Canada, the Corporate Services Community), http://www.on.ec. gc.ca/core-competencies/pdf/Questionnaire-e.pdf (accessed May 21, 2012); "Employability Skills Self-Assessment Part 2: Teamwork Skills," http://www.edu.gov.mb.ca/k12/cur/ cardev/gr9_found/blms/blm18b.pdf (accessed May 2, 2012); and "Team Self-Assessment" (Constructive Choices, Inc.), http://www.performancexpress.org/0807/Images/Team% 20SelfAssessment%20Tool.pdf (accessed May 21, 2012).

20. See Richard A. Swanson, *Analysis for Improving Performance: Tools for Diagnosing Organizations and Documenting Workplace Expertise* (San Francisco: Berrett-Koehler, 1996).

12

LIBRARY IMPACT AND OUTCOMES ASSESSMENT

Peter Hernon and Niels Ole Pors

Any historical analysis of academic and public libraries, regardless of the country in which they operate in, would suggest that managers compiled and reported input metrics (the distribution of resources through the budget) through annual and other reports. Such data might not be used to improve services, but they might be used to justify budget increases or reallocate funds from one budget line to another. In the mid-20th century, interest in metrics shifts to outputs (indicators of the volume and type of program activities) or performance metrics, which represents a combination of inputs and outputs. With the emergence of digital collections, the concept of outputs expands to include more usage statistics. In the late 20th century, interest in a new kind of metric emerges and results in a focus on outcomes or impacts. However, in such instances, outcomes and impacts represent more than a relationship between two variables, which can be reduced to a ratio and a percentage. Regardless of the type of metric and whether it could be cast as a ratio, the value of such evidence was greatest when managers could collect them over time and draw comparisons useful for planning and decision making.

When libraries and the stakeholders to which they report focus on inputs and outputs, there is little need for the professional staff to understand and apply research characterized as an inquiry process and do little more than institute a routine data collection procedure. For instance, managers might want to know the number of questions reference staff answered over a day or a week, so the metric is the number of questions answered in relation to the number asked.[1] Staff might merely record the results on a tally sheet.

In the 21st century researchers begin to develop a more expansive set of metrics, ones that go beyond the library perspective and embrace the perspective of customers, the broader organization or institution, and stakeholders (e.g., government, parents or community residents, and accreditation organizations). *Viewing Library Metrics from Different Perspectives* introduces multiple perspectives and provides an extensive set of metrics.[2] Counting Opinions takes those metrics and incorporates them into a management information system applicable to academic and public libraries in North America.[3] Still, these metrics do not deal with outcomes or impacts, unless these concepts are defined in terms of user satisfaction and economic efficiency of library services. Further, with increased focus on how the library supports institutional and broader organization affordability, there is renewed interest in economic efficiency defined in terms of the library's value or return on investment (ROI). ROI is series of ratios indicating that for each dollar invested in the library, the institution, the broader organization, or a stakeholder receives *$ZZZ* in benefits from library services.[4]

Academic libraries are also engaging more in outcomes assessment or impact assessment but mostly at an introductory level. The focus of outcomes assessment is driven by stakeholders, in particular government and accreditation organizations. In fact, governments pressure accreditation organizations to hold institutions, and, by extension, their libraries more accountable.

Although this chapter focuses on outcomes assessment as practiced in the United States and Europe, it is important to emphasize that a missing component of the literature is how institutions transform and perhaps involve libraries in that process of setting, implementing, and using outcomes for accountability and service improvement. More likely, there might be a desire to use library input and output metrics (those relating to staff, collections, use, and services) to demonstrate the library's contribution to student learning and institutional accountability. Using input and output data, Mark Emmons and Frances C. Wilkinson conclude that "when controlling for race/ethnicity and socioeconomic status, a linear regression finds that a change in the ratio of library professional staff to students predicts a statistically significant positive relationship with both retention and graduation rates."[5] Such a conclusion assumes frequent use of the library across the entire student body and ignores any analysis or role of outcomes assessment in influencing retention and graduation rates. Further, satisfaction, an unanalyzed variable, may contribute to both rates. Clearly, impact assessment requires new data sets (often ones generated from qualitative research) and skill sets beyond what the existing library staff may possess. Adding to the complexity, such assessment requires the development of partnerships with teaching faculty and a realization that libraries do not contribute to all areas subject to such assessment—or they are not seen as contributing to such assessment. Two questions arise in this context:

1. In what areas do libraries want to play a role?
2. How do libraries go about creating and nurturing that role?

THE UNITED STATES

Writing about impact assessment, David Streatfield and Sharon Markless conclude,

> Working in a UK [United Kingdom] and European context, we have readily adopted the nomenclature of impact evaluation, which we have interpreted as largely dependent on qualitative research evidence about effectiveness and as broadly complementary to "traditional" performance measurement, seen as quantitative and largely focused on monitoring service efficiency. In this broad context, assessment is primarily a term used in gauging performance of students.[6]

As this section explains, such a characterization neither reflects the U.S. scene nor addresses the differences between academic and public libraries in their application of outcomes assessment. These differences are largely due to how stakeholders perceive accountability and what evidence they want reported to them. Moreover, in the United States, the literature of library and information science confuses evaluation and assessment, and the terms *impact evaluation* and *impact assessment* are not synonymous. In fact, the scholarly work in library and information science focuses mostly on outcomes assessment and views it as gauging the extent to which an academic program causes change in the desired direction; however, the goal is to meet requirements set by the government or accreditation organizations. Assessment, which is a subset of evaluation, therefore reflects the perspective of stakeholders and their mechanisms for holding institutions accountable. Assessment might involve the ongoing process of establishing clear, measurable outcomes of student learning; gathering, analyzing, and interpreting evidence to determine how much of a gap exists between actual student learning and what they are expected to learn; and using the resulting evidence to improve student learning. As will be discussed, however, gap analysis might be applied to more than student learning; it might also be applied to the types of services that public libraries offer. The resulting evidence might be either quantitative or qualitative, or most likely both types of data might be collected.

Higher Education

According to the Higher Education Act of 2008 (Public Law 110-315), all institutions of higher education must place *net price calculators* on their websites to inform students and their parents about the approximate cost of an education after grants and scholarships are taken into account. The purpose of the calculator is to inform potential students before they apply whether a particular institution is within reach financially. Those calculators may not be easy to locate on the homepage, and they may contain questions (e.g., about student's religion) that discourage application. To help students, the National Center for Education Statistics, U.S. Department of Education, created the College Navigator (http://nces.ed.gov/collegenavigator/), which allows them to sort institutions in terms of average net price. The Obama administration is also developing a *college scorecard* that will inform students about how an institution compares to other ones on affordability and value. The administration has also proposed the creation of a shopping sheet that includes data on graduation rates and students' debt burdens.[7] The sheet follows President Barack Obama's proposal to limit tuition increases by punishing those institutions of higher education that increase their prices too quickly. Among other things, he also wants to see increased enrollments and higher graduation rates (in a shorter time, time-to-degree), and data on student loan defaults.

This illustrates that increased attention is now focused on outcomes assessment and greater accountability for institutions of higher education to meet their stated mission. The accountability focuses on both financial accountability and learning effectiveness, each of which involves the application of outcomes assessment. In higher education, outcomes assessment consists of two different types of evidence gathering:

1. Student outcomes, which are aggregate statistics on groups of students (e.g., graduation rates; retention rates; course, and program completion rates; and job placement: employment rates for a graduating class). Such outcomes are institutional outcomes and are used to compare institutional performance. They do not measure changes among students as a result of their educational experiences, and these outcomes reflect what the institution has accomplished; they do not reflect what (or how much) students learn.

2. Student learning outcomes, which focus on the development of student over time, such as the duration of an undergraduate or graduate program of study. Such outcomes focus on active learning, the demonstrable acquisition of specific knowledge and skills, and how well students transfer and apply concepts, principles, ways of knowing, and problem solving throughout their program of study; integrate their core curriculum, general studies, or liberal studies into their major problem or field of study; and develop understanding, behaviors, attitudes, values, and dispositions that the institution and their program of study asserts they develop.

The purpose of assessing student learning outcomes is to examine the level of achievement of program- or institutional-level learning goals. These goals relate to conceptual issues—such as leadership, civic engagement, critical thinking, creative thinking, literacy (information or visual), global citizenry, quantitative reasoning ability, values, and the foundation for lifelong learning—or skills—such as communication (oral, written, or presentation) for impact, foreign language communication, and technological abilities. Assessment, therefore, involves processes by which the program or institution gathers direct evidence about the attainment of those goals for the purposes of judging and improving overall instructional performance.

An effective assessment program should be structured (organized to have a recognizable conceptual framework), systematic (conceived and implemented according to a written plan that is regularly updated), ongoing (continuing rather than episodic), and sustainable (able to be maintained with the structures, processes, and resources allotted). The institution's mission, together with planning documents, documents what the institution seeks to accomplish and its commitments. Assessment indicates the extent to which the institution is successful in those accomplishments and commitments. As a result, for more than a decade, assessment has focused inside an institution and has not been used to compare institutions. However, in 2012, nine states are trying to move assessment across institutions in order to compare programs and institutions on a larger scale.

The assessment program should emerge from and be sustained by a faculty and administrative commitment to effective learning; provide explicit and public statements regarding the institution's expectations for student learning; and use the evidence gathered to document and improve student learning. More explicitly, the evidence should be used to plan for and implement changes in pedagogy, course content, the curriculum, student services, academic advising, and instructional services, including the role of the library.

Accreditation organizations view institutional effectiveness in terms of their evaluation of overall institutional processes, policies, practices, programs, function areas, and resources. They then view the assessment of learning as a process to assess and determine the congruity between intended learning outcomes and actual student performance. As such, they now expect the assessment of student learning to go beyond individual courses and to be evident at the program and institutional levels. Further, as faculty become more aware of such assessment and embrace its use, they expect more sophisticated means of collecting information that go beyond self-reporting and indicate what students actually learn. Playing a role, leadership or other, in outcomes assessment will require libraries to settle on what areas they want to concentrate their contribution to student learning outcomes and to move from involvement at the course level to acceptance at the program and institutional level, as well as finding ways to apply more sophistical means of collecting data.[8]

With the increased emphasis on outcomes assessment, higher education administrators are making decisions about the funding of programs and units, and they are questioning investments in libraries. At the same time, libraries are searching for new ways to contribute to the institutional mission and to "demonstrate their value in clear and measurable ways."[9] The Value of Academic Libraries project of the Association of College and Research Libraries encourages greater focus on value and identifies key areas associated with it.[10] As Peter Hernon, Robert E. Dugan, and Danuta A. Nitecki conclude,

> The literature concerning the impact and value of libraries is still developing. Researchers and practicing librarians are finding it more difficult to determine the impact and value of the library, its services, and its programs, in large part because the results of interacting with library resources are intangible. . . . Value is subjective and based, in part, on the perspective held by the person at the time. Despite these difficulties, researchers and practitioners are exploring and experimenting with impact and value, and new knowledge and conceptual frameworks will likely emerge.[11]

Public Libraries

Rhea J. Rubin introduced outcomes assessment to public libraries and adopted a broader perspective, in part because public libraries serve more than students and faculty. Still, she does not fully distinguish between outputs and outcomes.[12] Her coverage is in line with the definition of outcomes advanced by the U.S. Institute of Museum and Library Services (IMLS):

> Outcomes—Benefits or changes for individuals or populations during or after participating in program activities, including new knowledge, increased skills, changed attitudes or values, modified behavior, improved condition, or altered status (e.g., number of children who learned a finger play during story time, number of parents who indicated that they gained new knowledge or skills as a result of parent education classes, number of students whose grades improved after homework clinics, number of children who maintained reading skills over the summer as a result of a summer reading program, number of people who report being better able to access and use networked information after attending information literacy classes).[13]

Comparing this definition to the previous section underscores differences with practices in public libraries and higher education. This definition suggests that outcomes might be characterized as outputs and in the form of ratios and percentages. Further, higher education focuses more on direct methods of observing actual improvement whereas public libraries rely more on indirect methods—self-reported improvement.[14]

IMLS has funded two studies, which collectively form the U.S. impact study. First, based on 3,176 responses to a national telephone survey, 44,881 web survey responses from users of more than 400 public libraries, and 319 interviews, a project team from the University of Washington showed "that public libraries are a key element of America's digital infrastructure, and that large numbers of people are using libraries' public access services to meet their needs in health education, employment, and other important areas."[15] They compiled and reported on a series of outcomes associated with the IMLS definition provided above, mostly comprising evidence gathered from using indirect methods, but this compilation contains significant errors (e.g., the vague wording of numerous questions). Nonetheless, the findings are of interest to a number of public library stakeholders.

Second, the researchers selected four public libraries as case study sites and as representative of "the types of library environments most patrons encountered in U.S. public libraries as well as the range of issues and concerns faced by library administrators, librarians, and other staff in providing public technology."[16] The following are some of the recommendations:

- "Use of valid and reliable indicators as a basis of a performance evaluation and measurement system can improve performance and stimulate reinvestment in public access technology resources and services. Benchmarks can be used both locally and nationally to influence policymakers and funders by demonstrating the extent to which these resources are used and the important outcomes that result. They also help libraries better manage their resources and set appropriate motivating goals for librarians and other staff."

- "Communicating the value, both in terms of quality and quantity, that library computer access provides to the community is critical for expanding the library's base of support and increasing funding. Interviews with key stakeholders in funding and support organizations in the case studies showed that both data and stories were necessary for the message to engage their attention. Focusing on ways to package and deliver key messages about public access computing services to the right people and organizations in the community is an important activity for all libraries, no matter how they are funded. The combination of solid, outcome-based measures of public access technology results with stories from users who have taken advantage of the services and can articulate why it is important to the community is essential for building and maintaining the support of funders and influential backers in the community. Stories need to be specific and personal."[17]

Neither of these recommendations is original. The first focuses on outputs but should raise the issue of outcomes, whereas the second serves as a reminder that libraries should carefully consider how they package their metrics and present them to the public and other stakeholders. It might be most beneficial to relate them in the form of an organization story. Organizational storytelling, which has been linked to leadership, provides an effective way to communicate with stakeholders, influence organizational culture, and motivate staff and others to accomplish the stated vision.

Although not fully explored, the perspective on outcomes assessment from higher education is relevant to public libraries, for instance, with literacy and summer reading programs or with technology and parenting skills workshops. For a series of workshops focused on technology skill improvement, evaluators might determine the extent to which the skill set of participants has improved from workshop to workshop. In essence, do they experience the same problems as before, and have they gained new knowledge, skills, and abilities during the workshops they have attended?

EUROPE

Apart from the United Kingdom, European countries are confronted with problems when they engaged in cross-national work and translate the concepts they use. There exist some differences in the actual definitions of the core concepts of performance measurement, outcomes, and impacts. These metrics are viewed as interchangeable. Differences become even more marked when libraries in different countries employ different kinds of measurement tools and methods. In the end, concepts such as quality assurance, quality measurement, value, benefits, performance evaluation, performance assessment, quality assessment, and impact are synonymous.

Concepts are translated into different contexts. There is a huge difference working with concepts in a research setting or in a more practically oriented library setting. This is especially the case in some European countries and is probably related to educational traditions that existed in many of the countries before the so-called Bologna declaration was adopted.[18] The education of librarians in many European countries traditionally lies outside the university system. In many countries, librarians were educated at higher educational institutions with a more practical orientation, and these institutions did not issue PhD degrees, and they did not have research as a main objective. In some countries, education especially for public library librarianship took place in these types of institutions, and at the same time, universities ran programs in information science and information management. It is important to emphasize that the situation varies in the different regions, but overall European librarianship is more divided in relation to professional tasks and academic considerations. The fact that librarians educated in the last century in many, but not all, European countries received an education from institutions that did not have research obligations or a research orientation influences the profession's interpretation of research, definitions of concepts, and the whole outlook of adapting academic thinking into the practice. With the Bologna declaration this situation has changed and education for librarianship or information science now takes place in programs offering bachelor's degree, masters' degrees, and, in most cases, doctoral degrees.

The most important matter is that librarians use solid and validated knowledge to improve operations and procedures to deliver services in an effective, efficient way that demonstrate the significance of the organizations in which they work in different contexts. As a result, there is not that distinction between evaluation and assessment; however, there are major differences among the types of libraries that are interested in evidence-based practice (EBP). The differences also apply to evidence-based library and information practice (EBLIP). Ghislaine Declève indicates that interest in and knowledge about EBLIP is more pronounced in academic libraries in Europe than it is in public libraries.[19] Academic libraries, especially medical libraries, have promoted EBLIP. Looking at the contributors to the handbook, *Evidence-Based Practice for Information Professionals*, it can be seen that only 2 of the 19 contributors were not related to health care–, medicine-, and nurse-related institutions, libraries, and the like.[20] Awareness of EBLIP as a concept and as practice appears to be limited to Belgium health science librarians.

In the library sector, there are major national differences when we compare the development of EBP in different countries. On a global scale, England, Canada, and the United States assume prominent positions, and, within Scandinavia, Sweden and partly Norway are more advanced than is Denmark.

Declève, who studied the diffusion of EBLIP, investigated the participation and authorship at conferences arranged around the evidence-based approach.[21] It is not surprising that European countries appear to be underrepresented in relation especially to the U.S. dominance in the field. She examined the lists of delegates to the 4th and 5th EBLIP conferences that took place in Chapel Hill, North Carolina, and in Stockholm, Sweden, in 2007 and 2009. A total of 95 percent of the papers were in English. Of the 368 delegates to the two conferences, half of them came from North America, and the United Kingdom had 27 and 23 delegates at each conference respectively. Sweden had 68 delegates and Norway had 17. However, the 5th EBLIP conference in 2009, held in Sweden, had many participants from that country. Sweden, however, only had one delegate at the conference taking place in North Carolina. The 17 delegates from Norway all participated in the Sweden conference.

Other European countries also had delegates at the two conferences. Belgium had three at the two conferences; Denmark had six and five of them went to Stockholm; Finland had five, all of them participating in the Stockholm conference; Germany had three, and they also attended the Stockholm conference; and the Netherlands had three. Overall, the participation from Europe has been limited. However, the United Kingdom had 23 participants, 15 of which went to Stockholm. The conference participation indicates that the interest in EBLIP is most pervasive in Australia, Canada, the United Kingdom, and the United States. This is further emphasized if one looks at the members of the organization committees and keynote speakers. In both cases, the majority comes from the English-speaking countries.

The latest EBLIP conference took place in June 2011 in Salford, United Kingdom. It is interesting to look at the list of participants. The Scandinavian and European participation has not increased much compared to previous years. There were two participants from Denmark and approximately 14 participants from Sweden. The Norwegian number of participants amounted to 11, and a couple of professionals from Finland also participated. These figures indicate that the interest in the evidence-based approach is higher in Norway and Sweden. The participants from the Scandinavian countries are mainly affiliated with research institutions or university libraries. The number of delegates from all the other European countries excluding United Kingdom and the Nordic countries was less than 10 in total, and most of these came from the medical library sector.

As a matter of fact, we do see the same trends when we look in more detail at the conferences oriented toward performance measurement and assessment.

There are at least two conferences of interest here. There is the Library Assessment Conference in the United States, which really focuses on evaluation, and the International Northumbrian Conference on Performance Measurement and Metrics, in Northumbria, United Kingdom. The Library Assessment Conference took place in Baltimore in 2010, and there were over 75 presentations including keynotes but excluding posters. Five presentations came from outside the United States, and of these only three came from Europe: two from United Kingdom and one from Denmark. It should also be noted that the majority of participants indicated U.S. dominance at this conference.

The situation is more diversified when we take a look at one of the Northumbrian conferences. This biannual conference started as an international conference at Northumbria, in the northern part of England, as the venue, but from 2001 until 2009, it followed more or less the venues of the International Federation of Library Associations and Institutions (IFLA) conference. In 2009, the conference took place in Florence, Italy, and drew a larger number of European participants, and, of course, there was a rather good representation of people from the Italian library community. At that conference, more than 50 papers were presented and nearly 20 of them came from Europe, excluding the United Kingdom. There was especially a rather good representation of papers from the Baltic states. Hosting the conference in Italy obviously drew more European papers than it had before.

In 2011, the conference moved to its present location in York, England, and, at this conference, only 5 of the 60 papers came from Europe excluding Great Britain. The majority of papers came from United States and the United Kingdom. It is evident that librarians and researchers in library and information science have a rather limited participation in conferences at an international level in performance measurement and related areas like evidence-based practice. Still, we recognize that knowledge sharing takes place through a multitude of channels, conferences being only one. However, the results are probably indicative of the importance of the topic and practice in the different countries, or at least the importance assigned to international cooperation in the area.

It is also of interest to note that the requirements for measuring and evaluating the quality of services, including value, effectiveness, and efficiency vary from country to country. Less than 10 years ago, the official requirements in Great Britain concerning measurement and the employment of tools for management differed between the United Kingdom and Denmark, especially in the public library sector. In the United Kingdom, the libraries had to report to the national authorities on a number of services and activities. The requirements for measurement in Danish public libraries were at that time less demanding, and the strict requirements in the United Kingdom were one of the factors that reduced and minimized the latitude for independent decisions with the effect that library leaders and directors expressed a lower degree of job satisfaction than their Danish colleagues.[22]

European library associations, in some cases, play a major role along with other key players such as library authorities. In Scandinavia, several of the library associations have been involved in the development of different forms of metrics and performance measures and presented them in handbooks. In one of these, there is an overview of different European handbooks in and guides for performance measurement in a broad sense.[23] These handbooks follow closely the standards according to both the International Organization for Standardization

(ISO) and the IFLA handbook, which are similar in their description of measures and indicators.[24] Two of the handbooks follow more or less the structure and the conceptualization of the well-known balanced scorecard.[25] The IFLA handbook appears to have the greatest influence as it conforms to ISO standards and, to a certain degree, complies with national statistics.

In Germany during the last decade, libraries have worked with a measurement system named BIX, which was developed through cooperation among a number of German academic and public libraries; use of the system enables benchmarking activities.[26] The measurement system is available in two versions, one for public libraries and the second for academic libraries. The versions are not very different, but the system for academic libraries is based on the structure of the balanced scorecard. The system designed for public libraries does not differ much when one looks at single indicators, but its structure is related to factors such as resources, focus on users, processes, cost-effectiveness, and staff. Several hundred public and academic libraries use one of these systems to measure and report data, and engage in benchmarking without the presence of standards for goodness or the lack thereof. These systems are meant for measuring impact or outcomes in a direct sense, but both systems use ratios as a guiding method.

It is also worth noting the existence of what could be named a European version of the principles of total quality management (TQM). The European version is named the Business Model of the European Foundation for Quality Management. Like the balanced scorecard, it operates with some causal relations and the following factors contribute to quality:

- Leadership
- Strategy, goals, objectives, and policies
- Staff
- Partnerships and resources
- Processes.

The embedded quality and the combination of the factors contribute to results in the following areas:

- Customers
- Employees
- Society
- Critical areas, critical success factors, and key areas.

This model, however, has not really penetrated the European library sector. The balanced scorecard has been more successful in terms of impact on the profession. This could be a question of marketing the models, and it appears that the balanced scorecard has been perceived as a more flexible and adaptable model in which to incorporate many of the indicators and metrics already in use.

A number of studies, especially in the academic library sector in Great Britain, have analyzed the impact of libraries. The British studies have been presented at a number of international conferences and the studies include economic value studies like studies of the return in investment of the British Library, and they also include rather advanced studies concerning the economic value of loans in public libraries of different types of media.[27] Overall, the research tradition in Great Britain concerning impact research is rather strong and in many ways very similar to the tradition in the United States, even if the terminology differs.

There are some studies in Europe, and it is interesting to note that the Baltic states and, from southern Europe, Portugal are active in this area of research. Swedish librarians have produced a useful handbook on measurement and the value of libraries.[28] However, it is probably in Norway that the largest study took place as a part of a doctoral program. The study used the contingent valuation method to analyze how citizens in Norway perceived the value of public libraries in terms of willingness to pay and willingness to accept loss.[29]

The following two cases of measures of impact and value, and the interpretational discourse illustrate some of the dilemmas for a library leader. Several British universities conducted a comprehensive research project named Library Impact, which investigated the relationship between university libraries and students' academic performance, including student retention.[30] The researchers have access to sensitive data on an individual level, and they are able to look at a single student's grades, retention, and different forms of library use. This project has generated huge interest in at least parts of Europe and the reasons for that are simple. Preliminary results indicate strong correlations between different dimensions of use of university libraries and the students' achievements and retention rates. However, it is important to emphasize that there are correlations or associations among data and not causal relationships that have been verified.

The results are preliminary, but they indicate strong correlations between the number of loans and the grades obtained through examinations.[31] There also seems to be a strong correlation between use of the electronic resources and students' grades. In contrast, there does not appear to be any correlation between the number of visits to the library and the grades. Other results from the study also indicate correlations between use of library resources and retention rates. It is important to emphasize that the researchers do not overestimate the correlations, and they warn against drawing conclusions indicating causal relationships.

A nationwide study of the value of public libraries in Denmark funded by the Danish Library Association and conducted by a consultancy company was bolder in its statement about relationships between use of public libraries and educational level. Respondents were asked how often they as children used the public library, and the answers were cross-tabulated with the level of their education. The results were announced as demonstrating that use of public libraries caused people to take more education, thereby demonstrating the value of public libraries.[32]

The second project that deserves mention is a Norwegian research project oriented toward public libraries as generators of social capital. This project focuses on the softer values and the softer impact on the life of citizens. The project is still ongoing, but a number of very well researched papers have already appeared.[33] The project, named PLACE, analyzes libraries as generators of social capital, and one of the main goals of the project is to analyze the significance of the library as a place for citizens. The project employs a multitude of methods. The research project has already produced results that indicate the value of libraries for a number of groups, including female immigrants who come to the library and learn about the Norwegian society and educate themselves, and the immigrants express their perception of the public library as a place that builds trust. However, the perception of the research results and their use are more complicated as they tend to appear in headlines and the problem is like the one presented above. In the case of the Norwegian project, one of the questions that could be asked is what happens when a scientific concept like social capital clearly defined becomes a popular metaphor that is used in many contexts?

The leader's dilemma is rather interesting in this context. Data can be used to promote the services of the library as an argument for its impact on students' academic achievements and the success of retention, and this is probably the way it is often stated in press releases or similar forms of popular dissemination. However, it confronts the leader with a moral or ethical dilemma. Can that person treat a statistical correlation as a causal relationship? Is it possible to argue that libraries are more likely to foster social capital in terms of trust and adequate behavior to a higher degree than other publicly funded institutions? A more radical view of library impacts is that they can be socially constructed, which means that they are embedded in different kind of rhetorical configurations. As a matter of fact, library impacts ought to be important to library leaders.

LEADERSHIP

Outcomes or impact assessment might be linked to active learning when those engaged in teaching are less focused on imparting knowledge than in engaging students in such higher-order thinking tasks as analysis, synthesis, and evaluation. For librarians and academic departments, active learning associated with outcomes assessment applied at the program and institutional levels requires librarians and faculty members to assume new roles, and for leaders to change the organizational culture to value these new roles and to explain why staff are being reassigned to roles that require partnerships with other stakeholders (e.g., faculty in institutions of higher education). For both faculty and librarians, outcomes assessment introduces a type of problem solving that they most likely have not previously addressed. That problem solving may introduce types of research they have not previously done.

Another complication is that outcomes assessment might be associated with transformation and adaptive leadership, and focus on factors such as institutional and organizational culture, shared responsibility, problem solving, institutional support, and the efficacy of assessment. Outcomes assessment involves new relationships, knowledge, and abilities, especially when such assessment moves beyond the individual course or workshop and examines learning at the program or institutional levels, or across a series of workshops. Although they do not explicitly discuss leadership, Sandra Bloomberg and Melaine McDonald offer a case study of how Bloomberg as dean of the College of Professional Studies, New Jersey City University, got the faculty to accept and benefit from outcomes assessment. As they note,

> Given the growing complexity of facilitating learning in today's classroom and the fact that university faculty are prepared as disciplinary experts rather than educators, it is not surprising that faculty, both new and experienced, are sometimes perplexed by the challenges they face. It is these challenges and the frustration that result (when faculty input and quality of outcomes lack congruency) that gives rise to calls to action.[34]

The challenges they note are widely shared within academe but they realized that "in the fabric of reality are woven opportunities."[35] It is these challenges that leaders are prepared to seize. Their example offers a blueprint for others to follow in the application of transformational leadership to outcomes assessment.

Because outcomes assessment might involve professions from different disciplines (e.g., library and information science and subject disciplines), shared and everyday leadership become factors worthy of exploration. It is not realistic to expect that one party will impose its perspective (e.g., of information literacy) on others to achieve a program or institutional perspective on a learning goal and that librarians will have more than limited influence on much of classroom learning and on setting learning goals. Further, everyday leadership focuses on daily occurrences and how these relate to change management and active learning on a recurring basis. In this context, a good definition of everyday leadership "is the ability to create a vision for positive change, help focus resources on right solutions, inspire and motivate others, and provide opportunities for growth and learning,"[36] and such motivation and opportunities for growth and learning may involve shared leadership. Clearly, outcomes assessment is directly related to change management, but this relationship has not been explored.

CONCLUDING THOUGHTS

Unlike the other chapters of the book, this one focuses more on management and its connection to research, with leadership as a subtheme. In doing so, it shows more differences between the United States and the countries of Europe. Both geographical regions share common interests in the management of libraries and the gathering of evidence, quantitative and other. Still, there are substantial differences in terminology as stakeholders exert a major influence in what they expect especially when it comes to demonstrating accountability.

NOTES

1. For more examples see COUNTER (Counting Online Usage of Networked Electronic Resources), an international initiative serving librarians, publishers, which sets standards for the recording and reporting of online usage statistics in a consistent and compatible way. See http://www.projectcounter.org/ (accessed May 22, 2012).

2. Robert E. Dugan, Peter Hernon, and Danuta A. Nitecki, *Viewing Library Metrics from Different Perspectives* (Santa Barbara, CA: Libraries Unlimited, 2009).

3. See Counting Opinions, http://www.countingopinions.com/ (accessed May 22, 2012).

4. See Peter Hernon, Robert E. Dugan, and Danuta A. Nitecki, *Engaging in Evaluation and Assessment Research* (Santa Barbara, CA: Libraries Unlimited, 2011), 114–17; University of West Florida, Office of the Dean of Libraries, "Student Return on Investment (SROI): How Can I Get My Tuition Money's Worth from the Library" (2011), http://libguides.uwf.edu/content.php?pid=188487&sid=2183215 (accessed May 19, 2012); University of West Florida, Office of the Dean of Libraries, "Calculate Your Personal Return on Investment" (2011), http://libguides.uwf.edu/content.php?pid=188487&sid=2261667 (accessed May 19, 2012).

5. Mark Emmons and Frances C. Wilkinson, "The Academic Library Impact on Student Persistence," *College & Research Libraries* 72, no. 2 (2011): 128.

6. David Streatfield and Sharon Markless, "What Is Impact Assessment and Why Is It Important?" *Performance Measurement and Metrics* 10, no. 2 (2009): 135. See also Roswitha Poll and Philip Payne, "Impact Measures for Libraries and Information Services," *Library Hi Tech* 24, no. 4 (2006): 547–62.

7. White House, "College Scorecard" (Washington, DC: White House, 2012), http://www.whitehouse.gov/issues/education/scorecard (accessed May 21, 2012); Rachel Fishman, "Higher Education Needs a Flashlight," *The Quick & the Ed* [blog] (February 2, 2012), http://www.quickanded.com/about (accessed May 21, 2012).

8. Perhaps they should also know about different types of experimental research designs and associated reliability and validity issues. See Hernon, Dugan, and Nitecki, *Engaging in Evaluation and Assessment Research*, 71–95.

9. Lisa J. Hinchliffe and Megan Oakleaf, "Sustainable Progress through Impact: The Value of Academic Libraries Project," paper for the World Library and Information Congress, 76th IFLA General Conference and Assembly (2010), http://www.ifla.org/files/hq/papers/ifla76/72-hinchliffe-en.pdf (accessed May 22, 2012).

10. Association of College and Research Libraries, *Value of Academic Libraries: A Comprehensive Research Review and Report*, by Megan Oakleaf (Chicago: Association of College and Research Libraries, 2010).

11. Hernon, Dugan, and Nitecki, *Engaging in Evaluation and Assessment Research*, 119.

12. Rhea J. Rubin, *Demonstrating Results: Using Outcomes Measurement in Your Library* (Chicago: American Library Association, 2006).

13. Peggy D. Rudd, "Documenting the Difference: Demonstrating the Value of Libraries through Outcome Measurement," in *Perspectives on Outcome Based Evaluation for Libraries and Museums* (Washington, DC: Institute of Museum and Library Services, n.d.), 20, http://www.imls.gov/assets/1/workflow_staging/AssetManager/214.PDF (accessed May 21, 2012).

14. For coverage of direct and indirect methods see Peter Hernon and Robert E. Dugan, eds., *Outcomes Assessment in Higher Education: Views and Perspectives* (Westport, CT: Libraries Unlimited, 2004); Peter Hernon, Robert E. Dugan, and Candy Schwartz, eds., *Revisiting Outcomes Assessment in Higher Education* (Westport, CT: Libraries Unlimited, 2006).

15. Samantha Becker, Michael D. Crandall, Karen E. Fisher, Bo Kinney, Carol Landry, and Anita Rocha, *Opportunity for All: How the American Public Benefits from Internet Access at U.S. Libraries* (Washington, DC: Institute of Museum and Library Services, 2010), iv, http://www.gatesfoundation.org/learning/Pages/us-libraries-report-opportunity-for-all.aspx (accessed May 21, 2012).

16. Samantha Becker, Michael D. Crandall, Karen E. Fisher, Rebecca Blakewood, Bo Kinney, and Cadi Russell-Sauvé, *Opportunity for All: How Library Policies and Practices Impact Public Internet Access* (Washington, DC: Institute of Museum and Library Services, 2011), 5, http://impact.ischool.washington.edu/documents/OPP4ALL2_FinalReport.pdf (accessed May 21, 2012).

17. Becker et al., *Opportunity for All*, 7.

18. See "The Bologna Declaration on the European Space for Higher Education: An Explanation,"   http://ec.europa.eu/education/policies/educ/bologna/bologna.pdf (accessed May 22, 2012).

19. Ghislaine Declève, "Evidence-Based Library and Information Practice: Bridging the Language Barrier," *Journal of European Association for Health Information and Libraries* 7, no. 1 (2011): 12–17.

20. Andrew Booth and Anne Brice, eds., *Evidence-Based Practice for Information Professionals: A Handbook* (London: Facet, 2004).

21. Declève, "Evidence-Based Library and Information Practice."

22. Niles Ole Pors, Pat Dixon, and Heather Robson, "The Employment of Quality Measures in Libraries: Cultural Differences, Institutional Imperatives and Managerial Profiles," *Performance Measurement and Metrics* 5, no. 1 (2004): 20–28.

23. Niels Ole Pors, *Strategi, Værdi og Kvalitet: Teorier og metoder 1* (Valby, Denmark: Danmarks Biblioteksforening, 2007); Niels Ole Pors, *Strategi, Værdi og Kvalitet: Værktøjer og indikatorer 2* (Valby, Denmark: Danmarks Biblioteksforening, 2007).

24. Roswitha Poll and Peter te Boekhorst, *Measuring Quality: Performance Measurement in Libraries* (Munich, Germany: Saur, 2007).

25. Pors, *Strategi, Værdi og Kvalitet*; Poll and Boekhorst, *Measuring Quality*.

26. Sebastian Mundt, "BIX—The Bibliotheksindex: Statistical Benchmarking in German Public Libraries," in *Library Statistics for the Twenty-First Century World*, edited by Michael Heany (Munich, Germany: Saur, 2009), 188–97.

27. Anne Morris, Margaret Hawkins, and John Sumison, "Value of Book Borrowing from Public Libraries," *Journal of Librarianship and Information Science* 33, no. 4 (2001): 191–98.

28. Viveca Nyström and Linnéa Sjögren, *Nyttovärdering av Bibliotek* (Lund, Sweden: Se, BTJ–forlag, 2008).

29. Svanhild Aabø, *The Value of Public Libraries: A Methodological Discussion and Empirical Study Applying the Contingent Valuation Method* (Oslo, Norway: University of Oslo, 2005).

30. Society of College, National and University Libraries (SCONUL), "Impact Initiative," http://vamp.diglib.shrivenham.cranfield.ac.uk/impact/impact-initiative (accessed June 17, 2012).

31. Deborah Goodall and David Pattern, "Academic Library Non/Low Use and Undergraduate Student Achievement: A Preliminary Report of Research in Progress," *Library Management* 32, no. 3 (2011): 159–70.

32. Niels Ole Pors, "Evidens om Bibliotekernes Brugere," *Dansk Biblioteksforskning* 6, nos. 2–3 (2010): 65–81.

33. Ragnar Audunson, "The Public Library as a Meeting-Place in a Multicultural and Digital Context: The Necessity of Low-Intensive Meeting Places," *Journal of Documentation* 61, no. 3 (2005): 429–41.

34. Sandra Bloomberg and Melaine McDonald, "Assessment: A Case Study in Synergy," in Hernon and Dugan, *Outcomes Assessment in Higher Education*, 260.

35. Bloomberg and McDonald, "Assessment," 272.

36. André Martin, *Everyday Leadership*, a CCL Research White Paper (Brussels, Belgium: Center for Creative Leadership, 2007), 5, http://www.ccl.org/leadership/pdf/research/EverydayLeadership.pdf (accessed May 21, 2012).

Part IV

CONCLUSION

13

———✦———

AN INTERNATIONAL RESEARCH AGENDA

Peter Hernon

As the amount of research on leadership in library and information science (LIS) slowly increases, published studies still tend to rely on self-reporting and the perceptions of librarians, perhaps those recognized as leaders, about leadership characteristics and their use of particular leadership theories or styles. The goal of such research is to explore the most critical attributes of leadership and the association of these attributes with particular leadership theories or styles, as well as the application of particular theories in libraries. A secondary goal is to study ethical leadership and the role of character (ethical and moral beliefs, intentions, and behaviors) in it. With the economic recession of 2007–2009, and its lingering aftermath across the globe, librarians continue to adjust to new economic realities and to engage in change management. Most often the changes are incremental, but some directors envision the new realities as an opportunity to make fundamental changes to the organization and to expand their institutional role. Still, the focus on leadership within the profession should not be divorced from research reported in peer-reviewed journals in other disciplines and fields of study. After all, leadership is a set of concepts that applies across disciplines and types of work.

A perusal of journals such as *Leadership Quarterly* (Elsevier), the *Journal of Leadership & Organizational Studies* (Sage), *Harvard Business Review* (Harvard Business School), and *Leadership* (Sage) will suggest topics for exploration and methodologies that have yet to be applied to the study of library-related leadership. A number of published studies, except within LIS, cut across national boundaries and reveal an international, and perhaps comparative, focus, and indicate that the investigation of leadership may focus on national cultures and engage in cross-

This chapter builds from Peter Hernon, "A Research Agenda," in *Shaping the Future: Advancing the Understanding of Leadership*, edited by Peter Hernon (Santa Barbara, CA: Libraries Unlimited, 2010), chapter 6; Peter Hernon and Candy Schwartz, "Leadership: Developing a Research Agenda for Academic Libraries," *Library & Information Science Research* 30, no. 4 (2008): 243–49.

cultural comparisons. The relevant literature probes cultures based on Geert Hofstede's dimensions (see Chapters 1 and 14).[1] Research on national cultures does not
focus on leadership theories and styles, and any cross-cultural comparisons based
on them. That research adds another component or perspective on leadership, and,
of course, LIS researchers, like any researchers, have the choice whether or not to
pursue this direction.

This chapter does not go back to each chapter and incorporate any suggestions
for further research. The purpose here is to produce a stand-alone chapter that
offers some choices for those seeking research topics as well as putting chapter suggestions into perspective. In so doing, it expands the insights into how to examine
leadership across countries and continents; in different libraries, ones making incremental and more substantial changes, and in the daily work occurring in libraries.
Instead of probing leaders about particular theories or styles, research might focus
on the everyday activities that display leadership. In other words, if daily activities
were monitored within an organization, would any of those activities be directly
or indirectly related to leadership; what do they show about leadership and the visions set?

As Chapter 1 indicates, a number of different leadership theories and styles have
been discussed in the general literature and that of LIS. Adaptive leadership, for
instance, might mobilize people to thrive in changing and challenging environments, but how widely is this theory practiced in libraries, and how is it being applied? Instead of listing such questions for further investigation, this chapter links
different topical areas to a conceptual framework that lays out the components of
organizational leadership. It is not the purpose of this chapter to discuss each area
but rather to highlight certain features.

CONCEPTUAL FRAMEWORK

As noted in Chapter 2, Simmons College has a PhD program, Managerial Leadership in the Information Professions (MLIP), that revolves around a leadership
model adapted, with permission, from the National Center for Healthcare Leadership (NCHL) Leadership Competency Model, Version 2.0. As envisioned, that
program focuses on three broad areas of leadership, namely:

1. Transformation: Visioning, energizing, and stimulating a change process
   that coalesces communities, the public, and professionals around new models of managerial leadership. This area includes achievement orientation,
   problem solving/analytical thinking, and, to some extent, community orientation, financial skills, information discovery, innovative thinking, and
   strategic orientation.
2. Accomplishment: Translating vision and strategy into optimal organizational performance. This area encompasses communication skills, organizational awareness, domain knowledge (LIS), and, to some extent,
   accountability, change leadership, collaboration, management of information technologies, performance measurement, and project management.
3. People: Creating an organizational climate that values employees from various backgrounds and providing an energizing environment for them. This
   area also covers the leader's responsibility to understand his or her impact
   on others and to improve his or her capabilities, as well as the capabilities

of others. This area encompasses professionalism, team leadership, and, to some extent, human resources management, relationship building, self-confidence, and staff development.[2]

In total, 25 competencies associated with that conceptual model are connected to a curriculum model, which positions the program at the intersection of management and leadership in the discipline of library and information science. Examples of these competencies include innovative thinking, which is "the ability to apply complex concepts and develop creative solutions or adapt previous solutions in new ways" (transformation); relationship building, which is "the ability to establish, build and sustain professional contacts for the purpose of building networks of people with similar goals and that support similar interests" (accomplishment); and collaboration, which is "the ability to work cooperatively with others, to be part of a team, to work together, as opposed to working separately or competitively. Collaboration applies when a person is a member of a group of people functioning as a team, but not the leader" (people). Students in the program are expected to understand and demonstrate those leadership competencies within the disciplinary, temporal, spatial, and political contexts in which library and information enterprises operate. Some future studies might explore these competencies, their completeness, and their interconnections. Figure 13.1 suggests broad topics to explore these three leadership areas. Each area actually addresses both management and leadership, and for this reason we refer to the figure as covering *managerial leadership*, which involves setting the guiding vision and motivating others in the organization to achieve it.[3]

Accomplishment

This area covers both the internal organization and the external relationship between the library and its stakeholders. Internally, leaders deal with the organizational culture and climate, which is defined as an individual's perceptions of the organization and the nature of that person's relationship with others in the organization. Climate might be extended to the relationship of the library with stakeholders. Lee G. Bolman and Terrence E. Deal's have connected climate to leadership through four frame leadership styles.[4] Those frames include the following:

- Structural frame, which emphasizes organizational structure, authority, rules, roles, and priorities. Structural leaders make rational decisions, value efficiency, and strive to achieve established goals and objectives through coordination and control.

- Human resources frame, which focuses on the relationship between the organization and its workforce and which emphasizes "understanding people, their strengths and foibles, reason and emotion, desires, and fears."[5] Human resources leaders strive to achieve organizational goals through meaningful and satisfying work, and they recognize the importance of congruence between the individual and the organization.

- Political frame, which emphasizes conflict and competition. "Authorities have position power, but they must vie with many other contenders for other forms of leverage."[6] Political leaders engage in coalition building, negotiation, and compromise; recognize the diversity of individuals and interests; and compete for scarce resources.

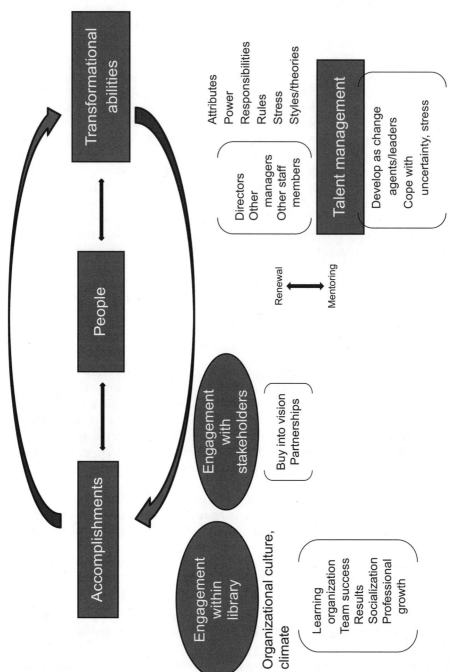

Figure 13.1: A Research Agenda for Leadership

- Symbolic frame, which embodies and expresses an organization's culture. Symbolic leaders recognize that symbols have meaning, and they strive to achieve organizational goals through inspiration, rituals, and ceremonies.

That the first two frames tend to focus internally on the organization, whereas the final two connect the library to its parent institution and beyond. Those applying for the position of director begin to read those frames and form conclusions about the institution and organization during their initial interview for the position. Still, little is known about how they read those environments and how their assessment might change over time.[7] Such research might go beyond the use of methods of gaining self-reports and involve, for instance, probing a set of scenarios that cover different situations and test how directors, in particular seasoned ones, go about reading the climates and deciding whether or not they would apply for a position.

Vinaya L. Tripuraneni surveys faculty, administrators, and librarians in private, nonprofit, doctoral universities about which of the four frames is important for library leaders. Faculty and administrators favor the structural frame for its inclusion of a well-managed organization that meets the institutional mission, whereas libraries prefer the human resources frame for its coverage of basic human needs.[8] Studies such as this one underscore that the four frames might serve as the basis for additional research that examines libraries in cross-cultural settings.

The broader leadership literature covers everyday leadership or the practice of leadership on a recurring—perhaps daily—basis. Everyday leadership is a sense-making process consisting of the following activities: interpretations, constant adjustments, and formulations of temporary solutions. Another striking feature is that everyday leadership is event-driven. Instead of looking at the application of a theory or a set of attributes in general terms, such research looks at the practice of leadership, perhaps in the work lives of those being led. One of its purposes is to examine those events and see how the vision is carried out, the challenges are faced, and any corrections are initiated. Are assigned leaders and staff focused on the vision or on management? What are they doing that qualifies as leadership in the context of Figure 13.1? Are particular theories more commonly practiced?

People

The typical assumption is that leadership is a positive activity. In fact, there is bad—unethical or ineffective—leadership.[9] What effects do such leadership have on organizations, and once such individuals leave the organization, how does the organization recover? What types of bad leadership appear in libraries? What strategies do new leaders implement when they follow bad leaders or the absence of leadership, how do they gauge the response to the changes they make, and how do they set priorities?

As discussed in Chapter 11, in the literature emanating from the United States, there are leaders and those who follow them, known as followers. Barbara Kellerman has characterized different types of followers and her model merits exploration.[10] How well does her typology, and that of others, apply to libraries in the United States, Europe, and elsewhere? In addition, Brian Crossman and Joanna Crossman, who review the literature on followership, show that there is no commonly accepted definition of the term and point out that "both managers and management academics appear to have assumed that individuals instinctively know how to follow and have not fully appreciated the potential for individuals to learn how to follow effectively."[11] This observation calls for the evaluation of the types of activities discussed in Chapter 12 to determine their effectiveness and the extent to which they create positive behaviors.

Much of the leadership literature, especially within LIS, focuses on the leaders—members of senior management teams—and those implementing the vision set. Research might probe leadership from the perspective of followers or staff. A problem might be the unwillingness of staff to be perceived as critical or judgmental of those who manage them.

Another topic relates to outstanding political and business leaders as they are frequently called upon to make high-stakes decisions. Because of the controversial and highly visible nature of these issues, they often face intense criticism. The responses of leaders to criticism not only impact employees, but also the successful resolution of the contested issue. It is possible that, if they are not careful, leaders might jeopardize the trust that staff place in them. Studies might, therefore, probe the reaction of library leaders to different types of criticisms that staff and perhaps others make to determine if trust in leaders diminishes.

Any discussion of people would be incomplete without mentioning resonant leadership (see Chapters 1 and 12) and how managerial leaders cope with the stress and pressures associated with the changes they are implementing as well as how their institutions and organizations cope with the recession and its aftermath. This topic might relate to positive or bad leadership and change management.

How important is it for leadership to be knowledgeable about different leadership theories and which ones do they practice in different situations? The context—or situation—in which leadership is applied merits examination. Finally, in modern society, which is multicultural, how does multiculturalism factor into leadership? How do learning organizations truly benefit from diversity? How are members of diverse communities given the opportunity to learn and grow, perhaps moving into leadership positions?

Transformation

A part of transformation is getting people to buy into the changes, especially if those changes are more than incremental. How do leaders go about gaining that buy-in and motivating staff to implement their visions? How do leaders cope with resistance to change? It might be relevant to probe those libraries becoming learning organizations and the leadership that takes place, perhaps on an everyday basis.

Those organizations that rely on teams to accomplish change might be the subject of research that examines the application of team effectiveness, as envisioned by J. Richard Hackman on academic and public libraries in different countries.[12] That research might build on Chapter 11 by examining the intersection among results and productivity, group socialization, and member professional growth.

With the recession and the slow global recovery from it, libraries are increasingly seeking new service roles and sources of revenue. As a consequence, there is greater interest in innovation and entrepreneurial activities. Do those interests result in new leadership theories, namely innovation leadership and entrepreneurial leadership?

TOPICS UNRELATED TO THE CONCEPTUAL FRAMEWORK

It is common for research studies to summarize a body of writing, discuss topics for further investigation, and review recent developments in the leadership literature, which are currently receiving attention regarding research, theory, and practice.[13] For this reason, dissertations are a good source of literature on the problem under investigation and on particular leadership theories or styles. There are also published literature reviews, such as Sharon G. Weiner's, who, writing in 2003, pointed out areas in which there was a dearth of research.[14] Although her conclusion may no longer be true in every instance, her article provides an excellent foundation for the exploration of potential topics to pursue.

In the literature, other than that portion related to LIS, there is likely a body of research on a particular theory or leadership style that might lend itself to meta-analysis, a set of statistical procedures used to summarize and integrate a body of literature. Those must have a sufficient number of similar characteristics to combine their results accurately and explore, for instance, the type of research design and methodologies used, the response rate, and similarities and differences among key findings. A goal of some studies might be to identify organizational and institutional leaders, who can lead effectively across national cultures, and to conceptualize and define differences and approaches to global leadership.

Some of the literature on leadership offers "highly romanticized, heroic views of leadership—what leaders do, what they are able to accomplish, and the general effects they have on our lives. One of the principal elements in this romanticized conception is the view that leadership is a central organizational process and the premier force in the scheme of organizational events and activities."[15] Probing the literature on leadership for the past 25 years, Michelle C. Bligh, Jeffrey C. Kohles, and Rajnandini Pillai cover a number of studies, highlight their findings, and identify areas for focusing future research. They note that

> transformational/charismatic leadership has been the primary focus of the RoL [romance of leadership] perspective, consistent with . . . [the] assertion that the prevailing emphasis on transformational/charismatic leadership represented a hyper-romanticization in itself. However, to what extent are perceptions of other leadership styles . . . [influencing the perception of RoL and] and interfollower processes? In other words, is there a generalized halo/horns effect when individuals romanticize leadership, in that once leadership is established as the preferred explanation for either positive or negative outcomes, leaders are either canonized or demonized accordingly?[16]

Based on research studies such as these two, it might be beneficial to examine the nonresearch literature in LIS and the characterization of leadership. Do these writings present a similar perspective on leadership, and how well do the authors understand the complex topic of leadership? After all, organizational effectiveness and success cannot be defined solely in terms of leadership. In fact, if that leadership is negative, leadership may not play any role.

As libraries engage in change management and assume roles and services not associated with traditional libraries, they most likely change the views or image that constituents form of them. As Joan Giesecke shows, for more than 100 years libraries have used metaphors, images of reality, to convey their roles as they shifted from warehouses and a focus on print collections. She notes that the themes "transitions, change, repackaging, [and] survival . . . dominate our field as libraries seek to reinvent themselves."[17] As libraries implement the vision set by leaders those metaphors change, but do constituents recognize and buy into these new, positive metaphors? Further, do library staff envision new metaphors that reflect the transformation of their positions?

Finally, a number of leadership theories focus on the vision that leaders set and its accomplishment. There are different definitions of a vision, but each offers a mental image or picture, a future orientation, and organizational direction. Some visions describe the means by which an organization achieves its strategic direction, but a vision also serves to inspire, motivate, and engage people. It provides meaning and purpose to the work of an organization. As important as it is to know what a vision is, it is also important to know what it is not. It is not static, a repetition of the mission statement, and focused on the present.

Burt Nanus maintains that the right vision

- "is a realistic, credible, attractive future;"
- identifies "the skills, talents, and resources to make . . . [the future] happen;"
- "attracts commitment and energizes people;"
- "creates meaning in workers' lives;"
- "establishes a standard of excellence;"
- "bridges the present to the future;" and
- "transcends the status quo."[18]

In contrast, John P. Kotter, who also provides an overview of a vision and what makes it effective, sees the characteristics of an effective vision as including:

- "Imaginable: Conveys a picture of what the future will look like
- Desirable: Appeals to the long-term interests of employees, customers, stockholders, and others who have stake in the enterprise
- Feasible: Comprises realistic, attainable goals
- Focused: Is clear enough to provide guidance in decision-[sic] making
- Flexible: Is general enough to allow individual initiative and alternative responses in light of changing conditions
- Communicable: Is easy to communicate; can be successfully explained within five minutes"[19]

Combining the perspectives of Nanus and Kotter with perhaps the work of other scholars, it is possible to develop a schematic that one can use to evaluate the visions of organizations, such as libraries, associated with the nonprofit sector. How well do the schematics that Nanus, Kotter, and others develop relate to libraries? Are there other or different characteristics? Might the different proposed characteristics be combined into one schematic?

Furthermore, Kotter and others offer examples of vision statements for the for-profit sector and discuss how to create such a statement. In contrast, what does a library vision look like? Is it similar to the statement that many libraries include on their homepage, and how well does that statement encompass the characteristics of a vision statement as captured in the schematic? Such homepage statements in fact might merely explain what the library does and thereby complement the mission statement, without challenging the organization to change and to lay out what it strives to become within the context of the vision set by the parent organization.

METHODOLOGIES USED IN THE STUDY OF LEADERSHIP

Some of the research is quantitative and involves the use of questionnaires, standardized tests administered to those in managerial and leadership positions, and content analysis of documents and the literature. Most of the research thus far in this century, however, tends to be qualitative and to rely on assorted methodologies. For example, content analysis, which can be either a quantitative or a qualitative method, might be applied to diaries that participants maintain for a set period of time or to the metaphors used to describe leadership; metaphors make messages more vivid and increase their retention. They also have emotional meaning and impact others. Researchers might ask study participants (either leaders or followers) to identify passages of text that they find most inspiring. Those passages might be checked for use of any metaphors.

Qualitative methodologies include participant observation and ethnography, semistructured and unstructured interviews, conversation and discourse analysis, phenomenological inquiry, and event history and life narrative analysis. Rarely do researchers rely on focus group or group interviews; or visual research, which, among other things, includes the study of relevant images (e.g., cartoons) for information about what it reveals about leadership.[20]

The research in LIS is more limited in the methodologies used. Typically a study uses a questionnaire or personal interview. Nonetheless, narrative inquiry, an interview protocol that enables subjects to recall a period of time and, from it, to select critical issues that the researcher can probe, is starting to be used in MLIP, and MLIP dissertations adopt multiple methods of data collection (see Chapter 2).

CONCLUDING THOUGHTS

With so many definitions of leadership and the number of the theories or subtheories continuing to expand, there seems to be little need to reach a consensus on a definition and to determine which theories and styles prevail. At the same time, a fuller understanding of particular theories is emerging from the research and reconceptualization of particular theories. Writing in 1985, Meindl, Ehrlich, and Dukerich concluded that "the concept of leadership remains largely elusive and enigmatic" and that the concept contains lofty imagery, mystery, and mythology.[21] Yet, there is an increasingly body of research, even within LIS, that relates leadership to organizational change and defining the direction that the organization is going. Much of that literature, however, does not have an international focus and include citations from different parts of the world. The major exception is the literature produced within Europe that makes reference to research produced in Europe, the United Kingdom, and elsewhere. Regardless, leadership is integral to change management and is rich in potential for further research. The methodological tool chest for that research continues to expand and is now becoming more qualitative than quantitative; and there are increased opportunities to apply multiple methods and combine quantitative and qualitative methods, thereby producing richer insights into leadership.

NOTES

1. See Geert Hofstede, *Culture's Consequences, International Differences in Work-Related Values (Cross Cultural Research and Methodology)* (Newbury Park, CA: Sage, 1980).

2. Simmons College Graduate School of Library and Information Science, "Managerial Leadership in the Information Professions: Models" (2006), http://www.simmons.edu/gslis/docs/phdmlip_models_new_permission.pdf (accessed May 21, 2012).

3. For an alternate model, see Husain al Ansari and Othman al Khadher, "Developing a Leadership Competency Model for Library and Information Professionals in Kuwait," *Libri* 61 (September 2011): 239–46. Much of this model focuses on management and does not group relevant competencies by areas of leadership such as transformation, accomplishment, and people.

4. Lee G. Bolman and Terrence E. Deal, *Reframing Organizations: Artistry, Choice, and Leadership*, 4th ed. (San Francisco: Jossey-Bass, 2008).

5. Bolman and Deal, *Reframing Organizations*, 21.

6. Bolman and Deal, *Reframing Organizations*, 209.

7. Peter Hernon, "Becoming a University Library Director," *Library & Information Science Research* 33, no. 4 (2011): 276–83.

8. Vinaya L. Tripuraneni, "Leader or Manager: Academic Library Leader's Leadership Orientation Considered Ideal by Faculty, Administrators, and Librarians at Private, Nonprofit, Doctoral Universities in Southern California," EdD dissertation, University of La Verne, 2010. Available from Dissertations & Theses Full-Text, AAT 3430266.

9. Barbara Kellerman, *Bad Leadership* (Boston: Harvard Business School Press, 2004).

10. Barbara Kellerman, *Followership: How Followers Are Creating Change and Changing Leaders* (Boston: Harvard Business School Press, 2008).

11. Brian Crossman and Joanna Crossman, "Conceptualising Followership: A Review of the Literature," *Leadership* 7, no. 4 (2011): 483.

12. J. Richard Hackman, *Leading Teams: Setting the Stage for Great Performances* (Boston: Harvard Business School Press, 2002).

13. See, for instance, Bruce J. Avolio, Fred O. Walumbwa, and Todd J. Weber, "Leadership: Current Theories, Research, and Future Directions," *Annual Review of Psychology* 60 (2009): 421–49, 10.1146/annurev.psych.60.110707.163621 (accessed May 21, 2012); Marcus W. Dickson, Deanne N. Den Hartog, and Jacqueline K. Mitchelson, "Research on Leadership in a Cross-Cultural Context: Making Progress, and Raising New Questions," *Leadership Quarterly* 14, no. 6 (2003): 729–68; Sonia Ospina and Erica Foldy, "A Critical Review of Race and Ethnicity in the Leadership Literature: Surfacing Context, Power, and the Collective Dimensions of Leadership," *Leadership Quarterly* 20, no. 6 (December 2009): 876–96.

14. Sharon G. Weiner, "Leadership of Academic Libraries: A Literature Review," *Education Libraries* 26, no. 2 (2003): 5–18.

15. James R. Meindl, Sanford B. Ehrlich, and Janet M. Dukerich, "The Romance of Leadership," *Administrative Science Quarterly* 30, no. 1 (1985): 79. See also http://www.jstor.org/pss/2392813.

16. Michelle C. Bligh, Jeffrey C. Kohles, and Rajnandini Pillai, "Romancing Leadership: Past, Present, and Future," *Leadership Quarterly* 22, no. 6 (2011): 1073.

17. Joan Giesecke, "Finding the Right Metaphor: Restructuring, Realigning, and Repackaging Today's Research Libraries," *Journal of Library Administration* 51, no. 1 (2010): 54–65.

18. Burt Nanus, *Visionary Leadership: Creating a Compelling Sense of Direction for Your Organization* (San Francisco: Jossey-Bass, 1992), 8, 17.

19. John P. Kotter, *Leading Change* (Boston: Harvard Business Review Press, 1996), 72.

20. For examples of works using these methodologies, see Peter Hernon, "A Research Agenda," in *Shaping the Future: Advancing the Understanding of Leadership*, edited by Peter Hernon (Santa Barbara, CA: Libraries Unlimited, 2010), 88–91.

21. Meindl, Ehrlich, and Dukerich, "Romance of Leadership," 79–80.

14

LEADERSHIP AS VIEWED ACROSS COUNTRIES

Peter Hernon and Niels Ole Pors

Although the global recession is now over, the economies of many countries have not recovered. Politically, the national focus is on reducing spending and reordering priorities. Further, the education sector in many European countries and somewhat in the United States faces severe budget cuts. The drastic cuts in public spending have generated considerable anxiety within the higher education community. Moreover, in such a climate, numerous academic and public libraries find they have declining budgets for the foreseeable future; the cuts may actually predate the recession starting in 2007. The result of these cuts might be reduced hours of being open; closing branches; consolidating services; releasing staff, especially those who are not working full time; engaging in greater collaboration for resource sharing; the declining availability of money to purchase items for the collection; increases in user fees; and, in some instances, privatizing services and library operations. Although these issues are normally associated with managing libraries in times of scarce resources, there are also implications for leadership. As a result, there is increased interest in the topic of leadership and the types of changes necessary for organizations to make to be more competitive with the services they offer. Those changes might go beyond incremental ones and involve the libraries in new ways of achieving greater effectiveness and efficiency in meeting the stated mission of the parent institution or organization. Another way to look at this is that "merely surviving this period of transition from analog to digital libraries is not sufficient to guarantee relevance to the academic . . . [or other] enterprise. Libraries will survive the transition, but whether they will be relevant to the primary mission of the larger institution and its faculty and students . . . [or other communities] is the real question."[1]

LEADERSHIP

Peter G. Northouse concludes that "there are many ways to complete the sentence, 'Leadership is . . .'"[2] The chapters in this book neither dispute his assertion nor concentrate on a definition, seeking consensus. Rather, the purpose is to report on leadership at both the theoretical and operational levels across academic and public libraries in a number of countries. Coverage concentrates on the organizational, as opposed to the institutional, context, but Chapter 13 encourages examination of leadership in a larger setting—the institutional level and linkage to the institutional mission and vision statements. Some library directors may be familiar with the literature on leadership, but not necessarily that emanating from library and information science, and in other instances they are unfamiliar with it.

The presumption is that, by position, a person is a leader. Northouse, among others, characterizes leaders as *assigned* or *emergent*. The former "is based on occupying a position in an organization," and the latter is "the most influential member of a group or organization, regardless of the individual's title."[3] What Northouse fails to address is that, when leadership is situational and is examined in an institutional setting, the same individual may move from emergent to assigned leadership. In other words, individuals are not simply one or the other; they can be both. At any rate, assigned versus emergent leadership is not a distinction that chapter authors make. In some instances, they do not distinguish between managers and leaders, and the study of leadership in some European countries is in its infancy. This does not mean that leadership is necessarily well developed in library and information science in any of the countries presented. The reason is that, as we learn more about leadership, new facets appear, especially if we view leadership from the perspective of managing complex organizations on a daily basis.

STATE OF KNOWLEDGE ABOUT ACADEMIC AND PUBLIC LIBRARIANS AS LEADERS

Chapter 1 offered the definition of leadership that guided chapter authors, but we did insist on its acceptance and use. Leadership, as the chapters indicate, tended to view leadership as "a process whereby an individual influences a group or individuals to achieve a common goal."[4] The first word in the definition, *process*, "implies that a leader affects and is affected by followers."[5] Influence might be the realm of the director as this person has the authority, mandate, and resources to achieve change. However, effective or truly transformational change will not occur unless subordinates and stakeholders buy into the change laid out by the director. When leadership is moved down the organization to the team level, the accomplishment of change might not relate to influence but rather to acceptance of that common goal. We do not support inclusion of *goal* in the definition because in planning and evaluation that word has a specific use—setting goals for which objectives enable managers to measure progress in the achievement of objectives. Goals therefore differ from a vision, which is broader in intent.

Although the term *follower* is common in the United Kingdom and the United States, it is not used throughout Europe; the preference might be for staff or employees. Either way, follower or worker implies someone who is motivated to carry out the vision, assuming that vision is clearly stated. This person should be willing to learn from others as well as share knowledge, skills, and abilities. Without effective followership, leaders cannot achieve organizational priorities—ones aligned with the vision statement.

Northouse believes that "influence is the sine qua non of leadership."[6] Influence might imply motivating, empowering subordinates, and supporting their development, but how leaders go about doing these things to make the organization effective has not been studied in library and information science on a cross-national basis of the magnitude of this book, especially during times of austerity. To influence others leaders must communicate effectively (connect with others) and demonstrate ethical behavior, but, again, research has not examined these attributes, especially regarding how leaders go about doing so on a daily basis. At this time of austerity, communication becomes more important and both managers and workers face interested uncertainty and stress. Yet, to date, the literature on leadership relates resonant leadership only to the United States and on a limited scale. As Annie McKee, Frances Johnston, and Richard Massimillan point out, "When leaders face power stress over the long term and cannot find ways to manage its downside, they risk becoming trapped in the Sacrifice Syndrome, a vicious circle leading to mental and physical distress, and sometimes even executive burnout. . . . Some people may even begin to act out; they may make rash decisions, act impulsively or do things that seem to contradict their values."[7]

There are different ways to characterize leadership, one of which is to view it as encompassing three areas as shown in the previous chapter: (1) transformation, (2) accomplishment, and (3) people.[8] If this characterization has validity and we think it does, the areas have received unequal treatment in the research literature. As presented in Chapter 13, each area has numerous research opportunities. As well, it is important to examine interactions across areas and national cultures.

One of the issues that emerges from the study of leadership in libraries in a cross-national comparison is between generic leadership and leadership embedded in a profession. To date, much of the literature on leadership has supported the approach toward generic leadership. This is understandable given the late arrival of the literature emanating from library and information science (LIS), the preponderance of writings—popular and scholarly—produced outside LIS, and the association that leadership was part of management. Support for the last point is based on the numerous management textbooks that included a chapter or part of a chapter on leadership. The presumption was that the leader headed the organization and got appointed perhaps on the basis of professional qualifications; this is especially true in Europe. Through the 1980s, a leader was perceived as a kind of primus inter pares, which meant that leaders often were perceived as spokespersons of the traditional values of a profession and change could be difficult to make. Leadership loyalty was firmly rooted in traditional values.

This situation changed dramatically in Europe with new public government and its focus on restructuring, efficiency, evaluation and assessment, change and innovation, and the need for effective leadership. The newer focus on leadership as an occupational position per se changed the situation and, in many public and private institutions, leadership took new forms, and organizations in Europe might find leaders outside the LIS profession.

Becoming a leader in a library could be difficult to achieve. A library is a knowledge-intensive organization with a staff consisting of experts who often identified closely with their specialty and educational background. Change could be extremely difficult to achieve because change often implies priorities that downgrade some specialties and upgrade others. This can have the effect that a change in strategy can be perceived as an attack on an expert's personality or identity.

Another difficult issue is that many professional experts in Europe appear to possess a negative attitude and perception toward management and managerial work. There is no doubt that it is difficult to lead professionals in a knowledge-intensive organizations as the respect that professionals tend to give is based on values and skills embedded in the profession. In many ways, leadership in an advanced organization such as a library or an information organization must be built on mutual respect and recognition.

Some people might argue that leadership in a knowledge-intensive organization must depart from the logic embedded in the profession, and this logic would normally imply that the quality of the work and work processes are important and that the employee often defines the criteria for the work. The managerial leadership challenge is to combine the logic embedded in the profession with that in the tasks. One way to unite the two is to develop leader authority and legitimacy. The leader receives real authority from the staff, and a prerequisite for authority is that the leader gives value to the organization through the creation of new positions, adding economic resources, and developing prestige, recognition, and organizational visibility. In other words, the leader has responsibility for organizational processes and recognition of individual employees. The organization must offer employees appreciation for their work and symbolic things that the organization values. Most of all, it is the responsibility of the managerial leader to ensure that proper professional competencies are recognized, developed, and used.[9]

There is no formula for achieving the type of leadership discussed in this section because organizational and national cultures are important factors in the process. The following example illustrates this. The authority of a leader is not assigned the same way in all countries as explained in Chapter 4. In some countries and organizations, it is necessary that a leader has a good grasp of professional content. In other countries, the authority embedded in the position as leader per se is very important. It would then be an important leadership ability to read and understand the environment, as well as reflect and take action on a personal and organizational level based on the reading of the environment.

Finally, it is important to be aware of the enormous diversity available in libraries, regardless of their size. In different countries the majority of libraries may be small, especially for public libraries and libraries attached to small educational institutions, and this fact poses leadership challenges that are omitted from the discourse on leadership. In Chapters 4, 6, and 7, it is clear that, for example, Greek and Norwegian public libraries tend to be small and have a very limited number of staff members. The formal leader of such a library has to participate actively in daily operations. Moreover, leading a small library is vastly different from, for instance, leading a large university library. Leading may imply having fully engaged management and blurring the dividing line between performing one's role as a manager and meeting leadership challenges. Perhaps the leadership challenges go unrecognized or unattended.

LEADERSHIP AS VIEWED FROM THE CONTEXT OF NATIONAL CULTURES

The concept of leadership does not always translate the same into the language of a national culture, as Felix C. Brodbeck and Michael Frese point out in their analysis of Germany.[10] Even when it does, different cultures may view leadership in organizations differently. At the same time leadership characteristics and behaviors may vary greatly across cultures. Culture is defined as learned or shared beliefs, values, symbols, and traditions common to (and transmitted to) a group of people. Until the emergence of the cultural approach to leadership and interest in the similarities and differences across cultures, the theories and corresponding research tended to focus on the adoption and practice of particular theories in the United States or, more broadly, Anglo-Saxon cultures.

Marcus W. Dickson, Deanne N. Den Hartog, and Jacqueline K. Mitchelson review the different frameworks for portraying cultural dimensions.[11] They show that the most widely recognized framework is the one advanced by Geert Hofstede.[12] For one of his dimensions, *power distance*, the extent to which a society accepts that power in institutions and organizations is distributed unequally, he created a power distance index, which measures the extent to which less powerful members of institutions and organizations accept the fact of unequal distribution. Germany, for instance, has a 35 on the scale and the United States a score of 40. The United States exhibits a more unequal distribution of wealth in comparison to Germany and, say, Denmark (a score of 18) and Sweden (a score of 31). On the other hand, France (68) and Poland (68) have a greater unequal distribution than is found in the United States.

The research on national cultures indicates that on most cultural dimensions there is considerable variance within Europe, thus there is no typical European pattern. However, there are cultural clusters; countries in Europe and elsewhere can be systematically clustered within culture clusters. One purpose of cross-cultural research is to make comparisons and generalizations with and across a cultural cluster. Audra I. Mockaitis, for instance, does so by focusing on the perceptions of managers and employees in culturally close countries (Lithuania, Estonia, and Poland). She shows that consensus among team members will take the longest to achieve in Estonia, where the opinions of each team member will be sought. Further, the "commitment to the team may not be as high as in the other two countries, as each group member also has individual interests to defend, however optimal solutions will be sought." Interestingly, "the highest commitment to the group was expressed in Poland, however, just as in decision making, group members may not be able to arrive at solutions without the guidance of someone in authority."[13]

A country likely has more than one culture and an organization such as a library likely has the same. As the chapters on Europe indicate, Hofstede studied how culture influences values in the workplace in more than 70 countries. His research and that known as GLOBE (Global Leadership and Organizational Behavior Effectiveness), for instance, provide cross-cultural research and enable comparisons within Europe and with other regions of the world. However, they do not reflect on leadership effectiveness; instead, they indicate how others perceive someone as a leader and not what leaders do as reflected through the leadership theories presented in the first chapter. Additional weaknesses with the cultural framework is that no single theory of how culture relates to leadership has materialized, there is no situational context to culture as there is for the leadership theories, and culture is not necessarily a component of various leadership theories.[14]

Cultural Dimensions

Chapter 1 presents the six dimensions of Hofstede, namely power distance, collectivism versus individualism, masculinity versus femininity, uncertainty avoidance, long-term orientation, and indulgence versus restraint. GLOBE, on the other hand, views culture from both the organizational and societal levels, recasts some of these dimensions, and adds new ones for a total of nine dimensions:

1. Assertiveness, which is the extent to which individuals are assertive and confrontational in their relationships with others
2. Gender egalitarianism, which is the extent to which a collective minimizes gender inequality
3. Future orientation, which is the extent to which a collectivity encourages and rewards future-oriented behaviors such as planning and delaying gratification
4. Humane orientation, which is the extent to which a society rewards individuals for being fair, friendly, generous, and caring
5. In-group collectivism, which is the degree to which individuals express pride, loyalty, and cohesiveness
6. Institutional collectivism, which is the extent to which institutional practices encourage and reward the collective distribution of resources and collective action
7. Performance orientation, which is the extent to which a community encourages and rewards innovation, high standards, excellence, and performance improvement. The level of performance orientation affects the degree to which leaders and leadership are viewed as effective.
8. Power distance, which is the extent to which institutions and organizations accept and endorse authority, power differences, and status privileges
9. Uncertainty avoidance, which is the extent to which a society relies on social norms, rules, and procedures to alleviate the unpredictability of the future. This dimension goes beyond assigned leaders and brings out team leadership.[15]

The research does not cover all national cultures. GLOBE, for instance, focused on 62 societies worldwide. The European countries were grouped into regions: Nordic Europe (Denmark, Finland, and Sweden), Germanic Europe (e.g., Austria, Germany, Netherlands, and Switzerland), Anglo cluster (e.g., England and Ireland), Latin Europe (e.g., France, Italy, Portugal, Spain, and Switzerland), and Eastern Europe (e.g., Albania, Greece, and Poland).

General Observations

The studies using cultural clusters do not necessarily use the same societies or countries but they report findings in terms of the cluster groups highlighted above. The Nordic Europe cluster, for instance, "is high on future orientation, gender egalitarianism, institutional collectivism, and uncertainty avoidance. The cluster falls in the middle range of scores on humane orientation and performance orientation. Its cores on assertiveness, in-group collectivism, and power distances are low."[16] The cluster scores for Germanic Europe are "high on assertiveness, future orientation, performance orientation, and uncertainty avoidance. It is in the mid-score range for gender egalitarianism and power distance. It scores low on humane orientation, institutional collectivism, and in-group collectivism."[17]

Although the Anglo cluster covers English-speaking countries outside our study population, there are high scores on performance orientation; mid scores for assertiveness, future orientation, gender egalitarianism, humane orientation, institutional collectivism, power distance, and uncertainty avoidance; and low scores on in-group collectivism.[18] This cluster includes the United States; however, as

Michael H. Hoppe and Rabi S. Bhagat indicate, the cluster approach does not sufficiently capture perceptions about leadership.[19] Undoubtedly the economic recession of 2007–2009 and the subsequent recovery, together with a shrinking middle class, a widening gap between rich and poor, and other factors, complicate extending comparisons of cultural dimensions to more recent times.

The Latin Europe cluster scores "low on humane orientation and institutional collectivism . . . and [were] in the middle range for all other dimensions."[20] And, finally, the Eastern Europe cluster rates "high on assertiveness, gender egalitarianism, and in-group collectivism. Its scores on humane orientation, institutional collectivism, and power distance were in the middle range. It scored low on future orientation, performance orientation, and uncertainty avoidance."[21]

Libraries

A key question is, How do libraries fit within the literature of national cultures, assuming that the concept applies well to such organizations? Chapter 7 is the first to address this question as the chapter authors examined some of Hostede's dimensions in libraries. They found some variation among Denmark, Norway, and Sweden (see Table 7.2). However, as the authors correctly note, it is premature to draw any conclusions. However, national cultures add an important component to the research agenda presented in Chapter 13; that agenda is merely suggestive.

LEADERSHIP THEORIES AND CHALLENGES

Our original intention was to compare the leadership theories presented in Chapter 1 and to determine which were most prevalent. Although subsequent chapters (especially those discussing the United States and the United Kingdom) make some reference to the theories, they do not become a focal point of any chapter. Chapters 3 and 4 provide an overview of Europe and provide the necessary context to the study of leadership. Clearly, at this time, it is more productive to focus on countries through the lens of both management and leadership. Chapter 7, for instance, reinforces the dearth of research into leadership, with that chapter taking a first step to conceptualize leadership in academic and public libraries from the perspective of the countries under review. Clearly, this book provides a foundation upon which others can build.

Many of the major issues and challenges that academic and public libraries face today and for the near future require more than the abilities that managers have to resolve. As libraries cope with the severe fiscal constraints, leadership will increasingly focus on service and management innovation and entrepreneurial enterprises—finding new resources of revenue from nontraditional markets; these markets may be willing to pay for these services. Libraries have long engaged in partnerships and collaboration, but these will continue to expand and involve new stakeholders. Another challenge relates to accountability, assessment, and evaluation. This challenge is greatest in countries such as England and the United States as more libraries must demonstrate their effectiveness and efficiency, most likely at the institutional level. Library metrics will continue to evolve into institutional metrics, but the United States perhaps has the most rigid framework for demonstrating accountability.

A third challenge is to maintain relevance to the mission of the parent institution or organization during times of uncertainty. A fourth challenge is to discard traditions when they are no longer relevant and embrace change; that change might be incremental or transformative. As libraries meet this challenge they may need to adopt organizational agility—shift and change quickly. A final challenge, as reflected in management theory, is that "organizations surviving in times of change move from an emphasis on economy to efficiency, and then to effectiveness. These organizations realize that they must not only make the best use of their resources (economy), and demonstrate excellence in how tasks are accomplished (efficiency), but must be sure they are doing the right things and are being effective."[22]

Chapters 8 through 12 highlight some of the important questions related to leadership, especially in Europe. Taken together, these chapters discuss the intricate relationship between factors such as personality, organizational culture, driving forces in the environment, and interpretations of that environment. That discussion continues with an examination of the relationship between leaders and those who follow them. This issue is important especially when organizations engage in measurement, evaluation, and assessment as part of the cognitive input to direct future orientation.

Two points are pertinent to an in-depth analysis of library directors. First, a detailed psychological profile of individual directors yields information that surpasses broader and less detailed profiling. For instance, one can examine openness to change, a psychological factor, that can take different forms, one of which would be an inclination to change through actions or doing. Another is openness to ideas and values. Depending on the inclination and mediated though the organizational climate, change processes also take different forms. The total psychological profiling of directors, in combination with semistructured interviews, including ones with staff members, provides valuable and otherwise unobtainable information about the role that personality plays in an organizational setting. It should be noted that all of the profiled library leaders conform to the general ideas of leaders. Some of these ideals are openness to change, extroversion, emotional stability, and a high degree of conscientiousness. However, the analysis also indicates that the specific configuration of all of the facets and attributes are extremely important for the way that leadership is performed and perceived. Further, psychological profiles are closely related to emotional intelligence.

Psychological profiling is much more than an academic exercise. It can have practical implications for the composition of leadership teams or teams in general. A psychological profile is also helpful for a leader who wants to reflect on his or her strengths and weaknesses and the relationship between emotions and modes of behavior. However, the interpretation of a psychological profile can only be stated as a kind of hypothesis about behavior in different situations.

An organization needs the capacity to interpret the environment and the data it collects. To do this, leaders need to develop throughout the organization an appreciation for planning and evidence-based management. The information culture that is established should be aware of (and avoid) blind spots, risk denial, and structural hindrances to change. Wrong decisions in a library are not likely to be fatal, but they can have dire consequences in the context of path dependency. Examples of managerial situations in which path dependency might arise relate to organizational restructuring, the acquisition of a library database, reaching an agreement with an information provider, or the selection and implementation of organizational recipes.

Organizational recipes (see Chapter 9), when they become a standard for libraries, involve both management and leadership. Such a recipe often originates in an academic setting but was often created in cooperation with others in the profession or with the business community. Further, it provides a blueprint for leading members of the academic and professional communities, is advanced by consultants, incorporates the promise to solve organizational problems, and is a framework for corrective action, and organizations can adopt or change them according to their culture and needs. Recipes are often connected to success stories, and the story behind a recipe often takes the form of a drama. Successful recipes often become part of a trend, and their use spans national boundaries and cultures. Some recipes, such as the balanced scorecard, have a long life, whereas others, such as business process reengineering, have a shorter life span. The balanced scorecard is widely used in Europe and only infrequently so in academic and public libraries in the United States for accountability and planning purposes at an institutional level.

Recipes might be incorporated into organizational operations, and, as a result, people no longer talk about them. Finally, recipes have content and symbolic aspects. It is interesting to see which recipes dominate the discourse of a profession and represent more than a fad. On the reverse side, it is interesting to see which recipes a profession does not include in its discourse. A given recipe might be adopted because the organization is forced to do so by the parent organization or stakeholders. Adoption might relate to the perception that the recipe is in accordance with the norms and values of a profession. Adoption might also be linked to the fact that comparable and prestigious organizations already use the recipe.

There is no doubt that the profession as a whole is focused on change, with some libraries more engaged in change than others. The catchphrase that "libraries stand on a burning platform" has been raised in the European discourse on leadership, and this catchphrase has served as a rational for change. Such change is the consequence of a special interpretation of the environment in which libraries function. However, there is no doubt that the ideology and need for change are deeply integrated in the professional identity of many academic and public library directors. Most likely, they see the status quo as unacceptable.

In summary, leadership is about leading people and interacting consciously with the organizational environment, the parent organization, and stakeholders in a reflective and mature manner to create an inspiring vision of the future and not to be overwhelmed with what austerity today brings. Directors and other leaders in an organization must be open to new intellectual experiences, try new innovations and change the organizational structures as needed, value the skill set needed to guide the organization forward, and adopt recipes that will enable them to monitor progress in achieving the new future.

CHANGE MANAGEMENT VS. CHANGE LEADERSHIP

These are not interchangeable concepts. Change management refers to a set of tools or structures intended to manage change—keep any change under control. Change leadership, on the other hand, concerns the vision, processes, and driving forces that lead to transformation, or large-scale change. Leadership focuses on the vision and influences others to make the necessary changes, and to do so in an urgent manner. Change leadership implies the type of theories or styles discussed in Chapters 1 and 2. For this reason, research might examine everyday leadership and the types of styles that emerge and compare them to the situations leaders describe.

When commenters define libraries in terms of providing computers and books, and hours open,[23] they present status quo management and, in such cases, the type of workforce becomes unimportant. It is possible to downgrade positions and be unconcerned about the knowledge, skills, and abilities that the future workforce will need. Fortunately, this sentiment did not arise in any of the chapters. It may represent the viewpoint of some in public libraries in the United States, but the thrust of this book and the literature on the future of academic and public libraries contradicts status quo management, which can lead only to decline or extinction.[24]

THE TYPICAL STUDY HIGHLIGHTED IN THIS BOOK

The average study covered in the various chapters reports the results gathered from a survey or questionnaire and/or relying on an interview. These surveys tend not to involve the use of predeveloped, behaviorally based leadership assessment tools. The questionnaires tend to be given to individuals working in an organization, mostly the library director, and ask them for a self-report assessment of themselves, their behaviors or activities, or their perceptions of something related to management or leadership. They focus on managers and perhaps leaders rather than followers, and these studies do not examine the interactions among managerial leaders and followers. There is no tendency to ask subordinates to report on the perceived behaviors of their supervisors due to the belief that subordinates would be unwilling to offer critical comments of their managers, presumably because those managers might not like the results, but would they retaliate? Another complication is the extent to which subordinates truly understand the concept of leadership.

There is an assumption in a number of studies that all managers are leaders. A second set of assumptions is leadership tends to be viewed as something positive, when in fact there is negative or bad leadership. Further, it is assumed (and perhaps incorrectly) that only positive leader actions are critical to the effectiveness or efficiency of the organization. No studies have explored leader errors and how such errors influence organizational success. The literature within library and information science frequently does not consider the context in which leader behaviors and actions occur as well as the extraneous variables that may be operating within that context.[25]

As previously discussed, leadership is a process in which leaders rely on a series of activities and exchanges over time and under varied circumstances. Such complexity tends to remain unaddressed in the literature of library and information science. The typical distribution of a single survey to a particular population or sample only produces a snapshot of what leaders think or what is occurring as leaders engage in some activity or interact with others. That leadership process therefore is not viewed as a complex issue, one that defies simple analysis and characterization.

It is critical that concepts and applications of leadership across national boundaries be developed and that library and information science researchers conduct longitudinal studies and control variables. The goal here is not to paint a negative view of research in library and information science, but to indicate the need for more research utilizing complex research designs and examining issues of causality. There are some excellent studies in the discipline of library and information science, and this base of research merits further development and showcasing in the broader leadership literature.

THE LEADERSHIP INDUSTRY

The focus on leadership varies among the countries studied. There is perhaps greater attention to it in the United Kingdom and the United States. This does not mean there is a lack of opportunities to read or hear about it in the other countries. Still, the leadership industry is probably the largest in the United States and, to a lesser degree, in the United Kingdom. That industry encompasses countless leadership institutes, centers affiliated with universities, courses and programs of study, workshops, books, blogs, webinars, conferences, consultants, and so on. The goal of much of the industry, even that within library and information science, is to teach people how to lead and the presumption is that effective leaders can easily be created. Barbara Kellerman challenges the industry to substantiate its claims that its offerings make a difference.[26] The industry, even where it is in its infancy, should accept the challenge and review the extent of success in achieving learning goals. Those goals might center on enhancing awareness of issues and how to cope with them, develop participants' skill set and knowledge, and differentiate between the roles and abilities of managers and leaders. We would add that problem solving requires greater knowledge about how to conduct research and identify researchable problems than many managers currently have. Leaders of the future will require greater training to do research, especially that associated with evaluation and assessment.

LIBER (Association of European Research Libraries) intends to engage in leadership development for the next generation of senior leaders in European research libraries, given "a shortage of people willing and ready to take leading positions in the research libraries of tomorrow." To offset the shortage, Julien Roche, Chair of the LIBER Steering Committee on Organisation and Human Resources, proposes that "in general, libraries will forsake the traditional profile in favor of more internationally oriented directors."[27] To avoid the mistakes common to the leadership industry which Kellerman notes, we encourage more concentration on transformation, accomplishments, and people, while devoting attention to the leadership attributes highlighted in this book, namely emotional intelligence, trust of subordinates, integrity, innovation, entrepreneurial activities, and collaboration with a wide set of stakeholders—new and old. For leaders to be able to see a new future toward which they will lead the workforce, they must be creative and have the ability to think differently and see things that others have not seen, and thus to give others a reason to follow.

The leadership attributes are complex and some are not easily mastered. However, they illustrate the demands that emerge from organizations that must respond to numerous communities and driving forces. To the list, we add problem-solving ability such as that associated with adaptive leadership (see Chapter 1). Chapter 12 reinforces that in times of austerity, for instance, demands for accountability will not lessen and they might take new directions, such as student and student learning outcomes as defined in the United States.

CONCLUDING THOUGHTS

Writing in 2010, Peter Hernon and Ellen Altman noted, "Progress implies change. Not all change is progress, but all progress requires change. Change can be planned or unplanned. Libraries have experienced some serious unplanned changes in the recent past."[28] Unplanned changes are not limited to the impact of the global

Issues	Components
Accountability and assessment	• Outcomes and evidence-based research and decision making • Performance standards and metrics • Transparency as an organizational value
Crisis management	• Disaster management • Crime • Election/funding loss • Financial crisis • Homelessness • Intellectual freedom challenges • Library closings/reductions in hours, etc. • Media relations
Ethical issues and values	• Contracting issues • Legal statutes/rules • Professional ethics
Fiscal/financial management and leadership	• Enterprise creation and management • Collaborations for fiscal efficiency • Resource allocation, enhancement, and reallocation (what to stop and start in tough times)

Interaction with stakeholders	• Building effective relationships
	   * Maintaining those in existence
	   * Creating new ones

Operating in the political environment	• Governing structures, governing bodies, and relationships • Statutory and legal issues
Planning for leading	• Strategic planning • Tactical implementation • Demographics of who is served: the aging, different generations, ethnicity, and language
Service development	• Evaluating/embracing trends and fads • Literacy (early childhood, adult, computer/technology, other) • Marketing and public relations—building a brand image
Staff development	• Collective bargaining • Succession planning • Turnover and training (and retraining)

Figure 14.1: Critical Issues Facing Academic and Public Librarians*

*Adapted from: Peter Hernon and Ellen Altman, "Embracing Change for Continuous Improvement," *American Libraries* 41, nos. 1–2 (2010): 53. Reprinted by permission American Library Association.

recession and subsequent recovery. They also cover topics such as the changing information-seeking behavior of library customers, the intense competitive environment in which libraries function, stakeholder demand for accountability (effectiveness and efficiency), and beginning the journey of continuous improvement, a worthy goal—one that metrics of *how many* and *how much* do not adequately address.

Service drives the library, not vice versa. For this reason, the leader's vision that guides the organization should stake out an innovative competitive service position that addresses future expectations related to customer service quality and satisfaction. Such a vision should be brief, clear, challenging, future-oriented, desirable, and perhaps inspiring. However, we recognize that such a vision would not apply to all of the countries in Europe and thus will require some readjustment.

Nonetheless, libraries should not assume the service they provide is exemplary or that they automatically know or can anticipate the expectations of their customers. They should set priorities, goals, objectives, and service targets; benchmark performance over time; commit themselves to adhering to best practices; and commit the resources necessary to maintain levels of exemplary service—that is, service that customers regard as exemplary. Clearly, the library manager of the future will likely different from that of today, and definitely from that of yesterday. It may well be that the manager is a leader who values adaptive leadership. Such persons adapt to internal changes in the organization such as adopting timely alterations in attitudes, values, behaviors, and styles of work. They ensure that the team members perform in accordance with accepted norms and values. They also are aware of the contextual environment and ensure that their decisions are relevant with respect to the problem; they are problem solvers. They are flexible and capable of accommodating to the changing environment. Adaptive leaders apply their perceptual knowledge in a given context to improve the productivity of the team or organization.

Figure 14.1 summarizes the areas in which many academic and public librarians need expertise as new challenges arise. To overcome those challenges will require more librarians who are both managers and leaders. Leadership, which centers on a common goal (the vision), is not a fad that will soon be displaced with some other fad. Without leadership that is future- and change-oriented, academic and public libraries as a whole would face dire consequences.

NOTES

1. Rush Miller, "Damn the Recession, Full Speed Ahead," *Journal of Library Administration* 52, no. 1 (2012): 4.

2. Peter G. Northouse, *Leadership: Theory and Practice*, 6th ed. (Thousand Oaks, CA: Sage, 2013), 2.

3. Northouse, *Leadership*, 8.

4. Northouse, *Leadership*, 5.

5. Northouse, *Leadership*.

6. Northouse, *Leadership*.

7. Annie McKee, Frances Johnston, and Richard Massimillan, "Mindfulness, Hope, and Compassion: A Leader's Road Map to Renewal," *Ivey Business Journal* 70, no. 5 (2006), 1. Available from General BusinessFile ASAP.

8. Simmons College, Graduate School of Library and Information Science, "Managerial Leadership in the Information Professions: Leadership Models" (Boston: Simmons

College, 2006), http://www.simmons.edu/gslis/docs/phdmlip_models_new_permission.pdf (accessed May 28, 2012).

9. Ole Anderson and Søren B. Rasmussen, *Sádan Leder du Medarbejdere der er Klogere end Dig Selv: Mulighedsledelse I udviklingsorganisationer* (Copenhagen: Børsens Forlag, 2005).

10. Felix C. Brodbeck and Michael Frese, "Societal Culture and Leadership in Germany," in *Culture and Leadership across the World: The GLOBE Book on In-Depth Studies of 25 Societies*, edited by Jagdeep S. Chhokar, Felix C. Brodbeck, and Robert J. House (New York: Taylor and Francis, 2008), 167–68.

11. Marcus W. Dickson, Deanne N. Den Hartog, and Jacqueline K. Mitchelson, "Research on Leadership in a Cross-Cultural Context: Making Progress, and Raising New Questions," *Leadership Quarterly* 14 (2003): 729–68.

12. Geert Hofstede, "The Influence of Organisational Culture on Business," http://geert-hofstede.com/organisational-culture.html (accessed May 28, 2012). For a list of publications by Geert Hofstede, see http://geert-hofstede.com/publications.html (accessed June 11, 2012).

13. Audra I. Mockaitis, "A Cross-Cultural Study of Leadership Attitudes in Three Baltic Sea Region Countries," *International Journal of Leadership Studies* 1, no. 1 (2005): 44–63 (p. 60).

14. Northouse, *Leadership*, 406, 421.

15. Jagdeep S. Chhokar, Felix C. Brodbeck, and Robert J. House, *Culture and Leadership across the World*.

16. Chhokar, Brodbeck, and House, *Culture and Leadership across the World*, 31.

17. Chhokar, Brodbeck, and House, *Culture and Leadership across the World*, 107.

18. Chhokar, Brodbeck, and House, *Culture and Leadership across the World*, 297.

19. Michael H. Hoppe and Rabi S. Bhagat, "Leadership in the United States of America: The Leader as Cultural Hero," in Chhokar, Brodbeck, and House, *Culture and Leadership across the World*, 475–543.

20. Chhokar, Brodbeck, and House, *Culture and Leadership across the World*, 765.

21. Chhokar, Brodbeck, and House, *Culture and Leadership across the World*, 545.

22. Joan Giesecke, "The Value of Partnerships: Building New Partnerships for Success," *Journal of Library Administration* 52, no. 1 (2012): 36.

23. Will Manley, "The Matter of the Master's," *American Libraries* 43, nos. 5–6 (2012): 96.

24. Peter Hernon and Joseph R. Matthews, *Reflecting on the Future: Academic and Public Libraries* (Chicago: American Library Association, 2013).

25. Gary A. Yunkl, *Leadership in Organizations*, 7th ed. (Upper Saddle River, NJ: Prentice Hall, 2009).

26. Barbara Kellerman, *The End of Leadership* (New York: HarperCollins, 2012).

27. Julien Roche, "LIBER Leadership Development Program: Building a High-Level Seminar for the Next Generation of Senior Leaders," *Library Connect*, http://libraryconnectarchive.elsevier.com/lcn/0903/lcn090306.html (accessed June 1, 2012).

28. Peter Hernon and Ellen Altman, "Embracing Change for Continuous Improvement," *American Libraries* 41, nos. 1–2 (2010): 52.

BIBLIOGRAPHY

ARTICLES

al Ansari, Husain, and Othman al Khadher. "Developing a Leadership Competency Model for Library and Information Professionals in Kuwait," *Libri* 61 (September 2011): 239–46.

Alire, Camila. "Diversity and Leadership: The Color of Leadership," *Journal of Library Administration* 32, nos. 3–4 (2001): 99–114.

Anglada, Lluis. "Collaborations and Alliances: Social Intelligence Applied to Academic Libraries," *Library Management* 28, nos. 6–7 (2007): 406–15.

Audunson, Ragnar. "Between Professional Fields Norms and Environmental Change Impetus: A Comparative Study of Change Processes in Public Libraries," *Library & Information Science Research* 21, no. 4 (1999): 523–52.

Audunson, Ragnar. "The Public Library as a Meeting-place in a Multicultural and Digital Context: The Necessity of Low-intensive Meeting-places," *Journal of Documentation* 61, no. 3 (2005): 429–41.

Avolio, Bruce J., William L. Gardner, Fred O. Walumbwa, Fred Luthans, and Douglas R. May. "Unlocking the Mask: A Look at the Process by Which Authentic Leaders Impact Follower Attitudes and Behaviors," *Leadership Quarterly* 15, no. 6 (2004): 801–23.

Balague, Nuria, and Jarmo Saarti. "Benchmarking Quality Systems in Two European Academic Libraries," *Library Management* 30, nos. 4–5 (2009): 227–39.

Barling, Julian, Frank Slater, and E. Kevin Kelloway. "Transformational Leadership and Emotional Intelligence: An Exploratory Study," *Leadership & Organization Development Journal* 21, no. 3 (2000): 157–61.

Barsh, Adele, and Amy Lisewski. "Library Managers and Ethical Leadership: A Survey of Current Practices from the Perspective of Business Ethics," *Journal of Library Administration* 47, nos. 3–4 (2008): 27–67.

Bligh, Michelle C., Jeffrey C. Kohles, and Rajnandini Pillai. "Romancing Leadership: Past, Present, and Future," *Leadership Quarterly* 22, no. 6 (2011): 1058–77.

Block, Lory. "The Leadership–Culture Connection. An Exploratory Investigation," *Leadership & Organizational Development Journal* 24, no. 6 (2003): 318–34.

Bradley, John H., and Frederic J. Hebert. "The Effect of Personality Type on Team Performance," *Journal of Management Development* 16, no. 5 (1997): 337–53.

Brown, F. William, and Nancy G. Dodd. "Utilizing Organizational Culture Gap Analysis to Determine Human Resource Development Needs," *Leadership and Organization Development Journal* 19, no. 7 (1998): 374–85.

Bundy, Alan. "A Window of Opportunity: Libraries and Higher Education," *Library Management* 24, nos. 8–9 (2003): 393–400.

Carpenter, Maria T. H. "Cheerleader, Opportunity Seeker, and Master Strategist: ARL Directors as Entrepreneurial Leaders," *College & Research Libraries* 73, no. 1 (2012): 11–32.

Castiglione, James. "Organizational Learning and Transformational Leadership in the Library Environment, *Library Management* 27, no. 4–5 (2006): 289–99.

Chapleo, Chris. "What Defines 'Successful' University Brands?" *International Journal of Public Sector Management* 23, no. 2 (2010): 169–83.

Chen, Jihong, Peter Y. T. Sun, and Robert J. McQueen. "The Impact of National Cultures on Structured Knowledge Transfers," *Journal of Knowledge Management* 14, no. 2 (2010): 228–42.

Clarke, Christopher, and Simon Pratt. "Leadership's Four-Part Progress," *Management Today* (March 1985): 84–86.

Collier, Mel. "Moving on: Transferability of Library Managers to New Environments," *Library Management* 28, nos. 4–5 (2007): 191–96.

Costa, Paul T., and Robert R. Mccrae. "Stability and Change in Personality Assessment: The Revised NEO Personality Inventory in the Year 2000," *Journal of Personality Assessment* 68, no. 1 (1997): 86–94.

Crossman, Brian, and Joanna Crossman. "Conceptualising Followership: A Review of the Literature," *Leadership* 7, no. 4 (2011): 483–99.

Declève, Ghislaine. "Evidence-Based Library and Information Practice: Bridging the Language Barrier," *Journal of European Association for Health Information and Libraries* 7, no. 1 (2011): 12–17.

Deiss, Kathryn J. "Innovation and Strategy: Risk and Choice in Shaping User-centered Libraries," *Library Trends* 53, no. 1 (2004): 17–32.

Dewey, Barbara I. "Leadership and University Libraries: Building to Scale at the Interface of Cultures," *Journal of Library Administration* 42, no. 1 (2005): 41–50.

Dickson, Marcus W., Deanne N. Den Hartog, and Jacqueline K. Mitchelson. "Research on Leadership in a Cross-Cultural Context: Making Progress, and Raising New Questions," *Leadership Quarterly* 14, no. 6 (2003): 729–68.

Düren, Petra. "Public Management Means Strategic Management: How Can Libraries Fulfil the Requirements of the New Public Management," *Library Management* 31 no. 3 (2010): 162–68.

Edwards, Vilas, and Niels Ole Pors. "International Co-operation: The West–East Relationship in EU Funded Projects," *Library Management* 22, no. 3 (2001): 124–30.

Emmons, Mark, and Frances C. Wilkinson. "The Academic Library Impact on Student Persistence," *College & Research Libraries* 72, no. 2 (2011), 128–49.

Epps, Sharon K. "African American Women Leaders in Academic Research Libraries," *portal: Libraries and the Academy* 8, no. 3 (2008): 255–72.

Eriksson, Catarina, and Angela Zetterlund. "Den Svenska Biblioteksgeografin," *Svensk biblioteksforskning/Swedish Library Research* 17, no. 1 (2008): 39–63.

Fein, Erich, Aharon Tziner, and Cristinel Vasiliu. "Age Cohorts Effects, Gender, and Romanian Leadership Preferences," *Journal of Management Development* 29, no. 4 (2010): 364–76.

Giesecke, Joan. "Finding the Right Metaphor: Restructuring, Realigning, and Repackaging Today's Research Libraries," *Journal of Library Administration* 51, no. 1 (2010): 54–65.

Gilstrap, Donald L. "A Complex Systems Framework for Research on Leadership and Organizational Dynamics in Academic Libraries," *portal: Libraries and the Academy* 9, no. 1 (2009): 57–77.

Goffee, Robert, and Gareth Jones. "Followership: It's Personal Too," *Harvard Business Review* 79, no. 11 (2001): 148.

Goleman, Daniel. "Leadership That Gets Results," *Harvard Business Review* 78, no. 2 (2000): 78–90.

Goodall, Deborah, and David Pattern. "Academic Library Non/low Use and Undergraduate Student Achievement: A Preliminary Report of Research in Progress," *Library Management* 32, no. 3 (2011): 159–70.

Goulding, Anne, Beth Bromham, Stuart Hannabuss, and Duncan Cramer. "Professional Characters: The Personality of the Future Information Workforce," *Education for Information* 18, no. 7 (2007): 7–31.

Grenness, Tor. "Scandinavian Managers on Scandinavian Management," *International Journal of Value-Based Management* 16, no. 1 (2003): 9–21.

Gundersen, Arne, and Magadalena Kubecka. "Polish–Norwegian Cooperation on Strategies for Regional Libraries," *Library Management* 33, nos. 1–2 (2012): 104–11.

Hansson, Joacim. "Just Collaboration or Really Something Else? On Joint Libraries and Normative Institutional Change with Two Examples from Sweden," *Library Trends* 54, no. 4 (2006): 549–68.

Hariff, Subnum, and Jennifer Rowley. "Branding of Public Libraries," *Library Management* 32, no. 4 (2011): 346–60.

Hautala, Tinna M. "The Relationship between Personality and Transformational Leadership," *Journal of Management Development* 25, no. 8 (2006): 777–94.

Heinström, Jannica. "Fast Surfing, Broad Scanning, and Deep Diving: The Influence of Personality and Study Approach on Students' Information-Seeking Behavior," *Journal of Documentation* 61, no. 2 (2005): 228–47.

Heinström, Jannica. "Psychological Factors behind Incidental Information Acquisition," *Library & Information Science Research* 28, no. 4 (2006): 579–94.

Hernon, Peter. "Becoming a University Library Director," *Library & Information Science Research* 33, no. 4 (2011): 276–83.

Hernon, Peter, Ronald R. Powell, and Arthur P. Young. "University Library Directors in the Association of Research Libraries: The Next Generation, Part One," *College & Research Libraries* 62, no. 2 (2001): 116–45.

Hernon, Peter, Ronald R. Powell, and Arthur P. Young. "University Library Directors in the Association of Research Libraries: The Next Generation, Part Two," *College & Research Libraries* 63, no. 1 (2002): 73–90.

Hewlett, Sylvia A., Carolyn B. Luce, and Cornell West. "Leadership in Your Midst: Tapping the Hidden Strengths of Minority Executives," *Harvard Business Review* 83, no. 11 (2005): 74–82.

Hood, David, and Kay Henderson. "Branding in the United Kingdom Public Library Service," *New Library World* 106, nos. 1–2 (2005): 16–28.

House, Robert J. "A Path-Goal Theory of Leadership Effectiveness," *Administrative Science Quarterly* 16, no. 3 (1971): 321–38.

Humphrey, Ronald. "The Many Faces of Emotional Leadership," *Leadership Quarterly* 13, no. 5 (2002): 493–504.

Hyldegård, Jette. "Collaborative Information Behaviour—Exploring Kuhlthau's Information Search Process-Model in a Group-Based Educational Setting," *Information Processing and Management* 42, no. 1 (2006): 276–98.

Ibarra, Herminia, and Morton T. Hansen. "Are You a Collaborative Leader?" *Harvard Business Review* 89, no. 7–8 (2011): 68–74.

Inglehart, Ronald, and Wayne E Baker. "Modernization, Cultural Change and the Persistence of Traditional Values," *American Sociological Review* 65, no. 1 (2000): 19–51.

Jackson, Sandra. "A Qualitative Evaluation of the Shared Leadership Barriers, Drivers, and Recommendations," *Journal of Management in Medicine* 14, nos. 3–4 (2000): 168–78.

Jepson, Doris. "Leadership Context: The Importance of Departments," *Leadership and Organization Development Journal* 30, no. 1 (2009): 36–52.

Johannsen, Carl Gustav. "Money Makes the World Go Around: Fee-based Services in Danish Public Libraries, 2000–2003," *New Library World* 105, no. 1–2 (2004): 21–32.

Johannsen, Carl Gustav, and Niels Ole Pors. "Library Managers and Management 2001: A New Danish Survey," *New Review of Information and Library Research* 7 (2001): 186–200.

Kaarst-Brown, Michelle L., Scott Nicholson, Gisela M. Von Dran, and Jeffrey M. Stanton. "Organizational Cultures of Libraries as a Strategic Resource," *Library Trends* 53, no. 1 (2004): 33–54.

Kekäle, Tauno, and Jouni Kekäle. "A Mismatch of Cultures: A Pitfall of Implementing a Total Quality Approach," *International Journal of Quality and Reliability Management* 12, no. 9 (1995): 210–20.

Kellerman, Barbara. "What Every Leader Needs to Know about Followers," *Harvard Business Review* 85, no. 12 (2007): 84–91.

Kerr, Robert, John Garvin, Norma Heaton, and Emily Boyle. "Emotional Intelligence and Leadership Effectiveness," *Leadership & Organization Development Journal* 27, no. 4 (2006): 265–79.

Koopman, Paul L., Deanne N. Den Hartog, Edvard Konrad, et al. "National Culture and Leadership Profiles in Europe: Some Results from the GLOBE Study," *European Journal of Work and Organizational Psychology* 8, no. 4 (1999): 503–20.

Kostagiolas, Petros, and Maria Korkida. "Strategic Planning for Municipal Libraries in Greece," *New Library World* 109 nos. 11–12 (2008): 546–58.

Littrell, Romie F., and Lapadus N. Valentin. "Preferred Leadership Behaviours: Exploratory Results from Romania, Germany and the UK," *Journal of Management Development* 24, no. 5 (2005): 421–42.

Lok, Peter, and John Crawford. "The Relationship between Commitment and Organizational Culture, Subculture, Leadership Style, and Job Satisfaction in Organizational Change and Development," *Leadership & Organizational Development Journal* 20, no. 7 (1999): 365–73.

Lynn, Lawrence E., Jr. "A Critical Analysis of the New Public Management," *International Public Management Journal* 1, no. 1 (1998): 107–23.

Magnier-Watanabe, Rémy, and Dai Senoo. "Shaping Knowledge Management: Organization and National Culture," *Journal of Knowledge Management* 14, no. 2 (2010): 214–27.

Magnusson, P., and Richard T. Wilson. "Breaking through the Cultural Clutter: A Comparative Assessment of Multiple Cultural and Institutional Frameworks," *International Marketing Review* 25, no. 2 (2008): 183–201.

Manley, Will. "The Matter of the Master's," *American Libraries* 43, nos. 5–6 (2012): 96.

Mathews, Brian P., Akiko Ueno, Tauno Kekäle, Mikko Repka, Zulema Lopes Pereira, and Graça Silva. "European Quality Management Practices: The Impact of National Culture," *International Journal of Quality and Reliability Management* 18, no. 7 (2001): 692–707.

Mavrinac, Mary Ann. "Transformational Leadership: Peer Mentoring as a Values-Based Learning Process," *portal: Libraries and the Academy* 5, no. 3 (2005): 391–404.

McCarthy, Grace, and Richard Greatbanks. "Impact of EFQM Excellence Model on Leadership in German and UK Organisations," *International Journal of Quality and Reliability Management* 20, no. 9 (2006): 1068–91.

McKee, Annie, Frances Johnston, and Richard Massimilian. "Mindfulness, Hope, and Compassion: A Leader's Road Map to Renewal," *Ivey Business Journal* 70, no. 5 (2006): 1–5.

McKnight, Susan. "The Expatriate Library Director," *Library Management* 28, nos. 4–5 (2007): 231–41.

Meindl, James R., Sanford B. Ehrlich, and Janet M. Dukerich. "The Romance of Leadership," *Administrative Science Quarterly* 30, no. 1 (1985): 78–102.

Metoyer, Cheryl A. "Leadership in American Indian Communities: Winter Lessons," *American Indian Culture and Research Journal* 34, no. 4 (2010): 1–12.

Morris, Anne, Margaret Hawkins, and John Sumison. "Value of Book Borrowing from Public Libraries," *Journal of Librarianship and Information Science* 33, no. 4 (2001): 191–98.

Mullins, John, and Margaret Linehan. "Are Public Libraries Led or Managed?" *Library Review* 55, no. 4 (2006): 237–48.

Mullins, John, and Margaret Linehan. "The Central Role of Leaders in Public Libraries," *Library Management* 26, nos. 6–7 (2005): 386–93.

Mullins, John, and Margaret Linehan. "It Can Be Tough at the Top: Some Empirical Evidence from Public Library Leaders," *International Journal of Business and Management* 3, no. 9 (2006): 132–40.

Mullins, John, and Margaret Linehan. "Leadership and Followership in Public Libraries: Transnational Perspectives," *International Journal of Public Sector Management* 18, no. 7 (2006): 641–47.

Neal, James G. "Advancing From Kumbaya to Radical Collaboration: Redefining the Future Research Library," *Journal of Library Administration* 51, no. 1 (2010): 66–76.

Neal, James G. "The Entrepreneurial Imperative Advancing from Incremental to Radical Change in the Academic Library," *portal: Libraries and the Academy* 1, no. 1 (2000): 1–13.

Neely, Teresa Y. "Assessing Diversity Initiatives: The ARL Leadership and Career Development Program," *Journal of Library Administration* 49, no. 8 (2009): 811–35.

Niehoff, Brian P. "Personality Predictors of Participation as a Mentor," *Group Development International* 11, no. 4 (2006): 321–33.

O'Connor, Steve. "The Heretical Library Manager for the Future," *Library Management* 28, nos. 1–2 (2007): 62–71.

Oliver, Gillian. "Information Culture: Exploration of Differing Values and Attitudes to Information in Organisations," *Journal of Documentation* 64, no. 3 (2008): 363–85.

Ospina, Sonia, and Erica Foldy. "A Critical Review of Race and Ethnicity in the Leadership Literature: Surfacing Context, Power, and the Collective Dimensions of Leadership," *Leadership Quarterly* 20, no. 6 (2009): 876–96.

Paul, Gerd. "Mobilising the Potential for Initiative and Innovation by Means of Socially Competent Management: Results from Research Libraries in Berlin," *Library Management* 21, no. 2 (2000): 81–85.

Politis, John D. "The Relationship of Various Leadership Types to Knowledge Management," *Leadership and Organization Development Journal* 22, no. 8 (2001): 354–64.

Politis, John D. "Transformational and Transactional Leadership Enabling Knowledge Acquisition of Self-managed Teams: The Consequences for Performance," *Leadership and Organization Development Journal* 23, no. 4 (2002): 186–97.

Poll, Roswitha. "Managing Service Quality with the Balanced Scorecard," *Advances in Library Administration and Organization* 20, no. 67 (2001): 213–27.

Poll, Roswitha. "Performance, Processes, and Cost: Managing Service Quality with the Balanced Scorecard," *Library Trends* 49, no. 4 (2001): 709–17.

Poll, Roswitha, and Philip Payne. "Impact Measures for Libraries and Information Services," *Library Hi Tech* 24, no. 4 (2006): 547–62.

Pors, Niels Ole. "Changing Perceptions and Attitudes among Danish Library Managers and Directors: The Case of Environmental Factors," *New Library World* 106, nos. 3–4 (2005): 107–15.

Pors, Niels Ole. "Evidens om Bibliotekernes Brugere," *Dansk Biblioteksforskning* 6, nos. 2–3 (2010): 65–81.

Pors, Niels Ole. "Globalisation, Culture and Social Capital: Library Professionals on the Move," *Library Management* 28, nos. 4–5 (2007): 181–90.

Pors, Niels Ole. "Management Tools, Organisational Culture, and Leadership: An Exploratory Study," *Performance Measurement and Metrics* 9, no. 2 (2008): 138–52.

Pors, Niels Ole. "Perceptions of the Quality of the IFLA Conference in Glasgow," *IFLA Journal* 28, no. 5–6 (2002): 328–35.

Pors, Niels Ole, and Carl Gustav Johannsen. "Attitudes towards Internalization in the Library Sector: The Case of Danish Librarians and Library Managers," *New Library World* 104, no. 7 (2003): 278–85.

Pors, Niels Ole, and Carl G. Johannsen. "Job Satisfaction and Motivational Strategies among Library Directors," *New Library World* 103, no. 6 (2002): 199–209.

Pors, Niels Ole, and Carl Gustav Johannsen. "Library Directors under Cross-pressure between New Public Management and Value-based Management," *Library Management* 24, no.1–2 (2003): 51–60.

Pors, Niels Ole, Pat Dixon, and Heather Robson. "The Employment of Quality Measures in Libraries: Cultural Differences, Institutional Imperatives and Managerial Profiles," *Performance Measurement and Metrics* 5, no. 1 (2004): 20–28.

Porter, Brandi. "Managing with Emotional Intelligence," *Library Leadership & Management* 24, no. 4 (2010): 199–201.

Psychogios, Alexandros G. "A Four-Fold Regional-Specific Approach to TQM: The Case of South Eastern Europe," *International Journal of Quality & Reliability Management* 27, no. 9 (2010): 1036–63.

Rothstein, Samuel. "Development of the Concept of Reference Service in American Libraries, 1850–1900," *Library Quarterly* 23 (January 1953): 1–15.

Rothstein, Samuel. "Reference Service: The New Dimension in Librarianship," *The Reference Librarian* 11, no. 25–26 (1989): 7–31.

Sadri, Golnaz, Todd J. Weber, and William A. Gentry. "Empathic Emotion and Leadership Performance: An Empirical Analysis across 38 Countries," *Leadership Quarterly* 22 (2011): 818–30.

Schäffler Hildegard. "How to Organize the Digital Library: Reengineering and Change Management in the Bayerische Stattsbibliothek, Munich," *Library Hi Tech* 22, no. 4 (2004): 340–46.

Schneider, Judith, and Romie F. Littrell. "Leadership Preferences of German and English Managers," *Journal of Management Development* 22, no. 2 (2003): 130–48.

Schwartz, Shalom H. "A Theory of Cultural Value Orientation: Explication and Applications," *Comparative Sociology* 5, nos. 2–3 (2006): 137–82.

Seleim, Ahmed, and Nick Bontis. "The Relationship between Culture and Corruption: A Cross-National Study," *Journal of Intellectual Capital* 10, no. 1 (2009): 165–84.

Simon, Elisabeth, and Karl A. Stroetmann. "Managing Courses in Countries of Central and Eastern Europe: Experiences during Two German Seminars about Library and Information Management," *Library Management* 16, no. 2 (1995): 40–45.

Smith, Lucy, and Jennifer Rowley. "Digitisation of Local Heritage: Local Studies Collections and Digitisation in Public Libraries," *Journal of Librarianship and Information Science* 44, no. 1 (2012), doi:10.1177/0961000611434760. http://lis.sagepub.com/content/early/2012/02/23/0961000611434760.full.pdf+html/. Accessed October 17, 2012.

Smollan, Roy, and Ken Parry. "Follower Perceptions of the Emotional Intelligence of Change Leaders: A Qualitative Study," *Leadership* 7, no. 4 (2011): 435–62.

Streatfield, David, and Sharon Markless. "What Is Impact Assessment and Why Is It Important?" *Performance Measurement and Metrics* 10, no. 2 (2009): 134–41.

Thorhauge, Jens. "Branding the Library," *Scandinavian Public Library Quarterly* 40, no. 4 (2007): 3.

Tidwell, Michael, and Patricia Sias. "Personality and Information Seeking: Understanding How Traits Influence Information-Seeking Behaviors," *Journal of Business Communication* 42, no. 1 (2005): 51–77.

Vakola, Maria, Ioannis Tsaousis, and Ioannis Nikolaou. "The Role of Emotional Intelligence and Personality Variables on Attitudes towards Organisational Change," *Journal of Managerial Psychology* 19, no. 2 (2004): 88–110.

Van Maanen, John, and Edgar H. Schien. "Toward a Theory of Organizational Socialization," *Research in Organizational Behavior* 1, no. 1 (1970): 209–64.

Warner, Linda, and Keith Grint. "American Indian Ways of Leading and Knowing," *Leadership* 2, no. 2 (2006): 225–44.

Webster, Duane E., and DeEtta Jones Young. "Our Collective Wisdom: Succession Planning and the ARL Research Library Leadership Fellows Program," *Journal of Library Administration* 49, no. 8 (2009): 781–93.

Weiner, Sharon G. "Leadership of Academic Libraries: A Literature Review, *Education Libraries* 26, no. 2 (2003): 5–18.

Williamson, Jeanine M., Anne E. Pemberton, and John W. Lounsbury. "An Investigation of Career and Job Satisfaction in Relation to Personality Traits of Information Professionals," *Library Quarterly* 75, no. 2 (2005): 122–41.

Williamson, Jeanine M., Anne E. Pemberton, and John W. Lounsbury. "Personality Traits of Individuals in Different Specialties of Librarianship," *Journal of Documentation* 64, no. 2 (2008): 273–86.

Wilson, Kerry, and Sheila Corrall. "Developing Public Library Managers as Leaders: Evaluation of a National Leadership Development Programme," *Library Management* 29, no. 6 (2008): 473–88.

Yeganeh, Hamid, and Diane May. "Cultural Values and Gender Gap: A Cross-national Analysis," *Gender in Management: An International Journal* 26, no. 2 (2011): 106–21.

BOOKS

Aabø, Svanhild. *The Value of Public Libraries: A Methodological Discussion and Empirical Study Applying the Contingent Valuation Method*. Oslo, Norway: University of Oslo, 2005.

Anderson, Ole, and Søren B. Rasmussen. *Sådan Leder du Medarbejdere der er Klogere end Dig Selv: Mulighedsledelse I udviklingsorganisationer*. Copenhagen: Børsens Forlag, 2005.

Argyris, Chris, and Donald A. Schon, eds. *Organizational Culture II: Theory, Method and Practice*. Cambridge, MA: Addison-Wesley, 1996.

Audunson, Ragnar. *Change Processes in Public Libraries: A Comparative Project within an Institutional Perspective*. Oslo, Norway: Högskolen i Oslo, 1996.

Bennis, Warren, and Burt Nanus. *Leaders: Strategies for Taking Charge*. 2nd ed. London: Harper Business, 1997.

Bolman, Lee G., and Terrence E. Deal. *Reframing Organizations: Artistry, Choice, and Leadership*. 4th ed. San Francisco: Jossey-Bass, 2008.

Booth, Andrew, and Anne Brice, eds. *Evidence-based Practice for Information Professionals: A Handbook*. London: Facet, 2004.

Boyatzis, Richard, and Annie McKee. *Resonant Leadership: Renewing Yourself and Connecting with Others through Mindfulness, Hope, and Compassion*. Boston: Harvard Business School Press, 2005.

Burns, James MacGregor. *Leadership*. New York: Harper and Row, 1978.

Cameron, Kim S., and Robert E. Quinn. *Diagnosing and Changing Organizational Culture: Based on the Competing Values Framework*. Reading, MA: Addison-Wesley, 1999; New York: Wiley & Sons, 2006.

Chhokar, Jagdeep S., Felix C. Brodbeck, and Robert J. House, eds. *Culture and Leadership across the World*. Mahwah, NJ: Lawrence Erlbaum Associates, 2008.

Costa, Paul T., and Robert R. Mccrae, *NEO PI-R: Professional Manual*. Odessa, Ukraine: Psychological Assessment Resources, 1992.

Det Danske Ledelsesbarometer: Dansk Ledelse anno 2000 (The Danish Leadership Barometer: Danish Leadership 2000). Copenhagen: Århus, Handelshøjskolen i Århus & Ledernes Hovedorganisation.

Dugan, Robert E., Peter Hernon, and Danuta A. Nitecki. *Viewing Library Metrics from Different Perspectives*. Santa Barbara, CA: Libraries Unlimited, 2009.

Fukuyama, Francis. *Trust: The Social Virtues and the Creation of Prosperity*. New York: Free Press, 1995.

Gärdén, Cecilia, Anette Eliasson, Eva-Maria Flöög, Christina Persson, and Angela Zetterlund. *Folkbibliotek och Vuxnas Lärande: Förutsättningar, Dilemman och Möjligheter i Utvecklingsprojekt*. Borås, Sweden: Valfrid, 2006.

Goethals, George R., Georgia J. Sorenson, and James MacGregor Burns. *Encyclopedia of Leadership*. Thousand Oaks, CA: Sage, 2004.

Goleman, Daniel. *Emotional Intelligence*. New York: Bantam Books, 1995.

Goleman, Daniel, Richard Boyatzis, and Annie McKee. *Primal Leadership: Realizing the Power of Emotional Intelligence*. Boston: Harvard Business School Press, 2002.

Grancelli, Bruno, ed., *Social Change and Modernization: Lessons from Eastern Europe*. New York: Walter de Gruyter, 1995.

Hackman, J. Richard. *Leading Teams: Setting the Stage for Great Performances*. Boston: Harvard Business School Press, 2002.

Hansson, Joacim. *Libraries and Identity: The Role of Institutional Self-Image and Identity in the Emergence of New Types of Libraries*. Oxford, UK: Chandos, 2010.

Heifetz, Ronald A., Marty Linsky, and Alexander Grashow. *The Practice of Adaptive Leadership: Tools and Tactics for Changing Your Organization and the World*. Boston: Harvard Business Press, 2009.

Heinström, Jannica. *Fast Surfers, Broad Scanners, and Deep Divers—Personality and Information Seeking Behaviour*. Åbo, Turkey: Åbo Academi University Press, 2002.

Hernon, Peter, ed. *Shaping the Future: Advancing the Understanding of Leadership*. Santa Barbara, CA: Libraries Unlimited, 2010.

Hernon, Peter, and Robert E. Dugan, eds. *Outcomes Assessment in Higher Education: Views and Perspectives*. Westport, CT: Libraries Unlimited, 2004.

Hernon, Peter, Robert E. Dugan, and Danuta A. Nitecki. *Engaging in Evaluation and Assessment Research*. Santa Barbara, CA: Libraries Unlimited, 2011.

Hernon, Peter, Robert E. Dugan, and Candy Schwartz, eds. *Revisiting Outcomes Assessment in Higher Education*. Westport, CT: Libraries Unlimited, 2006.

Hernon, Peter, Joan Giesecke, and Camila A. Alire. *Academic Librarians as Emotionally Intelligent Leaders*. Westport, CT: Libraries Unlimited, 2008.

Hernon, Peter, and Joseph R. Matthews. *Reflecting on the Future: Academic and Public Libraries*. Chicago: American Library Association, 2013.

Hernon, Peter, Ronald R. Powell, and Arthur P. Young. *The Next Library Leadership: Attributes of Academic and Public Library Directors*. Westport, CT: Libraries Unlimited, 2003.

Hernon, Peter, and Nancy Rossiter. *Making a Difference: Leadership and Academic Libraries*. Westport, CT: Libraries Unlimited, 2007.

Hersey, Paul, and Kenneth H. Blanchard. *Management of Organizational Behavior*. Englewood Cliffs, NJ: Simon & Schuster, 1993.

Hersey, Paul, Kenneth H. Blanchard, and Dewey E. Johnson. *Management of Organizational Behavior: Leading Human Resources*. 9th ed. Upper Saddle River, NJ: Prentice-Hall, 2008.

Hofstede, Geert. *Culture and Organisations: Software of the Mind*. London: McGraw-Hill, 1991.

Hofstede, Geert. *Cultures and Organizations*. New York, McGraw-Hill, 2010.

Hofstede, Geert. *Culture's Consequences, International Differences in Work-related Values*. Newbury Park, CA: Sage, 1980.

House, Robert J., Paul J. Hanges, Mansour Javidan, Peter W. Dorfman, and Vipin Gupta. *Culture, Leadership, and Organizations: The GLOBE Study of 62 Societies*. Thousand Oaks, CA: Sage, 2004.

Inglehart, Ronald M., Michael Basanez, Jaime Dies-Medriano, Loek Halman, and Ruud Luijkx. *Human Beliefs and Values: A Cross-Cultural Sourcebook Based on the 1999–2002 Values Surveys*. Mexico City: Siglo XXI, 2004.

Jackson, Charles. *Understanding Psychological Testing*. London: Blackwell, 1996.

Johannsen, Carl Gustav. *Firmabiblioteker I Danmark 1945–2007* (Special libraries in Denmark 1945–2007). Copenhagen: Dansk Bibliotekshistorisk Selskab, 2009.

Johannsen, Carl Gustav, and Niels Ole Pors. *Ledere og ledelse i danske biblioteker—Bibliotekarforbundets lederundersøgelse 2001* (Leaders and leadership in Danish public libraries—The leadership survey of the Union of Danish Librarians 2001). Frederiksberg, Denmark: Bibliotekarforbundet, 2001.

Johannsen, Carl Gustav, and Niels Ole Pors. *Udfordringer og forandringer* (Challenges and change). Copenhagen: The Danish Library Association, 2002.

Kaplan, Robert, and David Norton. *Balanced Scorecard: Translating Strategy into Action*. Boston: Harvard Business School Press, 1996.

Kellerman, Barbara. *Bad Leadership*. Boston: Harvard Business School Press, 2004.

Kellerman, Barbara. *Followership: How Followers Are Creating Change and Changing Leaders*. Boston: Harvard Business School Press, 2008.

Kolb, David A. *Experiential Learning: Experience as the Source of Learning and Development*. London: Prentice-Hall, 1984.

Kotter, John P. *Leading Change*. Boston: Harvard Business Review Press, 1996.

Kouzes, James M., and Barry Z. Posner. *Credibility: How Leaders Gain and Lose It, Why People Demand It*. San Francisco: Jossey-Bass, 2003.

Kuhlthau, Carol C. *Seeking Meaning: A Process Approach to Library and Information Services*. 2nd ed. Westport, CT: Libraries Unlimited, 2004.

Lewin, Kurt. *Field Theory in Social Science*. New York: Harper & Row, 1951.

Mech, Terrence F., and Gerard B. McCabe. *Leadership and Academic Libraries*. Englewood, CO: Libraries Unlimited, 1998.

Mintzberg, Henry. *Structure in Fives: Designing Effective Organizations*. Englewood Cliffs, NJ: Prentice Hall, 1983.

Nanus, Burt. *Visionary Leadership: Creating a Compelling Sense of Direction for Your Organization*. San Francisco: Jossey-Bass, 1992.

Northouse, Peter G. *Leadership: Theory and Practice*. 6th ed. Thousand Oaks, CA: 2013.

Nyström, Viveca, and Linnéa Sjögren. *Nyttovärdering av Bibliotek*. Lund, Sweden: Se, BTJ—forlag, 2008.

Oliver, Gillian. *Organisational Culture for Information Managers*. Oxford, UK: Chandos, 2011.

Parsloe, Eric, and Monika Wray. *Coaching and Mentoring: Practical Methods to Improve Learning*. London: Kogan Page, 2000.

Poll, Roswitha, and Peter te Boekhorst. *Measuring Quality: Performance Measurement in Libraries*. Munich, Germany: Saur, 2007.

Pors, Niels Ole. *Ledere og ledelse i danske biblioteker—Bibliotekarforbundets lederundersøgelse 2007* (Leaders and leadership in Danish libraries: The leadership survey of the Union of Danish Librarians 2007). Frederiksberg, Denmark: Bibliotekarforbundet, 2007.

Pors, Niels Ole. *Ledere og ledelse i danske folkebiblioteker—Bibliotekarforbundets lederundersøgelse 2004* (Leaders and leadership in Danish public libraries—The leadership survey of the Union of Danish Librarians 2004). Frederiksberg, Denmark: Bibliotekarforbundet, 2004.

Pors, Niels Ole. *Strategi, Værdi og Kvalitet: Teorier og metoder 1.* Valby, Denmark: Danmarks Biblioteksforening, 2007.

Pors, Niels Ole. *Strategi, Værdi og Kvalitet: Værktøjer og indikatorer 2.* Valby, Denmark: Danmarks Biblioteksforening, 2007.

Riggs, Donald E. *Library Leadership: Visualizing the Future.* Phoenix, AZ: Oryx Press, 1982.

Robbins, Stephen P., and Timothy A. Judge. *Organizational Behavior.* Upper Saddle River, NJ: Prentice-Hall, 2009.

Roberts, Sue, and Jennifer Rowley. *Leadership: The Challenge for the Information Profession.* London: Facet, 2008.

Røvik, Kjell Arne. *Moderne Organisasjoner: Trender i Organisasjonstenkningen ved Tusenårsskiftet.* Bergen, Norway: Fagbokforlaget, 1998.

Rubin, Rhea J. *Demonstrating Results: Using Outcomes Measurement in Your Library.* Chicago: American Library Association, 2006.

Schein, Edgar H. *Organizational Culture and Leadership.* San Francisco: Jossey-Bass, 1992; 4th ed., San Francisco: Jossey-Bass, 2004.

Schramm-Nielsen, Jette, Peter Lawrence, and Karl H. Sivesind. *Management in Scandinavia: Culture, Context and Change.* Cheltenham, UK: Edward Elgar, 2004.

Schroeder, Jonathan, and Miriam Salzer-Morling, eds. *Brand Culture.* Abingdon, Oxon, UK: Routledge, 2006.

Stueart, Robert D., and Barbara B. Moran. *Library and Information Center Management.* Westport, CT: Libraries Unlimited, 2007.

Stueart, Robert D., and Maureen Sullivan. *Developing Library Leaders: A How-to-Do-It Manual® for Coaching, Team Building, and Mentoring Library Staff.* New York: Neal-Schuman, 2010.

Svendsen, Tinggaard Gert, and Gunnar Lind Haase Svendsen. *Social Kapital: En Introduktion.* Copenhagen: Hans Reitzel, 2006.

Swanson, Richard A. *Analysis for Improving Performance: Tools for Diagnosing Organizations and Documenting Workplace Expertise.* San Francisco: Berrett-Koehler, 1996.

Thorhauge, Jens, and Monika Segbert, eds. *Public Libraries and the Information Society.* Luxembourg: European Commission, 1997.

Trompenaars, Fons, and Charles Hampden-Turner. *Riding the Waves of Culture: Understanding Cultural Diversity in Business.* London: McGraw-Hill, 1997.

Wenglén, Robert. *Från dum till klok? En studie av mellanchefers lärande.* Lund, Sweden: Business Press, 2005.

Winston, Mark D. *Leadership in the Library and Information Science Professions: Theory and Practice.* Binghamton, NY: Haworth Information Press, 2001.

World Development Indicators 2004. Washington, DC: World Bank, 2004.

BOOK/PROCEEDING CHAPTERS

Anderson, A. J. "AJ's Problem-Solving Model—The Steps to Be Followed," in *Shaping the Future: Advancing the Understanding of Leadership,* edited by Peter Hernon. Santa Barbara, CA: Libraries Unlimited, 2010.

Audunson, Ragnar. "Folkebibliotekenes Rolle i en Digital Framtid: Publikums, Politikernes og Bibliotekarenes Bilder," in *Det Siviliserte Informationssamfunn: Folkebibliotekernes Role vid Ingangen til en Digital Tid,* edited by Ragnar Andreas Audunson and Niels Windfeld Lund. Oslo, Norway: Fagbokforlaget, 2001.

DiMaggio, Paul J., and Walter W. Powell. "The Iron Cage Revisited: Institutional Isomorphism and Collective Rationality in Organizational Fields," in *The New Institutionalism in Organizational Analysis,* edited by Walter W. Powell and Paul J. DiMaggio. Chicago: University of Chicago Press, 1991.

Hackman, J. Richard, and Richard W. Walton. "Leading Groups in Organizations," in *Designing Effective Work Groups*, edited by Paul S. Goodman and Associates. San Francisco: Jossey-Bass, 1986.

Jablin, Fred M. "Organizational Communication: An Assimilation Approach," in *Social Cognition and Communication*, edited by Michael E. Roloff and Charles R. Berger. Beverly Hills, CA: Sage, 1982.

Johannsen, Carl Gustav, and Niels Ole Pors. "Between New Public Management and Ethics: Library Management under Cross-Pressure," in *New Frontiers in Public Library Research*, edited by Carl J. Gustav Johannsen and Leif Kajberg. Lanham, MD: Scarecrow Press, 2005.

Khalil, Omar E. M., and Ahmed Seleim. "National Culture Practices and Societal Information Dissemination Capacity," in the *Proceedings* of the 2009 International Conference on Information Science, Technology and Applications. New York: AMC, 2009.

Landøy, Ane, and Angela Repanovici. "Managing and Managers of e-Science," in *E-Science and Information Management: Third International Symposium on Information Management in a Changing World, IMCW 2012, Ankara, Turkey, September 19–21, 2012. Proceedings*, edited by Serap Kurbanoğlu, Umut Al, Phyllis Lepon Erdoğan, Yaşar Tonta, and Nazan Uçak, 119–27. Berlin: Springer-Verlag, 2012.

Landøy, Ane, and Angela Repanovici. "What Challenges Are Library Leaders Facing?" in *Information in e-Motion*, Proceedings BOBCATSSS 2012, 20th International Conference on Information Science, Amsterdam, edited by Wolf-Fritz Riekert and Ingeborg Simon. Bad Honnef, Germany: Bock+Herchen Verlag, 2012.

Luthans, Fred, and Bruce J. Avolio. "Authentic Leadership: A Positive Development Approach," in *Positive Organizational Scholarship: Foundations of a New Discipline*, edited by Kim S. Cameron, Jane E. Dutton, and Robert E. Quinn. San Francisco: Barrett-Koehler, 2003.

Mackenzie, Maureen L., and James P. Smith. "How Does the Library Profession Grow Managers? It Doesn't—They Grow Themselves," in *Advances in Librarianship 33*, edited by Anne Woodsworth. Bingley UK: Emerald, 2011.

Mayer, John D., David R. Caruso, and Peter Salovey. "Emotional Intelligence as Zeitgeist, as Personality, and as a Mental Ability," in *The Handbook of Emotional Intelligence: Theory, Development, Assessment, and Application at Home School and in the Workplace*, edited by Reuven Bar-On and James D. A. Parker. New York: Jossey-Bass, 2000.

Moreland, Richard L., and John M. Levine. "Socialization in Small Groups: Temporal Changes in Individual-Group Relations," in *Advances in Experimental Social Psychology*, edited by Leonard Berkowitz, vol. 15. New York: Academic Press, 1982.

Mundt, Sebastian. "BIX—The Bibliotheksindex: Statistical Benchmarking in German Public Libraries," in *Library Statistics for the Twenty-First Century World*, edited by Michael Heany. Munich, Germany: Saur, 2009.

Ørom, A. "Folkebiblioteket i samfundet: Et rids af 100 års historie" (The public library in the society—A history of 100 years), in *Det stærke folkebibliotek—100 år med Danmarks Biblioteksforening* (The strong public library—100 years with the Danish Library Association), edited by M. Dyrbye Jørgen Svane-Mikkelsen, Leif Lørring, and Anders Ørom. Copenhagen: Danmarks Biblioteksforening og Danmarks Biblioteksskole, 2005.

Pors, Niels Ole. "Dimensions of Leadership and Service Quality: The Human Aspect in Performance Measurement," in *Proceedings of the Fourth Northumbrian International Conference on Performance Measurement in Libraries and Information Services: Meaningful Measures for Emerging Realities*, edited by Joan Stein, Martha Kyrillidou, and Denise Davis. Washington, DC: Association of Research Libraries, 2002.

Schwartz, Shalom H. "Beyond Individualism/Collectivism: New Dimensions of Values," in *Individualism and Collectivism: Theory Application and Methods*, edited by Uichol

Kim, Harry C. Triandis, Cigdem Kagitcibasi, Sang-Chin Choi, and Gene Yoon. Newbury Park, CA: Sage, 1994.

Zetterlund, Angela. and Cecilia Gärdén. "Why Public Libraries Have Problems Sharing a Vision of Joint Use Libraries: Experiences from a Program concerning Adult Learners," in Proceeding of Joint Use Libraries: An International Conference. Manchester UK, June 2007. Blackwood, South Australia: Auslib Press, 2007.

DISSERTATIONS

Paul, Gerd. *Leitung und Cooperation in Wissenschaflichen Bbibliotheken Berlins: Eine Empirische Untersuchung*, Dissertation des Grades eines Doktors der Philosophie, Humboldt-Universität, Berlin, 1999.

Tripuraneni, Vinaya L. *Leader or Manager: Academic Library Leader's Leadership Orientation Considered Ideal by Faculty, Administrators, and Librarians at Private, Nonprofit, Doctoral Universities in Southern California*, EdD dissertation, University of La Verne, 2010. Available from Dissertations & Theses Full-Text, AAT 3430266.

REPORTS

Association of College and Research Libraries. *Value of Academic Libraries: A Comprehensive Research Review and Report*, by Megan Oakleaf. Chicago: Association of College and Research Libraries, 2010.

Pors, Niels Ole. *Mellem Identitet og Legitimitet: Forandringer, Kultur og Ledelse i Danske Folkebiblioteker* (Between identity and legitimacy: Changes, culture and leadership in Danish public libraries), Research Report. Copenhagen: Royal School of Library and Information Science, 2005.

Pors, Niels Ole. *Mellem Identitet og Legitimitet: Ledelse, Kultur og Forandringer i Danske Biblioteker* (Between identity and legitimacy: Leadership, culture and change in Danish libraries), Research Report. Copenhagen: Danmarks Biblioteksskole, 2006.

WEB SOURCES

American Humanist Association. http://www.americanhumanist.org/What_We_Do/Education_Center/HELP/6_Peace_and_Social_Justice/6.1_A/Conflict_Resolution_Teaching_Tips. Accessed May 20, 2012.

American Library Association. "ALA Emerging Leaders Program." http://wikis.ala.org/emergingleaders/index.php/Main_Page. Accessed June 1, 2011.

American Library Association. "Library Leadership Training Resources." http://www.ala.org/ala/aboutala/offices/hrdr/abouthrdr/hrdrliaisoncomm/otld/leadershiptraining.cfm. Accessed June 1, 2011.

Association of Research Libraries. "Leadership Development" [Research Library Leadership Fellows (RLLF) Program]. http://www.arl.org/leadership/rllf/index.shtml. Accessed June 1, 2011.

Authenticity Consulting. LLC®, Free Management Library. http://managementhelp.org/personaldevelopment/self-assessments.htm; http://www.quintcareers.com/SWOT_Analysis.html (Quintessential Careers™). Accessed May 21, 2012.

Avolio, Bruce J., Fred O.Walumbwa, and Todd J. Weber. "Leadership: Current Theories, Research, and Future Directions," *Annual Review of Psychology* 60 (2009): 421–49. 10.1146/annurev.psych.60.110707.163621. Accessed May 21, 2012.

Becker, Samantha, Michael D. Crandall, Karen E. Fisher, Rebecca Blakewood, Bo Kinney, and Cadi Russell-Sauvé. *Opportunity for All: How Library Policies and Practices Impact Public Internet Access*. Washington, DC: Institute of Museum and Library

Services, 2011. http://impact.ischool.washington.edu/documents/OPP4ALL2_
    FinalReport.pdf. Accessed May 21, 2012.

Becker, Samantha, Michael D. Crandall, Karen E. Fisher, Bo Kinney, Carol Landry, and
    Anita Rocha. *Opportunity for All: How the American Public Benefits from Internet
    Access at U.S. Libraries*. Washington, DC: Institute of Museum and Library Ser-
    vices, 2010. http://www.gatesfoundation.org/learning/Pages/us-libraries-report-
    opportunity-for-all.aspx. Accessed May 21, 2012.

"The Bologna Declaration on the European Space for Higher Education: An Explanation."
    http://ec.europa.eu/education/policies/educ/bologna/bologna.pdf. Accessed May
    21, 2012.

Counting Opinions. http://www.countingopinions.com/. Accessed May 21, 2012.

Dahl, Stephan. "Intercultural Research: The Current State of Knowledge," Middlesex Uni-
    versity Discussion Paper no. 26 (January 12, 2004). http://www.alanisguzman.
    com/archivos/Culture.pdf. Accessed July 21, 2011.

"Employability Skills Self-Assessment Part 2: Teamwork Skills." http://www.edu.gov.
    mb.ca/k12/cur/cardev/gr9_found/blms/blm18b.pdf. Accessed May 21, 2012.

"Employee Self-Assessment Instrument: Core Competencies" (Environment Canada, the
    Corporate Services Community). http://www.on.ec.gc.ca/core-competencies/
    pdf/Questionnaire-e.pdf. Accessed May 20, 2012.

Fishman, Rachel. "Higher Education Needs a Flashlight," *The Quick & the Ed* [blog] (Feb-
    ruary 2, 2012). http://www.quickanded.com/about. Accessed May 21, 2012.

Gates, Robert. "In Commencement Speech, Gates Shares Thoughts on Leadership," *Wash-
    ington Post* (May 30, 2011). http://www.washingtonpost.com/politics/gates-on-
    leadership-a-rare-and-precious-commodity/2011/05/27/AGNamIEH_story.html?wprss=
    rss_politics. Accessed July 22, 2011.

Goleman, Daniel. http://danielgoleman.info/purchase/. Accessed May 21, 2012.

The Greenleaf Center for Servant Leadership. "About Us." http://www.greenleaf.org/
    aboutus/. Accessed June 1, 2011.

Grove, Cornelius N. "Introduction to the GLOBE Research Project on Leadership World-
    wide" (2005). http://www.grovewell.com/pub-GLOBE-intro.html. Accessed May
    24, 2012.

Grovewell LLC. "Leadership Style Variations across Cultures: Overview of GLOBE Re-
    search Findings." 2005. http://www.grovewell.com/pub-GLOBE-leadership.
    html. Accessed May 29, 2012.

Heinström, Jannica. "Fast Surfing for Availability or Deep Diving into Quality-Motivation
    and Information Seeking among Middle and High School Students," *Information
    Research* 11, no. 4 (2006). http://Informationr.net/ir/11-4/paper265.html. Ac-
    cessed May 21, 2012.

Heinström, Jannica. "Five Personality Dimensions and Their Influence on Information Be-
    haviour," *Information Research* 9, no. 1 (2003). http://Informationr.net/ir/9-1/
    paper165.html. Accessed May 21, 2012.

Hill Model. http://www.nwlink.com/~donclark/leader/team_leadership.html. Accessed
    May 21, 2012.

Hinchliffe Lisa J., and Megan Oakleaf. "Sustainable Progress through Impact: The Value of
    Academic Libraries Project," paper for the World Library and Information Congress,
    76th IFLA General Conference and Assembly (2010). http://www.ifla.org/files/
    hq/papers/ifla76/72-hinchliffe-en.pdf. Accessed May 22, 2012.

Hollander, Henryk. "Who Will Take over the Libraries of the New Europe," *LIBER Quar-
    terly* 17, nos. 3–4 (2007). liber.library.uu.nl/publish/issues/2007-3_4/index.
    html?000207. Accessed June 12, 2012.

Journal of Library Innovation. "Editorial Policies." http://www.libraryinnovation.org/
    about/editorialPolicies#focusAndScope. Accessed May 21, 2012.

"Karin Wittenborg—Future of Librarians Interview." http://www.collegeonline.org/
    library/librarians-online/karin-wittenborg. Accessed June 12, 2011.

LibEcon. "Database." http://www.libecon.org/database/default.asp. Accessed June 13, 2012.

Management Research Group®. Management & Leadership Development. http://www.mrg.com/Solutions/Management.asp. Accessed May 19, 2012.

Martin, André. *Everyday Leadership*, a CCL Research White Paper. Brussels, Belgium: Center for Creative Leadership, 2007. http://www.ccl.org/leadership/pdf/research/EverydayLeadership.pdf. Accessed May 21, 2012.

Mediate.com. http://www.mediate.com/articles/taylor.cfm. Accessed July 15, 2011.

Neal, James G. "Raised by Wolves: Integrating the New Generation of Feral Professionals into the Academic Library," Library Journal.com (February15, 2006). http://www.libraryjournal.com/article/CA6304405.html. Accessed June 3, 2011.

Neal, James G. "Raised by Wolves: The New Generation of Feral Professionals in the Academic Library," ACRL Twelfth National Conference. http://www.ala.org/ala/mgrps/divs/acrl//events/pdf/neal2-05.pdf. Accessed June 3, 2011.

Oxford English Dictionary (Oxford University Press, 2010), subscription database. http://www.oxforddictionaries.com

Patterson, Fiona, and Maura Kerrin. *Innovation for the Recovery: Enhancing Innovative Working Practices*. London: Chartered Management Institute, 2009. https://www.managers.org.uk/sites/default/files/user28/Innovation_for_the_Recovery_Dec_2009_0.pdf. Accessed May 21, 2012.

"Peter Senge and the Learning Organization." http://www.infed.org/thinkers/senge.htm. Accessed May 20, 2011.

Peters, Helen, and Robert Kabacoff. "GLOBAL or LOCAL: The Impact of Country Culture on Leadership Style in Europe" (Management Research Group®, 2010). http://www.mrg.com/documents/Euro_Culture.pdf . Accessed May 22, 2011.

Project COUNTER. http://www.projectcounter.org/. Accessed May 22, 2012.

Reilly, Anne H. and Tony J. Karounos. "Exploring the Link between Emotional Intelligence and Cross-Cultural Leadership Effectiveness," *Journal of International Business and Cultural Studies* 1 (February 2009). http://www.aabri.com/manuscripts/08134.pdf. Accessed July 15, 2011.

Rudd, Peggy D. "Documenting the Difference: Demonstrating the Value of Libraries through Outcome Measurement," in *Perspectives on Outcome Based Evaluation for Libraries and Museums*. Washington, DC: Institute of Museum and Library Services, n.d. http://www.imls.gov/assets/1/workflow_staging/AssetManager/214.PDF. Accessed May 21, 2012.

Simmons College. Graduate School of Library and Information Science. "Managerial Leadership in the Information Professions: Models" (2006). http://www.simmons.edu/gslis/docs/phdmlip_models_new_permission.pdf. Accessed May 22, 2012.

Society of College, National and University Libraries (SCONUL). "Impact Initiative." http://vamp.diglib.shrivenham.cranfield.ac.uk/impact/impact-initiative. Accessed June 17, 2012.

Tannenbaum, Robert, and Warren H Schmidt. "How to Choose a Leadership Pattern," *Harvard Business Review* (May/June 1973). http://www.elcamino.edu/faculty/bcarr/documents/How%20to%20choose%20a%20leadership%20pattern.pdf. Accessed May 29, 2012.

"Team Self-Assessment" (Constructive Choices, Inc.). http://www.performancexpress.org/0807/Images/Team%20SelfAssessment%20Tool.pdf. Accessed May 21, 2012.

Thorhauge, Jens *Danish Library Policy: A Selection of Recent Articles and Papers*. Copenhagen: Danish National Library Authority, 2002. http://www.bs.dk/publikationer/english/library_policy/pdf/dlp.pdf. Accessed May 19, 2012.

University of West Florida, Office of the Dean of Libraries. "Calculate Your Personal Return on Investment" (2011). http://libguides.uwf.edu/content.php?pid=188487&sid=2261667. Accessed May 19, 2012.

University of West Florida, Office of the Dean of Libraries. "Student Return on Investment (SROI): How Can I Get My Tuition Money's Worth from the Library" (2011). http://libguides.uwf.edu/content.php?pid=188487&sid=2183215. Accessed May 19, 2012.

White House. "College Scorecard." Washington, DC: White House, 2012. http://www.whitehouse.gov/issues/education/scorecard. Accessed May 21, 2012.

World Values Survey. http://www.worldvaluessurvey.org/. Accessed May 19, 2012.

UNPUBLISHED MATERIAL

Burton, Lois, and Deborah Dalley. *Beyond Influencing*, Leadership Seminar, Manchester, UK, 2007.

INDEX

ABOUT THE EDITORS AND CONTRIBUTORS

PETER HERNON is a professor at Simmons College (Graduate School of Library and Information Science, Boston, MA, peter.hernon@simmons.edu) and the principal faculty member for the doctoral program Managerial Leadership in the Information Professions. He received his PhD from Indiana University, Bloomington; is the 2008 recipient of the Association of College and Research Libraries' (ACRL) award for Academic/Research Librarian of the Year; is the coeditor of *Library & Information Science Research*; and has taught, conducted workshops, and/or delivered addresses in 10 countries (Canada, Denmark, England, Finland, France, Greece, New Zealand, Norway, Portugal, and South Africa). He is the author or coauthor of 53 books, including the award-winning books *Federal Information Policies in the 1980s* (1986, with Charles R. McClure), *Assessing Service Quality* (1998, 2010, with Ellen Altman), and *Viewing Library Metrics from Different Perspectives* (2009, with Robert E. Dugan and Danuta A. Nitecki).

NIELS OLE PORS is a professor at the Royal School of Library and Information Science (Copenhagen, Denmark, http://www.iva.dk/nop, nop@iva.dk). He has previously been dean at the school, with responsibilities for both research and education. He has written several books and research reports on user studies and information behavior, research methods and statistical analysis, organizational theories and leadership, quality management, and educational questions concerning the profession. He has written more than 250 papers and articles in academic and professional journals. He is also a member of the Danish Ministry of Culture's Research Council and has been research director of the Nordic–Baltic PhD program called NORSLIS. He is a member of the editorial boards of several academic journals. He also has comprehensive international experience. He has lectured in many different countries and has participated in many library development projects.

CARL GUSTAV JOHANNSEN is associate professor at the Royal School of Library and Information Science, Copenhagen (cgj@iva.dk). He has previously been head of the Research School of Cultural Heritage, 2004–2011. He has a PhD in quality management from the Business School of Aarhus. His published works include several books and research reports on evidence-based professional practice, public library issues, special librarianship, competitive intelligence, organizational theories and leadership, quality management, and educational questions concerning the profession. In total, more than 125 of his papers and articles have appeared in academic and professional journals. He is a member of the editorial boards of several academic journals and has lectured in different countries and participated in many library development projects in, for example, the Nordic countries, the Baltic states, Hungary, Egypt, and South Africa. Johannsen has been a member of government research councils and has also had chairman and other key positions in several Danish library associations concerned with public, research, and special libraries.

ANE LANDØY (cand. philol. in history from the University of Bergen, 1990) has worked as an academic librarian in charge of the social science, arts and humanities, and law libraries at the University of Bergen Library, Norway, since 2002. She is also currently enrolled in the PhD program of the Royal School in Copenhagen with a project about leaders and leadership in libraries in Norway. She contributes and presents at LIS conferences nationally and internationally, such as IFLA and IFLA satellites, QQML, and the Norwegian biannual library meeting. Her research interests include the teachings of information literacy, library use of statistics and indicators, and leadership of libraries. She co-edited the book *Aspects of the Digital Library* (2006). Internationally, she has co-coordinated library development projects in South Sudan, funded by the Norwegian Ministry of Foreign Affairs. She collaborates with libraries in Greece, Uganda, and Romania and is part of a large European Union–funded Tempus project for delivering information literacy training to the western Balkans.

JENNIFER ROWLEY is a professor in information and communications, Manchester Metropolitan University, UK (j.rowley@mmu.ac.uk). She has previously held a number of other academic posts in the United Kingdom. Her research interests are wide-ranging and embrace information and knowledge management, e-marketing, branding, and relationship marketing. She has been published widely, including recent articles in the *Journal of Marketing Management, Marketing Theory, Journal of the American Society for Information Science and Technology, Journal of Information Science, International Journal of Information Management*, and *Internet Research*. Her recent books include *Being an Information Innovator* (Facet, 2011) and *Leadership: The Challenge for the Information Profession* (with Sue Roberts, Facet, 2008). She is editor of the *Journal of Further and Higher Education* and associate editor of the *Journal of Marketing Management*.

ANGELA ZETTERLUND is an associate professor at Linneaus University, in the section for library and information sciences (Angela.zetterlund@lnu.se). She is head of the section and program coordinator for the LIS program and courses at the undergraduate and graduate level. She has been involved in and responsible for education directed to LIS management both in Sweden and in Nordic countries.

She has a PhD from the University of Gothenburg, with a specialization in evaluation and local change, at the Faculty of Social Sciences. She has been involved in collaborative projects in Central Europe, North America, Indonesia, and the Nordic Baltic area. She has had several articles published on library change, evaluation, decision making, student information behavior, adult learning, project management, and organizational aspects of joint-use libraries. Zetterlund has reviewed research work at different levels both nationally and internationally. She is a member of international networks such as Nordplus and IFLA. She is also an elected member of the Royal Library National Expert group for quality development and evaluation. She is involved as researcher in many development projects at both the local and national levels, and she collaborates in different types of libraries and between science and the field of professional practice. She is also a requested speaker and researcher outside the LIS community.